STORIES OF THE
BEGINNING

STORIES OF THE
BEGINNING

Genesis 1-11 *and* Other Creation Stories

Ellen van Wolde

MOREHOUSE PUBLISHING

Translated by John Bowden from the Dutch
*Vehalen over het begin. Genesis I-II en andere
scheppingsverhalen*, published 1995 by Uitgeverij Ten
Have b.v., Baarn

© Uitgeverij Ten Have b.v., Baarn 1995

Translation © John Bowden 1996

First published in the U.S.A. 1997 by
Morehouse Publishing
Editorial Office
871 Ethan Allen Hwy
Ridgefield, CT 06877

Corporate Office
P.O. Box 1321
Harrisburg, PA 17105

First British edition published 1996
by SCM Press Ltd,
9-17 St Albans Place, London NI ONX

A catalog record for this book is available
from the Library of Congress

ISBN: 0-8192-1714-X

Printed in the United States of America

Contents

For my parents
they were my beginning
and gave me a story of the beginning

Preface

A book is like a flower: you have to have good ground in which you can sow, you have to have good seed, and you need people for sowing so that the seed can shoot up. After that comes patient work: weeding, maintaining, watering, and having the patience to wait and continue to work on it. Then, one day, there is the flower. Beautiful! Or perhaps it is rather smaller, rather poorer than you had intended. Be that as it may, it needs someone to notice it and have an eye for it. Every flower will wither, and so will every book, but it is pleasant for it to be admired in bloom or to wait as a seed in the ground until it bears better fruit in the future.

This book, *Stories of the Beginning*, is the flower which has grown in a seedbed laid long ago by my parents. The seed sown in that bed not only shaped my beginning, but at the same time created possibilities for me to blossom. They are my constant inspiration. So this book is dedicated to my parents.

For the spadework, the fertilizer and the daily maintenance of my garden the theological faculty of Tilburg, where students and teachers work together in an stimulating way, has been very important. This book is certainly a product of that. Above all the real gardeners have been indispensable to me. They have joined in reading the text, correcting it and thinking about it, and helped by stimulating and supporting me. I am most grateful to all of them: Anneke Pieck, Yvonne van den Akker, Ron Pirson, Ton van der Worp and Frans Geerts.

Introduction: The Beginning

This is the beginning. Everything is silent, motionless. Everything is empty. There is no life: no bird sings, no fish glistens in the water, no people fill the air with noise. Pure silence reigns over everything. No wind blows and no spirit hovers over the waters. There is nothing to be seen of creation. Without a beginning there is nothing, no time and space, no life and air. Without a story there is no image and no idea with which to fill space. With God's creation and its re-creation by human beings in language and story, history has a beginning.

Without a story about the beginning, human beings face chaos, and their origin seems to be an abyss. In order to provide a foundation for existence, the beginning was filled with meaning. Moreover, every culture attaches a meaning to the beginning, often in the form of stories. These are not stories in the sense of tales, but realities in which people live. These are stories which give people roots. In Western culture Genesis is *the* story of the beginning. Other cultures tell different stories of how it all began, and we read them with great amazement. We follow their traces with fascination into the past. Where no person ever was, what no ear ever heard, we create by constantly reading afresh the story of our own beginning.

In our own time there are some who believe that the great stories have had their day. Most people even believe that only the facts count. For them, only perceptions of what is directly visible form the basis for scientific views and world-views. Above all people who live by common sense know that there are only hard facts, and that these facts usually take the form of a pound or a dollar. The rest is fantasy, fiction; at most an amusing distraction. Nevertheless, story-tellers and poets can be closer to experiences and feelings and in an important way express what a 'fact' is. And on the other hand 'objective' economic or scientific explanations, too, often seem to be more a matter of selection and perspective than thought. Both aspects, the explanatory power of narratives and the narrative power of explanations, will be at the forefront of this book.

First of all we are concerned here with the 'great' stories of Western culture: the creation stories in Genesis 1–11 and what people have read into them in the course of history. These Bible stories have exercised a great deal of influence on the formation of the Western view of human beings and the world. Then 'stories of the beginning' will be illuminated from other, non-Western cultures. They offer a wide range of images, a host of experiences and a reservoir of insights which can enrich our own images. Finally, we shall discuss some elements of modern twentieth-century views of the beginning. These scientific approaches to the beginning are so familiar to us that we no longer notice their narrative character.

At the same time it will become clear that the beginning itself preceded every story and every explanation of the beginning. No matter how original and creative a story or explanation may be, nothing can begin without a beginning outside that particular story or explanation.

From primal time to Ur: Genesis 1–11

Stories about the past usually begin at the beginning. But what is the past? Is it a series of facts and events or a narrative which reproduces human images and experiences? The book of Genesis shows both aspects: a series of genealogies and a series of stories. The lists of generations or genealogies in Genesis are always introduced by the words *elle toledot*, 'this is the history' of heaven and earth; 'this is the history' or 'this is the list of the generations' of Adam, Noah, the sons of Noah, Shem or Terach. These genealogies are a summary form of history-writing. In them the past is condensed to its biological nucleus, to the transmission of ancestral material. Life is described as survival, and history as the preservation of 'genes'. Therefore Genesis is primarily gene-sis. This is expressed by the word *toledot*, which means fatherings, but also births, begettings, becomings or generatings. *Toledot* is history regarded as a bio-logical-physiological process. Next, history can be experienced as a series of transmitted experiences: parents tell their children about their lives, about their backgrounds and their enthusiasms, about their motives, ideals and achievements. Through this, parents and children gain new strength, and historical and biological facts gain significance within the structure of the story. In Genesis these stories appear between the genealogies: these two aspects together, both the historical and biological facts and the meanings attached to them, define the human past. Precisely by combining the two, Genesis shows the two levels of history.

The first eleven chapters of Genesis tell the story of the creation and primal history of the world and of the first generations of human beings. They begin in primal time, in the time which precedes ordinary time and in the space which precedes ordinary space, and continue up to Ur, the birthplace of Abraham. From Genesis 12 onwards this universal history is focussed on the descendants of Abraham: the Hebrews, or the people of Israel. The stories of the patriarchs, Abraham and Sarah, Isaac and Rebecca, Jacob and Rachel and Leah, in Gen. 12–50 are about the formation of this people. These stories conclude with the blessing of the twelve sons of Jacob/Israel, and the book of Genesis itself ends with this blessing and with the sons of Jacob living in Egypt.

Since the beginnings of scientific exegesis in the nineteenth century, there has been a good deal of discussion about the dating of Genesis. The majority begin (or began) from the hypothesis that four redactional strata form its basis: the Yahwist, or J (960–930 BCE), a group of authors who have remained anonymous and who call God YHWH, writing in Judah in the reign of king Solomon; the Elohist, or E (850 BCE), the anonymous group of authors who call God Elohim and who wrote in the Northern Kingdom after the division of Solomon's kingdom; the Deuteronomist or D (620 CE), the anonymous author who wrote and edited at the time of Josiah's reform; and the Priestly Writing or P (550–450 BCE), the anonymous group of authors who arranged the earlier writings in one great whole, which we now have. All the texts of Genesis have been analysed with the help of this hypothesis about its authors, who at the same time are a kind of redactor. Thus the mosaic of the text is explained in terms of the stones from which it has been built up, by taking apart bits of the whole. Once they have identified these bits, scholars can put together loose stones of the same kind and it becomes possible to write 'a theology of J' or a 'theology of P'. In this way the text of Genesis is analysed.

From the middle of the 1970s this approach came increasingly to be questioned. Shouldn't far more attention to be paid to the mosaic as a whole? Once the question had been raised, people increasingly began to see the unity behind the differences. No longer were the little stones taken from the mosaic and studied; attention was paid to the mosaic itself. The present book stands in this more recent line. Here Genesis 1–11 will be read as a composition put together with care. Following the most recent investigations, I shall begin by assuming that elements of this composition go back to oral traditions from the second millennium BCE, which were only written down between 1000 and 500 BCE. It is by no means clear when the final redaction came into being. However, it may be assumed that during or soon after the Babylonian exile (587–538 BCE) the present version of Gen. 1–11 was accepted as an authoritative or normative text.

On the basis of the text of Gen. 1–11 as we now have it, we can discover new patterns and images. Looking attentively at words and units of texts, I want to bring out a new main theme which has so far escaped attention. So here is the scheme of this book. First, the basic Hebrew text will be given in a very literal translation. The translation will indicated the sentence-units – i.e. sentences with one subject and one predicate – and direct speech will be indicated by indentations. Secondly, the translation will make a typographical distinction between the two words in Hebrew for 'earth'. Hebrew *erets*, i.e. the earth in the sense of the whole earth or world, will be indicated as 'earth'; Hebrew *adama*, i.e. earth in the sense of land which can be or has been cultivated or inhabited, or agricultural land, is printed in italics, *earth*. After this, the text of Genesis will be discussed in depth chapter by chapter, usually ending with an account of the way in which these texts have been read in the course of history. Because all people read texts on the basis of the questions of their own time, the significance attached to the texts often changes considerably. So stories of the beginning seem to be in a continuous process of becoming, and are not static, as is often supposed. Perhaps that can create openness for revising our own reading of Gen. 1–11 and developing a new picture of the beginning.

From the Urals to the Andes: non-Western stories of the beginning

Stories of the beginning are similarly transmitted in other cultures. These creation stories are to be found in a particular culture at the grass roots of the social and religious community, and have also been determinative in shaping its social language. They functioned and still function as pointers, indicating the lines along which people have to explain their lives. The narrative form indicates that this way is filled not only with rationality but also with imagination. Stories of the beginning in other cultures are usually called myths. However, one's own story – which in Western history is Genesis – is not called a myth. To avoid value judgments I shall use the term 'stories of the beginning' for both the Hebrew text about creation in Genesis and the texts about the beginning from other cultures.

Usually creation stories from other cultures are told only so that they can be compared with Genesis. It seems to me better to let the stories speak for themselves, so here I shall not be making any comparisons. Moreover, such comparisons have often led to a quest for parallels, for what is 'universal' (as if the 'universal' could get us closer to God!). If we act in this way we fail to do justice to the distinctive character of the story and the context. The selection of stories offered here is based on their distribution throughout the world, so that here we have a picture of stories 'from the Urals to the Andes'. To achieve this, stories have been included from Babylonia, India, China and Australia, and from South and North America, Africa, Iceland and Finland.

5

From the Big Bang until now: the natural sciences and the beginning

In our day, at the end of the twentieth century, the scientific approach to the present and the past has become the dominant view of existence. When we begin to reflect on the beginning, we usually do so in the form of the theories of the Big Bang or of evolution. Although these theories have similarly brought order and cohesion by combining loose, controllable facts in a single context, we regard such scientific views of the beginning as coming closest to the truth. Consequently they do not point many of us to arbitrariness, like stories, tales or myths, but give us a glimpse of what really happened. These views are no longer seen as images of the world, but as an objective account of it. We have also become accustomed to the idea that the story of creation and the theory of evolution offer opposing views, and assume that one or the other is true, as if both could not be true at the same time. In the last part of this book I shall examine some scientific approaches to the beginning and demonstrate that they are not mutually exclusive, but supplementary.

Conclusion

The emphasis in this book is on a closer reading of Genesis 1–11. This is not only because I am more expert in this field than in the two others, but also because this story of the beginning has had the greatest influence on our Western culture and history. But at the same time that presents a problem. Precisely because Genesis has had so much influence, its significance is most fixed: the reading is settled; everyone already knows what is in it and is less inclined to develop a new view. One can approach an unknown story from Guatemala openly, but that is more difficult with Genesis. There is usually less readiness to read these texts as new. So a certain form of 'de-automation' is required for reading these stories of the beginning from Genesis. What is required is not only a readiness to revise one's own views, but also a sense of wonder, since this can make new questions and insights possible. In our time, when automation is rated so highly, I want to suggest that we should get away from an automated approach, from the familiar way of looking at things, in order to discover afresh what is distinctive about the stories of the beginning.

Part I

Genesis 1–11

Genesis 1: The Story of the Creation of Heaven and Earth[1]

1. 1   In a beginning God created the heaven and the earth.
   2   The earth was desolate and empty,
      darkness lay over the primal ocean,
      and God's spirit hovered over the waters.
   3   God said,
        Let there be light.
      And there was light.
   4   God saw the light,
      that it was good.
      God made a division between the light and the darkness.
   5   God called the light day
      and the darkness he called night.
      It became evening
      and it became morning,
      day one.
   6   God said,
        Let there be a vault in the middle of the waters,
        let there be a division between waters and waters.
   7   God made the vault
      and made a division between the waters below the vault
      and the waters above the vault.
      So it happened.
   8   God called the vault heaven.
      It became evening
      and it became morning,
      a second day.
   9   God said,
        Let the waters under the heaven gather in one place
        and let the dry land become visible.
      So it happened.
  10   God called the dry land earth
      and the gathering together of waters he called seas.
      God saw that it was good.
  11   God said,

Let the earth bring forth young green plants
that bear seed
and fruit-bearing trees with fruits after their kind
that have their seed in them
over all the earth.
So it happened.

12 Young greenery came up out of the earth,
bearing seed after its kind,
and fruit-bearing trees,
which have their seed in them after their kind.
God saw that it was good.

13 It became evening
and it became morning,
a third day.

14 God said,
Let there be lights in the vault of heaven
to make a division between the day and the night.
Let them be signs for the appointed times,
for the days and the years.

15 Let there be lights in the vault of heaven
to give light on the earth.
And so it happened.

16 God made the two great lights,
the greater light to rule over the day
and the lesser light to rule over the night,
and the stars.

17 God put them in the vault of the heaven
to give light on the earth,

18 to rule over the day and over the night,
and to make a division between the light and the darkness.
God saw that it was good.

19 It became evening
and it became morning,
a fourth day.

20 God said,
Let the waters teem with swarms of living creatures
and let birds fly over the earth across the vault of the heaven.

21 God created the great sea creatures and every living creature
that swarms,
which the waters make to teem after their kind,
and all the birds flying after their kind.

God saw that it was good.

22 God blessed them, saying,
>Be fruitful,
>become numerous,
>fill the waters in the seas
>and let the birds become numerous on the earth.

23 It became evening
and it became morning,
a fifth day.

24 God said,
>Let living creatures come forth from the earth after their kind,
>cattle, creeping things and animals of the earth after their
>kind.

So it happened.

25 God made the animals of the earth after their kind,
the cattle after their kind,
and all that creeps on the *earth* after its kind.
God saw that it was good.

26 God said,
>Let us make a human being in our image, like us,
>and let them rule over the fishes of the sea,
>over the birds of the heaven, over the cattle, over all the earth
>and over all the creeping things that creep on the earth.

27 God created the human being in his image,
in the image of God created he him,
male and female created he them.

28 God blessed them
and God said to them,
>Be fruitful,
>become numerous,
>fill the earth,
>subdue it
>and rule over the fishes of the sea, over the birds of the
>heaven,
>and over all creatures that creep upon the earth.

29 God said,
>Look,
>I give you all vegetation
>that bears seed
>and that is dispersed over all the earth
>and all trees with fruits

that bear seed,
they shall be your food.

30   And to all the animals of the earth and to all the birds of
the air
and to everything that creeps on the earth
in which there is the breath of life
(I give) all the green vegetation for food.
So it happened.

31   God saw all that he had made.
And look,
it was very good.
It became evening
and it became morning,
a sixth day.

2. 1   When the heaven and earth and all with which they were
furnished had been finished,

2   God had completed on the seventh day his work
that he had done.
And he rested on the seventh day from all his work
that he had done.

3   God blessed the seventh day
and sanctified it,
for on that day he rested from all his work
that God created by doing it.

4a   This is the history of the heaven and the earth in their being
created.

The very first word of the story, *bereshit*, 'in a beginning', indicates that here a beginning is made even on beginning. This
word is almost always translated 'in the beginning'. But there is
no definite article in the Hebrew. This beginning is still undetermined; no other beginnings have gone before it. Moreover, how
can you speak of 'the' beginning when there is as yet no time?
People can only think by relating experiences, feelings, actions
to phenomena which are situated in time and space. But there
was as yet no one to tell the story to, no place to connect the
events with. There is not even an eternity, for that would be
'lasting for an indeterminate time'. Only with the creation do
time and space come into being. The first day has its origin in
the creation of light. Creation does not take place at a moment

in time; time is created *with* the world. Here a start is made even with the phenomenon of time, with the beginning and what goes on after it. And God? God was always there. God did not exist so much before time, since without time there is nothing that can go 'before'; God is outside time. Creatures only come into being in time. In a beginning before all beginnings, God makes a beginning in time by creating.

This is what everything begins with: the Bible, history and the stories of this beginning. At first there is still no light and pitch darkness prevails. Then the light glimmers and light and darkness, black and white, come into being. Later, heaven and water are made and we see the blue of the air and the waves. Then vegetation springs up on the earth and greenery shoots up before our eyes. Finally, red makes the spectrum complete, when human beings come to life on the earth, the *adam* on the *adama* (both come from the root *adam*, be red). They give the palette of creation a blood-red glow. Creation appears from the moment that the beginning is coloured.

The outline of the story

1.1 In a beginning	God created	the heaven and the earth
2.4a These are the	the heaven and the	in their being created
toledot of	earth	

The creation story of Gen. 1.1–2. 4a has an opening verse and a closing verse which clearly correspond. They indicate that three components are central in this story: God's creating; the time which extends from *bereshit* to *toledot*, from beginning to history; and the heaven and the earth.

Before God begins creating, verse 2 describes the situation as God finds it: the earth is still empty and uninhabited, and pitch darkness prevails. Against the background of this primal state God begins with the creation of light, the basic condition for all life. Without light there would be no time and no life: plants, animals and human beings need light to grow and live. God divides this light from the darkness that already existed, so that day and night come into being. For the first time there is a day: day one.

Of the two great spatial components of creation, God begins with heaven. He makes a vault between the waters, which produces a division between the waters above and the waters below. And he calls this vault 'heaven', in Hebrew *shamayim*, a plural form which is very like the plural form *mayim*, waters. So here heaven is not the abode of God, far less the place of angels or part of the hereafter, but a dam or division between the waters. The name *shamayim* literally means 'what relates to (*sha*) the waters (*mayim*)': heaven, *sha-mayim*, divides the *mayim* above from the *mayim* below. With the creation of heaven, a day passes. Evening and morning come, a second day.

The next day God turns to the part under the heaven. He makes the waters gather together in one place so that the dry land becomes visible. God calls the dry land 'earth' and the wetness he calls 'seas'. The world above and the world below are similar, since heaven comes about through the ordering of the waters above and earth comes about through the ordering of the waters below. Moreover it is striking that while it is said that God creates the heaven and the earth, it is not said that God makes the water. God makes plants shoot up on the dry land under the heaven, i.e. the earth. God gives the heaven the task of dividing the waters and the earth the task of bringing forth plants. This is not a one-off event for either, but requires continuity. Thus the vegetation which grows from the earth can reproduce itself according to its kind; young greenery propagates itself by means of loose seed, and trees reproduce themselves by fruit with seeds in, so that their own kind is preserved. When the heaven and the earth have thus been distinguished and provided with names and functions, God gives them his approval. Evening and morning come, a third day.

The heaven and the earth form the skeleton of the story, which is now given 'flesh and blood'. Here again, first all attention is focussed on heaven. God makes the lights in the vault and at the same time states their functions: the greater light is to rule over the day and the lesser light to rule over the night. The heavenly bodies make a distinction in time possible; they order time in years and days and indicate the appointed times at which festivals fall. The question is, though, whether the heavenly bodies exist purely and simply in the service of the earth. Most people are inclined to argue in the way that suits them best. From the statement here in v. 16 that the heavenly bodies have to rule over the earth, it is concluded that the heavenly bodies are in the service of the earth. By contrast, from the statement in Gen. 3.16 that the man has to rule over the woman, it is concluded that the woman is in the service of the man. So people mould the text to their own views. In Gen. 1, after the heavenly vault has been fitted out with sun, moon and stars, the fourth day is brought to an end.

Then 'everything under the vault of heaven' is fitted out. The sea and the air get their inhabitants on the fifth day and the earth its population on the sixth day. First God creates the sea creatures: these creatures, large and small, are so numerous that the water teems with them. At the same time God creates the birds which fly across the vault of heaven. And God blesses all these creatures and gives them the task of being fruitful and numerous and constantly filling the waters of the seas and the air. Just as the earth has plants which have the possibility of propagating new plants through seed or seed-bearing fruit, so too the waters give the sea creatures the possibility of propagation, for each according to its kind, and the air gives the birds the chance to fly; but the birds also need the earth in order to multiply. With this populating of water and air, evening and morning come, the fifth day.

Then the dry earth gets its inhabitants, God creates the animals, from great to small, from walking to creeping, each according to its kind. Like the plants, the animals also seem to come forth from the earth. The difference is that the plants are inextricably bound to the earth, while the animals (and human beings) are put on the earth. The animals can propagate themselves, like the plants, and are explicitly given the command to multiply. The human being is also part of this population of the earth, and is created last. Because of that, most people draw the conclusion that the human being is the 'crown' or climax of creation, under the motto 'last best'. However, these same people use a different criterion at the creation of the man and the woman in Gen. 2. From the fact that there the woman is created last, they conclude 'last worst'! And so again they bend the text to suit themselves.

The way in which the human being is created in Gen. 1 seems very like the creation of the animals. God gives the human being a blessing which is identical to that to the animals: 'be fruitful, become numerous, fill the earth' (2.28). The new development is that God speaks about 'the making' of the human being and the human being's rule over the animals. So far there had been talk of rule only at the creation of the heavenly bodies, which have to rule over the day and the night. Here in vv. 26–28 God says that human beings must subdue the earth and rule over the animals. It does not make much sense to ask whether the human being is in the service of the earth or the earth is in the service of the human being (just as it does not make much sense to ask whether the heavenly bodies are at the service of the earth or the earth is at the service of heaven), since the question here is about creation and the relations of all the parts to one another.

To conclude this creation of the living beings on earth, God gives the plants of the earth as food for the human beings and the animals. It is for that reason that the plants on earth have to be able to propagate themselves, each after its kind; otherwise the earth would be eaten bare after one session! Because propagation is guaranteed through seeds and fruits with seeds, the foodstuffs can continually remain available and the ongoing life of the other living beings is assured. The sixth day is completed by the populating of the earth with animals and human beings.

Then follows the conclusion of the whole creation (2.1–3). God completes his work, the creation of heaven and earth 'and all that is in them'. This last is a free translation of *tseba'am* (RSV 'all the host of them'), that is, everything with which the heaven and the earth are clothed or furnished. It seems as if the narrator cannot say this clearly enough: God completes (*kalal*) all (*kal*), he completes (*kalal*) his work, he stops all (*kal*) his work and he rests from all (*kal*) his work. The very last verse (2.4a) once again sums this up, with 'these are the *toledot* of heaven and earth in their being created'. This seems to have been done deliberately, so that both the word 'create' (*bara*) and the word 'make' (*asa*) occur seven times in all. Seven is the number of wholeness, perfection: the creative beginning is over. On the seventh day God rests from all his work and therefore blesses and hallows this seventh day. On this day he rests from the work that he has done.

One thing clearly emerges from this sketch of the construction of Gen. 1. This story is not just about the creation of human beings, far less about the creation of the earth, nor is it even about how human beings must behave on earth. Genesis 1 is primarily focussed on the heaven and on the earth, on the population of the heaven and the earth, and on the continuation of the 'inhabitants' of the heaven (sun, moon and stars, water above the heaven) and the inhabitants of the earth (plants, animals, human beings, waters on the earth). The heavenly bodies are permanent and do not propagate themselves. They indicate order and time on the earth. The 'bodies' on earth do propagate themselves, each after its kind: the plants through fruits which bear seeds, the animals and human beings as males and females. So Gen. 1 is not just about the creation of the beginning, but about creation and procreation, about the beginning of all things and the continuation of all things. That makes it surprising that in the discussion between supporters of the doctrine of creation and supporters of the theory of evolution a conflict is created which is not in the text. Genesis 1 is not about creation or evolution, but about creation *and* evolution in a non-technical sense. This text shows the beginning of all things as a creation of God which is aimed at continuation and development. Genesis 1 shows the beginning of creation as the beginning of the coming to be of the heaven and the earth. This is the story of the beginning of the beginning (*bereshit*) and of the beginning of the continuation of the beginning (*toledot*).

The situation at the beginning

For centuries there has been an exhaustive discussion about whether according to Gen. 1 God created from nothing (*creatio ex nihilo*) or from chaos. If the former, God is an absolute creator; if the latter, God is a kind of great organizer. To answer this question we must look more attentively at the beginning of the story and at what is written in v. 2.

After the announcement (1.1) of what is to come, namely the creation of the heaven and the creation of the earth, the narrator concentrates on the earth as readers know it. At this moment the earth does not yet exist. The earth is still *tohu wa-bohu*. *tohu* means 'desolate', 'void' and indicates the unproductive state of the earth. *bohu* means 'empty' and indicates its uninhabited state: the earth does not yet have any inhabitants, either animals or human beings. The not-yet-productive earth becomes productive the moment God says, 'Let the earth bring forth plants', and the empty earth becomes inhabited when God says, 'Let living beings come forth from the earth', and 'Let us make human beings'. The order of this creation is a given one, because first vegetation must grow to be food for these animals and human beings. The bare earth can become productive and inhabited only by God's fiat ('let there be'). The situation which precedes this and is described as *tohu wa-bohu* thus has nothing to do with chaos, and simply denotes the unproductive and uninhabited earth.

Not only is the situation of the beginning characterized by an earth without vegetation and without living beings; it is also characterized by a *tehom* veiled in darkness. This word is related to the general Semitic term *tiham*, primal ocean. The *tehom* is the abyss or the deep, the boundless surface of water which existed before the creation of the heaven made a divide between the waters above and the waters beneath. *tehom* denotes the waters which extend on all sides (especially vertically) and indicates the condition before there was heaven (*shamayim*). After the description of the earth, which is characterized by a lack of the properties that make up its later identity, the situation is now described before the earth existed. This not-yet-earth and not-yet-heaven conjure up the picture of a heaven and earth preceding creation.

Verse 2 presents the primal state as an extended surface of water which still covers the earth and is veiled in darkness. It is striking that the Sumerians, the Babylonians, the Egyptians and the Greeks all describe the beginning as one great primal sea.

Among the Greeks, '*okeanos*' is the father of all gods; the Babylonians start from the fact that in the beginning 'all lands were still sea', and the Assyrians describe how 'the waters above and beneath were there before the heaven and earth had their names'. The primal ocean and the waters in Gen. 1.2 can also be a reflection of this 'universal' view that the waters stand at the beginning of the cosmos. On the other hand, there is no indication in Gen. 1 that God himself emerges from the water, as in the other religions.

The other factor which characterizes the situation of the beginning is the *ruach elohim*, the spirit of God. But what is this spirit of God? All activities, characteristics or names by which people refer to God (*elohim*) are based on God's relation to what is created, and does not yet exist. To present God as someone who speaks or acts, as a person who sees and hears, is to regard God in human categories. The words *ruach elohim* denote God before he appears as creator and stands apart from creation. *ruach elohim* can be translated 'spirit of God', but in that case the spirit must not be contrasted with the body, nor must it take on the meaning of 'soul' or 'Holy Spirit', since these are all ideas from a later Christian tradition. It is said that this spirit of God 'hovers over the waters'. These waters comprise both the horizontal waters which cover the earth and the vertical *tehom*-waters which are there before heaven is. God's spirit hovers over this extended surface of water in the primal state. This hovering is not flying like a bird, but a vague indication of a 'moving presence': the *ruach elohim* is there and is in movement. The word *al-pene*, which literally means 'upon the face of ', indicates that apart from water there is nothing but God's spirit. In this situation of the beginning the *ruach elohim* stands for God as he is before he begins to create and for God who still does not have a relationship with 'beings', because these do not yet exist. The moment God begins to speak, God ceases to be *ruach elohim* and becomes *elohim*, the creator God.

In short, the creation story in Gen. 1.2 lets us see the situation of the beginning as a not-yet situation: the earth is not yet productive (without vegetation), not yet inhabited (without animals and human beings); the heaven is still a *tehom* or undifferentiated flood and covered in darkness; God (*elohim*) is active only as *ruach elohim* and not yet as a speaking, seeing, dividing, creating, making or naming God. When we see this, it is striking how rationally the first two verses of Gen. 1 have been constructed.

1. In a beginning	God created	the heaven and the earth
2. The earth	was	not yet distinct
The heaven	was	not yet present
God	was	not yet creating.

All the elements of the first verse recur in the second verse as phenomena which are not yet present: God does not yet create, the heaven is still *tehom*, the earth is still *tohu wa-bohu*. This is the primal situation: not 'nothing', far less a chaos which has to be ordered, but a situation of 'before everything' or 'not yet' in respect of what is to come. Even God is not yet the creator God, but still hovers over the waters as an indeterminate spirit of God.

Speaking and creating

In Gen. 1 God introduces everything, but God himself is not introduced. God is already present. Every day begins with God speaking. All eleven times that God speaks, he calls something into being. God's speaking constitutes something new. In a text or story it is usually the narrator who introduces the characters: he or she presents the information and represents the words, thoughts and emotions of the character, be this character a human or a divine figure. Similarly, the narrator of Gen. 1 introduces God as a character and makes him say things. As a creation story, however, Gen. 1 aims at something more: its value and function are based on the assumption that the border between the fictional and the real world is transcended. In the communication process between texts and readers God does not just function as a character locked up in the world of the text. God's speech acts are considered to be actions that not only take place in the inner textual world, but also are thought to have been constitutive for the outer textual world as well. Genesis 1 expresses this clearly. The narrator regularly confirms, classifies or evaluates what happened previously in God's speech. In so doing, he often echoes God's words. God's utterance, 'let there be light', for example, is a performative speech act: the phrase constitutes the coming into being of light. Only after God has said 'let there be light' does the narrator state 'there was light', as if the authority of the speech is God's, not the narrator's. In this sense the speech acts of God turn out to be constitutive for those of the narrator. Another feature confirms this special position of the divine character. The other characters are created by the words of God, although God is a character in the text. The narrator can only speak about these characters and can only let them use direct speech *after* God's creation. On the other hand, it is the narrator who presents what God says, who introduces God as a character, who presents the creatures made by God as characters and presents what they say. The significance of the story lies precisely in this ambiguity. The words of the narrator point to the words of God which point beyond the world of the text.

This is connected with a fundamental fact in the Hebrew Bible. The key question there is not how human beings deal with God but how God deals with human beings. It is not human beings who make a projection of God, but God who makes or 'projects' human beings. So the starting point in the Bible is different from that in our twentieth-century thought. Since the Enlightenment we have been accustomed to give the human subject a central place: human beings imagine a God, they make God in the human image. (Post-)Modern thought, the natural sciences, literature and art have in common the fact that they take human thought, perception and experience as a starting-point. Everything depends on the human perspective. Genesis 1 shows a fundamentally different way of looking. What is central is not the thinking, seeing or speaking human being, but the speaking and acting God. The initiative in speaking and creating and the starting-point lie with God, not with human beings.

The human being and God

Immediately afterwards, the narrator and God show what is important for them in the creation of a living being. Ten times they say that all creatures are made after their own kind, and bring forth seed after their own kind. God says this once about the vegetation of the earth, and the narrator confirms it twice. Only twice does the narrator put 'after its kind' in God's mouth in speaking of the population of the sea and the air. When it comes to the population of the earth God twice says that he is making the animals of the earth 'after their kind', and the narrator confirms this with 'after their kind' three times. Thus the origin and ongoing life of all species lie in their own kind. In other words, from their creation onwards, the point of reference for these plants and animals lies in the later ongoing existence of their own kind.

Then the human being is created.

26 God said:
Let us make a human being in our image, like us,
and let them rule over the fishes of the sea,
over the birds of the heaven, over the cattle, over all the earth
and over all the creeping things that creep on the earth.
27 God created the human being in his image:
in the image of God created he him,
male and female he created he them.

Human beings are the only ones which are not made after their own kind. Instead of 'their' kind we have 'our image', and in the case of the human being the possessive pronouns which in the case of the other living creatures refer to the creatures themselves refer to God. That means that human beings, unlike other creatures, do not have their point of reference in themselves, but in God. The human species is made to point to God.

God's language speaks volumes. He creates the plants and animals and in so doing constantly speaks in the third person; only in the case of the human being does God speak in the first person. In so doing he uses the word 'us' or 'our' three times: 'let us make', 'as our image', 'in our likeness'. God speaks and addresses himself, just as in other creative sayings he is always addressing someone. His creation takes place in communication, though here that communication is with himself. The plural 'us' in this internal monologue corresponds to the plural 'they' that God uses for human beings. In both cases ('let us make' and 'let them rule') God or the human being in the singular are connected with a verb in the plural. God, who defines the other creatures in relation to the earth, the air and the sea, defines the human being in relation to God. As readers we are so closely involved in this creation that we experience it from God's perspective. Looking through God's eyes we see that the human being is made to refer to God.

Genesis 1 does not give any concrete content whatsoever to the image of God that the human being is, so to speak, in order to avoid any 'image-building' of God. Human beings do not have the image of God, since God has no image, but are 'as' the image of God. Thus the text does not say anything about God's likeness to the human being, but only something about the human being who is in a relationship of likeness to God. However, this analogy does not offer any concrete information about God.

The image of God: a brief look at its history

There has been much discussion down history about the content of the 'image of God'. Some theologians in the tradition think that it expresses an essential likeness or relationship between God and human beings, but others think that there is a functional relationship. The first group says that 'image of God' indicates that human beings have something in their nature which is like God, that human beings have 'something' that God also has. The question then arises what this 'something' is: a physical correspondence or a spiritual likeness between God and human beings. To avoid thinking 'how ridiculous for human beings ever to have thought that corporeal human beings are like an incorporeal God', we ourselves could ask whether we have ever imagined God on four legs, or whether we haven't always assumed that God walks and stands upright. If we think it ridiculous to give God a body, why don't we think it odd to say 'God sees', 'God speaks' or 'God says'? Seeing, hearing, smelling, speaking, are all anthropomorphic descriptions of God's activities, derived from human behaviour. In other words, although already for the greater part of history emphasis has been placed on the fact that the likeness between God and human beings is not physical, nevertheless an anthropomorphic image of God has become fixed in our heads.

Thus the main line of the tradition has always emphasized that 'image of God' means that there is a spiritual likeness between human beings and God. To say that human beings are in the image of God means that they have the soul or life-principle of God, and in this sense have a share in the divine. At the present time the twentieth-century view of human beings is also influencing the discussion of the 'image of God'. Because people no longer think that the division between body and spirit is right and applicable, the dualism between body and spirit cannot be projected back on to Gen. 1 any longer either. Since we now see human beings as persons composed of body and spirit, the two indissolubly connected and influencing each other, the present-day view is generally that human beings are like God in their whole persons.

As well as this 'essentialist' notion, from antiquity there have been people who have thought that Gen. 1.26 is not about essential characteristics; human beings are like God in that they subdue the earth and rule over the fishes, the land animals and the birds. Thus the likeness between God and human beings is not essential but functional. This text does not indicate who or what human beings are, but what they must do: subject and rule. Only to the degree that human beings exercise this function are they the image of God. Thus the position of being like God amounts to human beings behaving as ruler of creation.

The problem with texts like Genesis is that a contemporary reader usually only knows the tradition or history of the interpretation and reads this history back into the text. Under the motto 'back to basics', I want to return to the basic Hebrew text itself.

Image and likeness

In Genesis 1 nothing is just by itself. Everything is made by God in relation to other things and everything is in a continuous process of becoming. This is evident not least from the double sentences with which God makes the vault, the earth, the lights and the human being. First God calls the phenomenon into existence ('let there be a vault', 'let there be lights'), and then he formulates its relationship to the other phenomena ('to make a division between the waters', 'to be a division, signs, lights'). This is also reflected by the Hebrew verb *haya*, which means both 'be' and 'become': it is really a 'being' that implies a 'becoming'. Moreover this being/becoming is essentially a 'relational being', a life of becoming in relation to others. Therefore it is wrong to separate essence from function or being from activity. These aspects are closely connected, without it being possible to reduce one to another. That is also the case with the human being as the image of God: in a specific way the human being both is and becomes the image of God, by what he or she is and by what he or she does in relation to the earth and the animals.

This emerges from the words used: 'image', *tselem*, and *demut*, 'likeness'. The word *tselem* is never used for a concrete visual representation, but only for the pure image that has no concrete content or form. It is a general word which denotes a relationship, indicates an analogy and makes present something that is absent. Thus for example the ark of the covenant stands for the footstool of YHWH on earth, and the portrait of Queen Elizabeth on British postage stamps indicates the monarchy. *tselem* can therefore best be rendered 'sign': a sign indicates something or someone that is absent. This means that according to Gen. 1.26–27, the human being is put in the world as a sign of God, to make God present. What makes the human being the image of God is not the corporeal person who stands for the (in)corporeal God, but the human being who makes God present in the world.

Throughout Gen. 1 the transcendence of God is evident: God precedes creation, stands above it and brings all things into existence. The only continuity, the only relationship between

God and the creation, is God's word and the creation which emerges from it: these point to God. The human being is created in order to be the image of God in a world in which God himself as transcendent creator cannot be present. In contrast to the neighbouring religions of the ancient Near East, Genesis does not present God as a nature god, a god who is present in nature. This is so that people do not begin to worship nature gods. Far less is the human being created in order to serve gods (as in neighbouring religions); the human being is created to make God present in his creation. Human beings are created as God's image so as to make this transcendent God visible in the world. The second word, *demut*, 'likeness', specifies this general character of the human being as sign. Thus image and likeness are not two separate concepts (in our image, and after our likeness); rather, the second term makes the first deeper. It is a particular quality which more closely defines the general character of the human being as sign. To see this closer definition we must turn to Gen. 5.3, in which the words *demut* and *tselem* also occur:

5.3   Adam lived 130 years
       and he fathered a son in his likeness after his image.

In 5.3, the order of the words *tselem* and *demut* is the opposite to that in 1.26. Here *demut* comes first, denoting the physical or genetic likeness between father and son which is primary in human procreation and which therefore comes first in 5.3. Perhaps even the choice of the word *demut* can be explained by its strong likeness to the word *dam*, blood; *demut* may have acquired the meaning of physical likeness because in Hebrew culture the life-principle is situated in the blood, *dam*. The second word in 5.3, *tselem*, indicates that the son is there to allow the father to go on living and to make his father's name present in later history. For ancient Hebrew culture this is the characteristic of children. Because there was no belief in a life after death, children and children's children were the only possible way of going on living. At the same time this illustrates the significance of the word *tselem*: children are the image of their parents not because of their physical or genetic likeness (that is indicated by the word *demut*), but to the degree that they make their parents present in later history. In this sense, human beings, as those who have come forth from God's creation, make God and his name present in the later history of creation.

But in the comparison between Gen. 1.26 and 5.3 it seems that there are also differences. In the relationship between human beings and their descendants the genetic bond (likeness, *demut*) comes first, and in the relationship between human beings and God it is being a sign (*tselem*) that comes first. And there is another difference. In 5.3 *tselem* has the preposition 'as', whereas in 1.26 there is the stronger preposition 'in, after'. This indicates that the sign/*tselem* character of human beings is stronger in relation to God than that of a son in relation to his father, whereas the likeness/*demut* character of the human being in relation to God is weaker than that between child and parent. From all this we conclude for the relationship between image and likeness in Gen. 1.26 that *tselem* indicates that human beings have been created to represent God in creation and that *demut* specifies this by describing the likeness between God and human beings. In contrast to the relationship of likeness between a father and a son, this relationship of likeness between God and human beings is not a genetic relationship but one of creation. The human being is a sign of God from the very beginning of creation to the present day.

This character of the human being through time as a sign who is like God by virtue of his/her createdness is true of all human beings: man and woman, heterosexual and homosexual, young and old. Only in so far as the human being is human can he/she be an image of God. Not only an Israelite, a Dutchman or an Englishman is an image of God. All human beings are images of God. In this sense every human being is in the world to make God present. Therefore all human beings are equal before God: the king and the commoner, the man and the woman, the Jew and the non-Jew, the Christian and the non-Christian, the Muslim and the non-Muslim. Every human being is created to represent God; every human being is a pointer to God for another human being.

The human being and the earth

28   God blessed them
and God said to them,
> Be fruitful,
> become numerous,
> fill the earth,
> subdue it
> and rule over the fishes of the sea, over the birds of the heaven,
> and over all creatures that creep upon the earth.

The human being is not a sign that refers to God, but only becomes a sign of God the moment that he/she behaves in this way towards the earth and the animals. That is expressed in the three instructions or tasks that God gives the human being in 1.28. The first is that human beings have to be fruitful and numerous and fill the earth. This cannot be understood too rigorously, since the human being is not the only species which may inhabit the earth; the animals have been given the same task. Secondly, human beings are instructed by God to subject (*kabash*) the earth: the human being has rule over the earth and can exercise control over it. But this subjection cannot just be seen as a one-sided mastery, for just as the earth is dependent on being subjected by human beings, so the human being is dependent on the fruits of the earth for his/her food supplies. The relationship between human being and earth is in a sense comparable with that between the heavenly bodies and the earth in v. 16: there the heavenly bodies are made to rule (here the even stronger word *mashal* is used) over the day and the night; here the human being is made to rule over the earth. In both cases the impression is confirmed that the issue is the establishment of a close bond among creatures; 1.28 is then about the relationship between human being and earth, which is not to be broken. The third instruction that the human being is given is to rule over the animals. This does not extend to the eating of animals, since it seems from v. 29 that the the first human being was vegetarian. The word *rada* that appears here means 'exercise lordship over'. That this lordship is relative emerges from the fact that the human being is master of birds and fishes only to a limited degree. But the human being has the power to kill these animals. Any form of rule, whether this is over the earth (*kabash*) or over the animals (*rada*), comprises a whole range of possibilities: from pure oppression, domination and trampling under foot, through rule or exercising mastery over, to care or bearing responsibility for. It is for human beings to fulfil their instructions towards the earth and animals in a way which accords with their being in the image of God.

The last aspect that God mentions is not an instruction but a gift. God gives to human beings and animals all the plants of the earth for food. Human beings get the seed-bearing vegetation and animals the green vegetation. Thus everything that has the breath of life is characterized in close connection with the earth and the plants of the earth. The instruction to live and survive is not just a task or duty; it is also a gift.

The seventh day

God also enjoys himself. He sees that everything that he has made is very good. And he takes a rest. He blesses and sanctifies the day on which he rests. Resting is evidently as important as working. There is a time to work and a time to stop working.

The seventh day is the day on which God rests (*shabbat*) from all the work. In the later tradition this became the reason for naming the seventh day sabbath. Some people even go so far as to make the seventh day the nucleus of the creation story in Gen. 1. In my view this fails to do justice to the text. Genesis 1 carefully describes the close connection between the days and the creatures. To take the seventh day from the story like a loose thread and weave one's own web with it is contrary to Gen. 1, which is itself already a network. And in this network 'being' and 'becoming', being created and becoming *toledot*, being and becoming an image of God in relation to the earth, concern and gift, working and stopping work, responsibility and enjoyment, form an indissoluble whole. It is no coincidence that after 'his work' three times and 'that he made' twice, we also twice have 'complete' and 'rest from all his work' The day of rest itself comes to bless and sanctify. Without working there would be no creation, but without rest and enjoyment one would fail to do justice to the whole of creation.

Conclusion and evaluation

A creation story has many aspects. In the light of the tradition we are accustomed to see one of them above all: the human being as the image of God and as ruler of creation. This side of the story is valuable because it can inspire us to see life as something given and not take it for granted, and in this way to respect all life. The story can inspire us as an ideal that prompts us to look after the earth and preserve it, which is considerably more than living on the basis of a balance of interests or self-preservation. But in the course of history this view has also shown its shadow sides: the human being as the crown of creation has been the occasion for seeing the human being as ruler of the world and the measure of all things. Measured by human criteria, everything is subjected, made capable of being controlled and understood. Thus the idea of the human being as ruler over creation led to an approach to creation as something made to meet human needs. Even in the modern version of stewardship, a view in which great importance is attached to environment and ecology, the starting-point still sometimes seems to be too much that the human being is a kind of anxious supervisor on whom the world (and the cosmos) depends. But neither the order of creation nor the order of things is dependent on human beings. God is not made in our image, nor is the world. The possibility of the world's survival is perhaps in part dependent on us, but the world is not our projection. It seems that whenever we find traces outside ourselves somewhere, we reduce these traces to 'us', to the ones who are seeking the traces. The others are delivered over to this human 'self'.

Genesis 1 seeks to present a fundamentally different approach: the starting point lies elsewhere than with human beings; the primacy lies outside us. The others exist in themselves and in relation to one another. The heaven is created in itself and the earth functions in relationship to it. The earth is created and characterized by the difference between seas and continents; it has a value of its own but functions only in a close relationship with heaven, its own substance and its inhabitants: the plants, animals and human beings. The plants shoot up from the earth and live in close conjunction with the sun, the rain, the animals and human beings. The animals live their own life, which is indissolubly bound up with plants and human beings. And what about human beings? They come into existence in their own distinct way, which consists in the fact that they are related both to God and to the earth, the plants and the animals. We exist to the degree that we are connected with others.

At the same time Gen. 1 also shows God as the one who stands outside the ties of creation. Therefore human beings can never see, hear or feel God directly, because that would presuppose that God is to be found within creation. Human beings can become signs of God to one another. By their behaviour and their way of living they can represent God to others, just as the whole of creation can also point to God. Because God is outside creation, God never coincides with creation and can never coincide with the images that people make of God. God is therefore also more than any human pictures in religions or stories can present of him. In this sense God escapes any religion.

This story of the beginning shows that the beginning is there before people could begin to speak: the beginning precedes the stories. It shows the primacy of what stands outside human beings and the primacy of the bond between what has been created. This insight can replace the view of the human being as the crown of creation. The question which then becomes acute is: on the basis of this story, how can we abandon anthropocentric thinking and find a different starting point for an ethic and a belief in which our own position has always been central?

Genesis 2–3: The Story of Paradise[2]

2.4b   On the day when YHWH God made earth and heaven

5   no vegetation of the field was yet in the earth,
     and no herb of the field had yet sprung up,
     for YHWH God had not caused it to rain upon the earth
     and there was not yet the human being to cultivate the *earth*.

6   And a flood arose on the earth
     and watered the whole face of the *earth*.

7   Then YHWH God formed the human being of the stuff of the *earth*
     and breathed the breath of life into his nostrils
     and the human became a living being.

8   YHWH God planted a garden in Eden in the east
     and there he put the human being
     whom he had formed.

9   YHWH God made to grow from the *earth* all the trees,
     pleasant to look at
     and good to eat from,
     and the tree of life in the middle of the garden
     and the tree of the knowledge of good and bad.

10   A river flowed out of Eden to water the garden,
     and from there it divided into four branches.

11   The name of the first was Pishon;
     this flowed round the whole land of Havilah
     where there was gold.

12   The gold of that land was good
     and bdellium and onyx stone were there.

13   The name of the second was Gihon;
     this flowed round the whole land of Cush.

14   The name of the third river was Tigris,
     this flowed east of Assyria.
     The fourth river was the Euphrates.

15   YHWH God took the human being
     and put him in the garden of Eden to cultivate it and watch over it.

16   YHWH God gave the human being a command, saying,

Of all the trees of the garden you may certainly eat,
17 but of the tree of the knowledge of good and bad you shall
   not eat,
   for on the day when you eat of it
   you will surely die.
18 YHWH God said,
   It is not good for the human being to be alone,
   let me make him a help suitable for him.
19 YHWH God formed from the *earth* all the animals of the field
   and all the birds of the heaven
   and he brought them to the human being
   to see how the human being would name them.
   And whatever the human being named every living creature,
   that was its name.
20 And the human being gave names to all cattle, and to all the
   birds of the air and to every animal of the field.
   But for the human being he did not find a help who suited him.
21 YHWH God brought a deep sleep upon the human being
   and he slept.
   He took one of his ribs,
   and closed up its place with flesh.
22 YHWH God built the rib
   which he had taken from the human being
   into woman.
   And he brought her to the human being.
23 The human being said,
   This now is bone of my bone
   and flesh of my flesh;
   this shall be called woman,
   because this was taken out of a man.
24 Therefore a man shall leave his father and mother
   and attach himself to his wife
   and they shall become one flesh.
25 They were both naked, the human being and his woman,
   but they were not ashamed.
3.1 The snake was the most cunning of all the creatures of the field
   which YHWH God had made.
   He said to the woman,
      Did not God certainly say
      that you may not eat from all the trees in the garden?
2 The woman said to the snake,

Of the fruits of the trees in the garden we may eat,
3 but of the fruits of the tree in the middle of the garden God
said,
You may not eat of it
and you may not touch it
so that you do not die.
4 The snake said to the woman,
You will not die at all.
5 Truly God knows
that on the day when you eat of it
your eyes will be opened
and you will be like God,
knowing good and bad.
6 The woman saw
that the tree was good to eat from,
that it was attractive to the eyes,
and that the tree was to be desirable for gaining insight.
She took of its fruit
and ate.
She also gave to her man with her,
and he ate.
7 The eyes of both of them were opened
and they knew
that they were naked.
They joined leaves from a fig tree together
and made themselves aprons.
8 And they heard the voice of YHWH God,
who was walking in the garden in the cool of the day.
The human being and the woman hid themselves before the face
of YHWH God under the trees of the garden.
9 YHWH God called to the human being
and said to him,
Where are you?
10 He said,
I heard your voice in the garden
and I was afraid
because I am naked
and I hid myself.
11 He said,
Who told you
that you are naked?

Have you eaten of the tree
from which I commanded you not to eat?

12 The human being said,
The woman whom you gave me,
she gave me from the tree
and I ate.

13 YHWH God said to the woman,
What have you done?
The woman said,
The snake led me astray
and I ate.

14 YHWH God said to the snake,
Because you have done this,
you are the most cursed of all cattle and all animals of the
field;
on your belly you shall go,
and dust you shall eat all the days of your life.

15 I will put enmity between you and the woman,
between your seed and her seed;
it will bruise your head,
and you will bruise its heel.

16 To the woman he said,
I shall increase the pain of your pregnancy,
in pain you shall bear children.
For your husband your desires will go out
and he shall rule over you.

17 To the human being he said,
Truly, you have listened to the voice of your woman
and you have eaten of the tree
of which I commanded you, saying,
You must not eat from it.
Cursed is the *earth* because of you,
with pain you shall eat of it all the days of your life.

18 Thorns and thistles it will bring forth for you,
and you shall eat the herbs of the field.

19 In the sweat of your face you shall eat bread
until you return to the *earth*,
for out of it you were taken.
For you are dust,
and to dust you shall return.

20 The man called the name of his woman Chawwa (Eve)

for she is the mother of everything that lives.

21 YHWH God made garments of skin for the human being and his
woman and clothed them with them.

22 YHWH God said,
Look,
the human being has become like one of us,
knowing good and bad;
and now, let him not stretch out his hand
and take from the tree of life
and eat
and live for ever.

23 YHWH God sent him out of the garden of Eden
to cultivate the *earth*
from which he had been taken.

24 He drove out the human being;
and at the east of the garden of Eden he placed the cherubs
and the flaming sword which turns to and fro
in order to guard the way to the tree of life.

Someone going on to read 2.4b, 'On the day when YHWH God
made earth and heaven', straight after Gen. 1.1–2.4, might
think that the thread of the story was begin taken up again and
spun further. When v. 5 then says that there was as yet no vegetation on the earth and that there was as yet no one to cultivate
the earth, and a bit later God creates the human being, it seems
as if the creation is beginning all over again. However, that is
not the case.

The situation at the beginning

2.4b On the day when YHWH God made *earth* and heaven,

2.5a no vegetation of the field was yet in the earth,
and no herb of the field had yet sprung up,
for YHWH God had not caused it to rain upon the earth

2.5b and there was not yet the human being to cultivate the *earth*.

2.6 And a flood arose on the earth
and watered the whole face of the *earth*.

The story of paradise begins with an indication of time, like the
story of creation in Gen. 1. This time there is no beginning in

time; rather, one moment from the process of creation which has just been described is illuminated, and more light is shed on it. We might compare it in a sense with a photograph, a particular part of which has been enlarged: Gen. 1 is then the whole photograph of the cosmos and Gen. 2–3 illuminates a small bit of it and enlarges that. The first lines at the same time show what the lens is focussed on, namely on the earth . . . earth . . . earth, and on the human being on this earth. After the opening sentence, heaven itself does not appear again, and everything turns on the earth in relation to the human being. In the first instance this relationship is above all characterized by 'not yet': the earth has not yet any vegetation and human beings are not yet engaged in cultivating the earth.

Here the text makes a distinction between the whole earth, *erets* (in the translation indicated as 'earth') and part of it: the earth which is cultivated or to be cultivated *adama* (in the translation indicated as '*earth*'). It is characteristic of the uncultivated part of the earth that the growth of plants is dependent on the 'water from above the earth' or the rain, which is attributed to God; it is characteristic of the cultivated part of the earth or *adama* that this is watered by 'water from below the earth' and is dependent for the growth of its plants on the human being (*adam*). In 2.6 the *adama* seems already to have acquired sufficient moisture quickly, since a subterranean flood which is not defined more closely wells up and waters it. Now all that the *adama* lacks is a human being (*adam*). After this beginning the text no longer speaks of the *erets*, but is solely concerned with the cultivable part of the earth, the *adama* and the *adam*.

Whereas Gen. 1 turned its attention to the heaven and the earth, Gen. 2–3 thus concentrates on the earth and the human beings on it. The chapters also differ in their names for God: in Gen. 1 God is called *elohim* (God) and in Gen. 2–3 *yhwh elohim* (YHWH God or Lord God). The name *elohim* in Gen. 1 points to God as the creator of heaven and earth. There he is the transcendent creator, the one who makes the whole cosmos, but himself remains outside the creation. In Gen. 2–3 another dimension of this God comes to the fore. The word *yhwh*, which is really a third-person masculine singular of the verb *haya*, 'become' or 'be' (thus, 'he is' or 'he becomes'), shows God in relation to the being and becoming of creation and especially of the earth and the inhabitants of this earth. Moreover, in Gen. 2–3 this God walks around in the garden on earth, explicitly comes into contact with the creatures on earth, talks about what is good for them and what is not, addresses man, woman and snake, is concerned with the growth of plants, and occupies himself with guarding the garden and cultivating the earth. Thus the name *yhwh* seems to indicate an immanent God or to point to that dimension of God which is concerned with the earth and with the history of the earth. As a combination of words, *yhwh elohim* shows that *yhwh* and *elohim* are indissolubly connected and cannot be separated. As one divine name, *yhwh elohim* therefore denotes at the same time both the transcendent and the immanent dimensions of God: God as creator who has made heaven and earth and stands outside creation, and God as the one who is and becomes in the history of the earth and the creatures on the earth. (In order to avoid constantly repeating the terms YHWH God in the text, however, from now on I shall always speak of 'God'.)

Thus these opening verses indicate what is characteristic of the story of Gen. 2–3 and how it differs from the story of Gen. 1. In Gen. 2–3, the general story of the creation of the heaven and the earth in Gen. 1 is focussed on one moment from the history of creation, namely the creation of the earth and of human beings on this earth. Here everything is concentrated on the earth; however, this is not the whole earth (*erets*) in contrast to the heaven, but the *adama*, the cultivable ground. Moreover this orientation on the earth and the people on this earth seems to correspond to the particularization of the general divine name *elohim* as *yhwh elohim*. For whereas in Gen. 1 God's general creative activity is described and God is denoted by *elohim*, in Gen. 2–3 this name is supplemented with the name *yhwh* so as also to express God's concern with the earth and the history of the creatures on earth.

The outline of the story

Against the background of an earth (*adama*, from now on referred to as 'earth') which is still bare and without vegetation, because there is no human being to cultivate it, the developments of the story begin. The opening is at the same time a climax: God makes the human being out of the stuff of the earth, *adam* from *adama*. He blows breath into the human being's nostrils and this becomes a living being. Now this human being has only to be put on the earth to cultivate it, and that should be the end of the story.

However, events take another turn. God plants a garden in Eden in the east and puts the human being whom he has formed in this garden. And he makes trees grow from the earth in the garden, attractive to look at and good to eat from. The garden in Eden forms part of the earth (*adama*), but differs from the rest of the earth which is to be cultivated by virtue of its plants and irrigation. Whereas the earth outside the garden is watered by an undefined flood, the garden itself is watered by a river. This is so richly provided with water that, just outside Eden, all the great rivers of the then known world flow out of it: the Pishon, the Gihon, the Tigris and the Euphrates. In order to show how favourable the situation there is, the narrator depicts at length the riches and abundance of the lands around which these four main rivers flow. Just before and after this description of lands and rivers, i.e. twice, the narrator reports that God takes the human being and puts him in the garden 'to cultivate it and watch over it'; here the word 'it' refers back to the earth in the garden.

The situation is perfect from the start: in the garden there is everything that the human being desires and everything that the ground desires. For the human being it is a pleasure palace of delights, and for the earth there is water in abundance and a human being to cultivate it and watch over it. There seems to be an everlasting happiness here, a paradise on earth (although the word paradise does not occur here; the word derives from the Persian). It could all have remained like this, had not God himself thought otherwise. In a situation which is characterized by sheer beauty and pleasure, he puts two trees in the middle of the

41

garden, the tree of the knowledge of good and bad and the tree of life. No one had asked for these; it would not have occurred to anyone to do so. And God issues a prohibition against eating from the tree of knowledge. By doing this, for the first time he introduces a negative aspect into a situation which was characterized by sheer goodness. He also imposes a sanction for transgressing this prohibition. The one who eats of the tree shall die. But the human being whom God has made and who has thus only just discovered life, does not yet know what dying is. In a situation which is characterized by creation and life, God himself introduces the possibility of death. It is alienating, even incomprehensible. Why is this tree put there? Why is the prohibition made? Why is death created?

God notices another lack in the garden. He says that it is not good for the human being to be alone. This is a striking remark, since hitherto from Gen. 1 we know God only as someone who says that things are good or very good. God has done everything himself and says that something is lacking in what he has made: the human being needs a help of equal status. God first makes the animals, but he does not find a companion or partner who is the human being's equal. From the rib or side of the human being God makes a woman, one who is a suitable partner. Man and woman are pleased with each other. A new rest has appeared in the garden: two people, in a garden with attractive trees and animals, but with one tree standing precisely in the middle, from which the human being has just been forbidden to eat.

A new phase begins the moment the snake opens its mouth. It is striking that it is explicitly stated that the snake was the most cunning animal that God had made. The snake is cunning enough to draw attention to the forbidden tree. By its questions, the snake opens the woman's eyes to this tree. And she sees that the forbidden tree is good to eat from, attractive to look at and desirable for gaining insight. She eats from it, her husband eats from it, and the result is that they notice that they are naked. Evidently they had not realized this previously, so it must be a direct consequence of eating from the tree of the knowledge of good and bad. But God comes along and asks, 'Have you eaten of the tree from which I forbade you to eat?' First they hide behind a fig leaf, the largest leaf that they can find, and after that they hide behind each other. But this does not really help. God discovers them and reacts to the transgression. He does not confront them directly with death, as was thought in the first instance, but with a kind of death on credit. Moreover the woman is told that she will suffer pain and an equally painful domination by her man. And the human being must begin to toil on the earth.

The human being has to go out of the garden. This is described as follows:

3.23 YHWH God sent him out of the garden of Eden
to cultivate the earth
from which he had been taken.
3.24 He drove out the human being;
and at the east of the garden of Eden he placed the cherubs
and the flaming sword which turns to and fro
in order to guard the way to the tree of life.

Punished for transgressing the commandment, the human being is driven out of the garden. This garden has become inaccessible and from now on is guarded by cherubs, a kind of angelic guard, and by a flaming and moving sword. No one can get in. The story ends with the same theme as that with which it began: the earth (outside the garden) which first had no one to cultivate it, now gets the human being to cultivate it, and from that moment can begin to bring forth plants.

Genesis 2–3 is a garden story with a clearly different framework, in which it is not the garden but the relationship between human beings and the earth that stands at the centre. The framework indicates that from the perspective of the earth it is necessary for human beings to come and cultivate it so that it can bring forth plants. From the perspective of the earth it is thus a positive development for the human being to be driven out of the garden, less so for the human being. The similarity between the words *adam* and *adama*, both from the root *adam*, 'be red', could already make the link and the reference clear. The earth (in Palestine) is red, and the principle of human life was thought to be located in the blood (*dam*), hence the fact that red blood is regarded as most characteristic of human beings. Human beings and earth resemble each other; they are bound to each other: the human being is an 'earth-being' and the earth is dependent on the human being. Moreover, this human being is made from the stuff of the earth and he/she eventually returns to the earth. Origin and name, name and surname, all this binds human beings to the earth: all the days of their life they will have to cultivate the earth in order to make it bear fruit. How could people ever have overlooked the fact that the framework of Gen. 2–3 is 'earth-centred' and that the lack of the *adam* on the *adama* is the decisive factor for the story?

It is within this framework that the garden story is played out. All the attention has always been focussed on this. Moreover, the tradition has led people to read the story in a human-centred way. From the human perspective here everything is just as it needs to be: the trees are there for the human beings, who may look at them and eat from them; the water in the river waters the garden and the human being has the task of cultivating and watching over the garden. Here God has done everything very well. The usual reading is that to test the human being God has put two trees in the middle and forbidden the human being to eat from the tree of the knowledge of good and bad. The situation is clear: the human being can remain eternal provided that he/she observes the prohibition against eating from one particular tree. In such an ideal situation is it too much to be obedient to God? Clearly it is, since the human being transgresses the commandment. Thereupon God punishes the guilty and drives the human being from the garden. The human being no longer gets attractive trees, as in the garden; from now on he has to work the earth with the sweat of his brow. In this human-orientated reading, cultivating the earth is a punishment and not God's intention.

But what if it should prove that the garden story also has important pointers towards another reading? It is striking that in a paradisal situation God creates all the conditions for the departure from the garden: he himself makes the tree of knowledge; he himself issues the prohibition against eating from the tree which he has put precisely in the middle and which must therefore draw all the attention to itself; he himself introduces the prohibition, a negative factor, into a situation which hitherto was solely positive; he himself devises the sanction of death in a garden which hitherto had been characterized by life; he himself creates help for the human being, which later proves to be a help in transgressing the prohibition: the animals with the snake as the most cunning of them, the woman as the one who desires insight . . . Could perhaps the intention have been for the human being to transgress the commandment and begin to eat of the tree of life? Who is now going against the grain: the human being who is transgressing God's prohibition or God who expressly makes all the conditions and means for the transgression of this prohibition? Might one not conclude from this that it was God's intention for the human being (after a first phase in the garden) to have to go out of the garden to cultivate the earth? That would mean that not only the narrative framework but also God in the garden story is more orientated on the earth and the place of human beings on the earth than on the human being in the garden.

The tension in this story is caused by the friction between the human-centred and the earth-centred reading. As readers we are influenced by a tradition which has read the story as a 'fall' and by our own humanity, in which we see ourselves as the centre of the world. It is perhaps difficult to take off these spectacles, to discard the assumption that in God's action everything turns on the human being and the interpretation that God punishes the human being overwhelmingly for transgressing a prohibition. However, the twofold line of the story reflects more than the simple 'disobedient human being versus the strict God' which it is often made out to be.

The tree of the knowledge of good and bad

If we look at the sub-divisions of this story, we see how at every level this double line translates into a certain ambiguity. So we shall look at the text again thematically, in particular at the tree of knowledge and the other trees, the snake and other animals, the man and the woman, and human beings and the earth.

The garden in Eden has only just been planted; God has made trees grow in it and a river waters it all abundantly. Then the human being is put in the garden, since the trees have been planted there for him. For whom else are the trees attractive to look at and good to eat? Certainly the worms will love them too, but they aren't there yet. Even the snake isn't there yet. Just one human being. For this one human being, two trees have been put in the middle of the garden: the tree of life and the tree of the knowledge of good and bad. God forbids the human being to eat of the tree of knowledge, but not of the tree of life. The story does not tell us whether the human being also actually ate of this tree of life.

The tree of the knowledge of good and bad has always stimulated the imagination. A bookcase full of literature has been written about it: all sorts of ethical insights and laws have been said to be part of this knowledge. Here I shall limit myself to this story and the Hebrew Bible; I think that an elucidation of the words can be already help to clarify it. The word *yada* denotes both a theoretical and a practical and existential knowledge; it is knowledge based on experience. Perception and experience lead to knowledge, to the ability to make a distinction and act on the basis of it. This knowledge relates to both subjects and persons; it can mean both knowing or understanding and also being acquainted with someone or knowing someone sexually. 'Good' and 'evil' are ethical terms in the Christian tradition, but in the Hebrew Bible in this context 'good' and 'bad' stand for the two poles of a totality (just as in English 'from head to foot' stands for 'the whole body'). Thus 'good and bad' stand for 'everything'; that is why the phrase is not translated with the ethically coloured 'good and evil' here. So purely on the basis of the terms, 'knowledge of good and bad' indicates a general capacity for discernment: an awareness of things, from good to bad; a knowledge which relates to everything, both persons and objects. This phrase 'knowledge of good and bad' occurs in two other passages in the Hebrew Bible. One is II Sam. 19.36, where an old man says, 'I am this day eighty years old; can I discern between good and bad? Can your servant taste what he eats or drinks?' So here we have someone whose capacity for discernment has been taken away because of his advanced old age. The other, Deut. 1.39, speaks of small children 'who this day have no knowledge of good and bad'; this refers to children who have not yet reached years of discretion. The Qumran scroll 1QSa 1.8–10 says: 'for ten years he will be counted among the boys. At the age of twenty . . . he will join the holy community. He shall not approach a woman to know her through carnal intercourse until he is fully twenty years old, when he knows good and bad'. The conclusion to be drawn from this is that 'knowledge of good and bad' refers to a general capacity for discernment that one gets when one is grown up, and that people can sometimes lose when they are very old; it is a mature knowledge or awareness of everything, from good to bad.

The human being may eat from all the trees except the tree of knowledge, but stimulated by the questions of the snake, the woman discovers that the tree is good to eat from, attractive to look at and desirable for 'gaining insight'. It is not said that she desires to gain insight into the tree; the text just says 'gain insight'. The woman associates the tree with knowledge, with understanding and insight generally. And when on the basis of this desire the woman then decides to eat from it (and the man joins her in eating without it being said explicitly that he has a desire to gain insight), the result is that 'the eyes of both of them were opened and they knew that they were naked'. The text does not say that they 'see' that they are naked, but that they 'know' (*yada*), become aware, realize that they are naked. They come as it were to years of discretion. Immediately after this, God is the one who first talks about 'having children'. It is as if God is always ahead of the things that happen; God's starting point is that attaining the capacity for discernment also comprises a sexual awareness and thus the possibility of having children. Perhaps the human himself had not yet got that far, but by eating the tree of the knowledge of good and bad the woman and the man have acquired a general capacity for discernment of which sexual knowledge is a part.

47

Another consequence of eating from the tree of knowledge is that the human being is driven out of the garden. From now on he/she must go to work outside the garden. In contrast to the garden with its many plants and trees, in which the human being saw little work rewarded, the earth outside the garden will produce little vegetation with much toil. So closely is the human being bound up with the earth that the transgression of the human being seems to have consequences for the earth itself: the earth is cursed and brings forth thorns and thistles. And the human being has to work hard to get even a reasonable sufficiency of food from the earth.

After all this, and right at the end of the story, God again forbids the human being to eat from the tree of life. For, he says, those who eat from it live for ever. And then all at once the connection between the two trees becomes clear. The tree of knowledge stands for the capacity for discernment, with sexual awareness as one of its exponents. By contrast, the tree of life represents eternal life; it stands for life without death. To eat of both trees at the same time would mean that the human being would have the capacity both to have children and to go on living for ever. That would be a bit too much of a good thing, and the earth would get over-populated. So the moment that the human being eats from the tree of knowledge, the tree of eternal life is prohibited. The way to the tree of eternal life is now barred for good by cherubs and a flaming and moving sword.

Finally, it can be concluded that much of the ambiguity of the story in Gen. 2–3 has been caused by God's command not to eat from the tree of knowledge. God puts a tree in the middle of the garden which stands for the capacity for discernment, and at the same time issues a prohibition against eating it. It could be argued that knowledge or awareness is not something that one gets immediately, but something that one must acquire. It comes from a degree of growth and a desire for insight, and requires a certain autonomy. Once acquired, the capacity for discernment cannot be got rid of again. For example, you cannot act as though you have not seen that there are men and women. But however negative the description of the acquisition of this knowledge may be, at the same time it shows that the knowledge creates the conditions for a life outside the garden. Without the capacity for discernment, which among other things forms the basis for procreation, human beings would not be able to cope on the earth. Thus on the one hand, in the eyes of God the human being needs this knowledge for a long-term cultivation of the earth, and on the other he seems to want to avoid this because of the pain and misery which are coupled with it. For pain and difficulty, misery and distress, labouring and toiling are the negative sides of the knowledge that has been acquired. Knowledge is not just the awareness of the continuity of existence but is at the same time the recognition of its discontinuity: differences emerge which can bring problems with them. The forfeiture of not-knowing is here imagined as a loss and in a certain sense it is. It is the loss of unity and simplicity. Plurality and complexity take its place. At the same time, what the human being loses is a gain for the earth. The story itself creates a tension here by playing off the points of loss on the human side against the points of gain on the side of the earth.

The snake and other animals

The snake and the animals also play their own role in this tense story. Let's go back to the garden the moment the human being is there: the trees are blossoming and the water is bubbling in the river. Without any directly visible reason, God says that 'it is not good for the human being' to be alone, and he goes to look for a suitable help for him. He forms all possible creatures out of the earth, walking, creeping and flying, and brings each of them to the human being to see what name he will give it. Here the linguistic capacity of the human being is evident: he can give names to whatever he sees around him. But it is no use, since God does not find a suitable help for the human being. As yet we do not know what this help is to be for, whether to help with the work or to banish loneliness (nor does the human being); that has to emerge from what follows.

Without a transition the story now goes on to speak about one creature: the snake.

2.25   They were both naked (*arummim*), the man and his woman,
      but they were not ashamed.

3.1   The snake was the most cunning (*arum*) of all the creatures of
      the field
    which YHWH God had made.

This snake is cunning or knowing (*arum*), whereas just beforehand the nakedness (*arummim*, plural of *arum*) of the man and the woman has been described. Really the word for naked is *erom* (and moreover we have it in 3.10, 11), plural *erommim* (which also occurs in 3.7), but in 2.25 the term *arummim* is clearly used deliberately to make a connection between naked and cunning or knowing. Both words, *erom* and *arum*, derive from the root 'or, 'be disclosed'. The relationship between naked and knowing/cunning seems to be a play on which the story turns.

By its questions the snake stimulates the woman to want to gain insight and to eat. She eats, and so does her husband. The effect is that they know that they are naked and that they are different from each other, something of which they were not yet aware before they ate. This knowledge of their difference is the basis for their capacity for procreation, for the possibility of renewing life. This transition is brought about through the mediation of the snake. Why a snake? Because the snake is the only creature that has a naked feel to it and constantly renews its skin. Consequently in the ancient Near East and elsewhere the snake became the symbol of the knowledge of a life that constantly renews itself. Here the snake mediates in communicating this knowledge to the woman. The reason why the snake addresses the woman emerges from what God says to the snake: 'I will put enmity between you and the woman, between your seed and her seed' (3.15). Moreover the snake does not address the woman in order quickly to lead her astray into consuming the fruit or because she is stupid, but because in Gen. 2–3 she represents the one who gives life: she can absorb the snake's knowledge and put it into practice. This is evident, first, from the very remarkable expression 'her seed'; normally the word 'seed' is only used of a man (the word seed occurs 220 times in the Hebrew Bible, 218 times of a man and twice of a woman: here in 3.15 and in Gen. 16.10). In this text the capacity for procreation is so coupled with the woman that this male characteristic, seed, is connected with her. That emerges, secondly, in v. 16, where God addresses the woman about her capacity to bear children: she is responsible for the bearing of children and thus human survival, however much pain and difficulty goes with that. And thirdly, in 3.20 her name specifically indicates this life-giving function: she is called Chawwa or Eve (in Hebrew *chawwa* is 'life'), since she is the mother of all that lives.

Up till now attention has been paid only to the positive side of the relationship between the human being and the snake. But there is also a negative side. The negative side of the snake is not that it tells untruths. Everything that the snake says proves to be true: the human being does not die through eating from the tree of knowledge; their eyes are opened and the result of this knowledge is that they seem like God. At least, this last is also confirmed by God in 3.22: 'Look, the human being has become like one of us, knowing good and bad.' The negative side of the snake is thus not that it tells untruths, but that it does not tell the whole truth. God makes clear precisely what part of the truth is missing. In v. 4 the snake puts the emphasis on a life without death. This seems to be right, in so far as no death directly follows the eating of the tree of knowledge, but God shows that later death does follow this life. In v. 5 the snake suggests that if the human beings eat from the tree they will become completely like God, but further on in v. 22 it seems that the human being is like God only so far as the knowledge of good and bad is concerned. The snake really presupposes a likeness between itself and the human being, and between the human being and God, whereas in 3.14–24 something completely different will prove to be the case: the snake has to bite the dust and be less than the human being, and God and human beings will not be like each other either. The snake proclaims an absolute equality and denies all differences: a life without death, no difference between God and human being, pure knowledge, no difference between human being and snake. The man and the women will become clear that this is not the case straight after their transgression, i.e. *before* the appearance of God. They discover that the knowledge that they have acquired does not disclose only similarities but also differences.

And so things can change. The snake, which was first a help to the human being, has now become the enemy. Right at the end of the story, other creatures also begin to play a role. That happens the moment when (in 3.21) 'God made garments of animal skin/hair for the man and the woman and clothed them with them.' At the beginning of the story it is said at the creation of the animals that the animals could be helpers of human beings, but it remained unclear in what way they could help. Now we see how they are helpful. They are providers of clothing: their wool or fleeces provide protection. In Hebrew this is made even plainer: the word for 'skin' is *'or*, which comes from the same root *'or*, 'be disclosed', as *arum* and *arom*. Whereas the snake helped human beings to become aware of their nakedness, the other animals help to cover their nakedness. Because the snake itself has a hairless smooth skin, this skin is not suitable for human clothing. But because it often renews its skin, the snake is suited *par excellence* as a mediator in handing down knowledge of a life which constantly renews itself. In Gen. 1 and in Gen. 2–3 only the plants serve human beings and animals for food; animals are not eaten. They provide human beings with their clothing, and so they have eventually become a help to human beings, though in an unexpected way.

The wonderful thing is that with the creation of the animals God has made helpers for the human beings which contribute to the possibility of the human beings leaving the garden. The snake, one of the creatures which God has made, helps the woman and the man to acquire the capacity for discernment and sexual awareness. The other animals ensure that the human being gets clothing which warms and protects him and her as they till the earth. These animals are not significant for the human being in the garden, but are all the more useful for a life on the earth outside the garden. In this sense one can say that God makes the animals as a help for the transition from a life in the garden to a life outside the garden. With a forbidden tree and animal help in transgressing the commandment, with providers of clothing for a life outside the garden, the story once again shows the tension between competing forces. Is there no mention here of the 'intolerable ambiguity of existence' in the garden of Eden?

Man and woman, human being and earth

The first human beings have come to be known under the names Adam and Eve. But that isn't really right. The first human being is called 'the human being' (*ha-adam*, with the emphasis on the last syllable). The word *adam* occurs twenty-two times, always with the definite article, so there is no question of this being a proper name, Adam; it is a generic name, human being. Moreover we already knew this earlier because the term *adam* for human being was also used in Gen. 1.26–28: 'God created the human being (*ha-adam*) in his image: after the image of God he created him, male and female he created them.' Here likewise it seems that *ha-adam* comprises both man and woman, and that both are like God.

At the beginning of the story in Gen. 2–3 we see that the human being is still an undivided being: made by God from stuff of the earth, *apar min ha-adama*. It is really impossible to speak of a 'he', 'she' or 'it', but because one has to use some personal pronoun, here I am using 'he' as a so-called 'gender-neutral term'. In 2.18 God takes the initiative in seeking help for this human being. The word *ezer* means a vitally important 'help' or 'helper'. Thus God is often called an *ezer*, help, for human beings in the Psalms. In itself this term denotes neither superiority nor inferiority, but here people often typically argue on the basis of something that they already have in mind: when God is called 'help', the word 'help' is seen as an indication of a superior (God as the great bestower of help); when the woman is called 'help', then this is regarded as the indication of an inferior (the woman as the man's helper). Here in 2.18, 20 *ezer*, help, is combined with *kenegdo*, a composite word in which *neged* means 'over against', 'appropriate', or 'corresponding to' and *ke* 'as', so that as a whole it means 'an appropriate, corresponding help'. Together the words indicate 'a help which suits him', 'a similar, corresponding help'. Thus God wants to divide the human being, who is still undivided and only distinct from the earth, into two equal and corresponding parts. To do this God makes the human being fall into a deep, trance-like sleep and takes 'one of his ribs (or sides), and closes up its place with flesh' (2.21). The term *tsela*, side or rib, indicates that this help is 'on the same level'. As the rabbis attractively put it: 'The woman was not taken from the head of man, that she should not stand above him; nor from the feet of man, that she should not stand below him; but she was taken from the side of the man, that she should stand on the same level.'

God has divided the human being into two partners which are so equal that the man gives himself and the new being the same name, using the male form *ish* for himself and the female form *issha* for the woman. Following the text very closely you could say that the name 'woman', *issha*, occurs before (v. 22) the name 'man', *ish* (v. 23). On the basis of the fact that the woman is created last here, some interpreters have felt able to conclude that she is therefore the best, others think that the man who is created here first is therefore the best; however, both opinions probably reflect preconceived views rather than the text. What Gen. 2.21–23 in fact shows is that the man comes into being only at the moment when the woman comes into being, and that the woman comes into being the moment that the man comes into being. It is really the species human being that is divided into two genders, man and woman. It is striking that after this creation the man above all delights in his equality with the woman: 'This now is bone of my bone and flesh of my flesh; this shall be called woman, because this was taken out of a man' (2. 23). He celebrates the equality, not the difference; and seeing that he himself is now changed, he says that she has come out of him, the *ish*. This last is not, of course, wholly true, since the woman has come out of the human being, *adam*, but in his delight the man clearly no longer remembers his previous undivided existence.

In short, God himself arrives at the insight that a simple and undivided human being is not enough. Therefore he constructs a woman out of part of the human being, so that the human being is distinct and plural. In his relation to the woman, *issha*, the human being no longer refers to himself as human being, *adam*, and thus no longer as a being that is bound to the earth, but as *ish*, man, as a being who is bound to the woman. This is the crucial point: the human being is a relational being who as human being derives his identity from his relationship to the earth, who as man derives his identity from his relationship to the woman and who as woman derives her identity from her relationship to the man.

Verse 24 follows immediately after the song of praise from the man to the woman:

2.24 Therefore a man shall leave his father and mother
and attach himself to his wife
and they shall become one flesh.

This verse is exceptional because there are no fathers and mothers at all; here we are talking about the first human beings. This indicates that the narrator is addressing the reader directly, outside the framework of the narrative. And of course this reader knows what fathers and mothers are. This narrative verse announces what the help is that the woman means to the man: she frees him not only from being alone but also from deadly danger, namely the threat of no ongoing existence. The sexual intercourse which the narrator anticipates results in one flesh or one child. An undifferentiated human being cannot have an ongoing existence because for this, human beings must be divided into male and female parts. It is God who sees the need for difference, for the creation of the plural human being, because he envisages an ongoing life and an ongoing cultivation of the earth. The narrator introduces this into the text by standing outside the course of the story and addressing the reader. Only the man and woman in the narrative have not yet got this far. They are still naked and ignorant, and their eyes have not yet been opened. So there is not yet any sexual intercourse in the garden, nor is there any question of a monogamous marriage. Only after the man and the woman have become aware of their nakedness, the difference in their sexuality, can there be something like an 'engagement'. It is as if the narrator in v. 24 is getting ahead of himself in the story and indicating where it is going. But nothing has yet happened.

The word *adam*, human being, does not occur again in 3.1–8. Only the terms *issha*, woman, and *ishah*, her husband, are used, words which are very similar. And although the snake and the woman have already been engaged in conversation, the subject is always 'you' or 'we', woman and man ('you may not eat', 'we may eat', followed by another ten verbs in the plural). But whereas during the discussion and the eating all the emphasis is on the unity between man and woman, that changes immediately after the eating of the forbidden fruit. Man and woman are immediately aware of their mutual differences. Whereas formerly there was constant talk of 'we', now they speak only of 'I' (the man seven times, the woman twice, in 3.10–13), and the man calls the woman 'the woman that you gave me' and 'she'. All solidarity has disappeared. After this God gives the relationship between man and woman its definitive form. First he addresses the woman:

3.16 To the woman he said,
    I shall increase the pain of your pregnancy,
    in pain you shall bear children.
    For your husband your desires will go out
    and he shall rule over you.

What God says consists of two parts. The first is about the relationship between the woman and her children: she shall bring them forth, but this will not be without pain and difficulty. The second part shows her relationship to the man: her (sexual) desire shall go out to her husband (otherwise there would also perhaps be fewer children) and he shall rule over her. The word *mashal* used here also occurs in Gen. 1.16 for the heavenly bodies. As was said earlier in the discussion of Gen. 1, no one presupposes that in 1.16 the heavenly bodies are the masters of the earth or that the earth is in the service of the sun and the moon. However, that is presupposed on the basis of the same formulation in 3.16. Both instances describe a relationship. That means that in 3.16 the woman is described in relation to her man in her individuality and in her relationship.

After this God addresses another conversation partner:

3.17 To the human being he said,
    Truly, you have listened to the voice of your woman
    and you have eaten of the tree
    of which I commanded you, saying,
    You must not eat from it.
    Cursed is the *earth* because of you,
    with pain you shall eat of it all the days of your life.
18   Thorns and thistles it will bring forth for you,
    and you shall eat the herbs of the field.
19   In the sweat of your face you shall eat bread
    until you return to the *earth*,
    for out of it you were taken,
    For you are dust,
    and to dust you shall return.

In 3.16 God addressed the woman, and now in 3.17–18 he addresses the *adam*, so most readers assume that these verses in their totality relate to the man. However, if these verses related only to the man, that would mean that the cultivation of the earth, the eating of the products of the earth and the return to the earth or dying would not apply to the woman. But even a woman does not have eternal life. We find a comparable situation in 3.22–24. In it God first says that *ha-adam* is like God as far as knowledge of good and bad is concerned, and this refers back to the verses in which the man *and* the woman eat from the tree of knowledge. Then God drives *ha-adam* out of the garden of Eden. No one has the idea that the woman remains behind in the garden. It is obvious that these verses relate to man and woman.

But what precisely is said in 3.17–19? In the first sentence (3.17a), God criticizes the man for having listened to the voice of his woman and not to God, and this criticism must relate to the man. The second part of what God says (3.17b–19) is about the relationship between the human being and the earth. Thus

God connects the relationship between man and woman with that between the human being and the earth and that between the human being and God. At the same time he introduces a hierarchy: the relationship between man and woman in which the woman has her own task (3.16) is embedded in the relationship between the human being and the earth in which the human being has his own task (3.17b–19) and this is embedded in the relationship between God and human beings in which the human beings has his own knowledge (3.22–24). The connection between all these relationships is represented graphically by the Hebrew: the words *adam* and *adama* and the words *ish* and *issha* show that both the human being and the earth and the man and the woman are closely related to each other. Furthermore, a visible line also runs between *adama* and *issha* on the one hand and *adam* and *ish* on the other. The text describes *issha* or the woman as the one who brings forth children and is the mother of everything that lives, and *adama* or the earth as that from which plants, trees, animals and human beings come forth. The similarity is clear: the feminine ending –*a* in *adama* and *issha* depicts the life-giving character of both. Thus the male forms *ish* and *adam* also express their own functions: the man is the one who has rule over the woman and the human being is the one who has rule over the earth. So the mutual relations in Gen. 2–3 seem to be very closely interwoven. This is to be indicated as follows:

adam: *adama* = *ish*: *issha* = rule: give life

In the network of relationships woven by Gen. 2–3, man and woman and human being and earth are both distinguished from each other by tasks and functions and necessarily bound up with each other. In that network, man as a human being is dependent on the earth, since this is his beginning and end-point and his source of food, and as man he is dependent on the woman, since she is the one who gives new life. As a human being the woman is dependent on the earth, since this is also her starting and ending point and source of food, and as a woman she is dependent on the guidance and control of the man. The earth is dependent for the production of plants on the human being who cultivates it.

The life in the singular with which the text began, an earth in the singular and a human being in the singular, has evolved steadily into a plural life. This is a life of mutual distinctions but also of components which are essentially dependent on one another: man and woman, human being and earth. In 2.23 the man celebrated the woman and in particular praised what the two of them had in common. Their relationship was based only on that in which they corresponded to one another. Only when they have become aware of their differences is a real partnership possible: a partnership on the basis of similarities and differences.

The narrator

The narrator in Gen. 2–3 is omniscient: he knows what God thinks, what God says, what the characters say, that the snake speaks, what the garden looks like, what rivers flow where, what the trees in the garden are called. He knows everything, but like most narrators he keeps outside the story and does not appear as a figure in it. Only once does he come forward and address the reader directly:

2.24   Therefore a man shall leave his father and mother
and attach himself to his wife
and they shall become one flesh.

The personal view with which the narrator interrupts the story comprises three components. The first is 'his father and mother'. These terms imply that the persons denoted by them precede the man, that they are present at the beginning of his life and bring him up as an independent being. The second component is 'leave': the man wants to leave his father and his mother to stand on his own feet. Just as the father and mother indicate the years of childhood, so leaving them expresses the man's transitional phase from years of childhood to a more independent form of life. The third component is 'attach himself to his wife' and 'become one flesh', which marks the man's adulthood; he can have sexual intercourse with his wife and they in turn can become father and mother. Moreover it is striking that whereas the whole story is written from the perspective of the human being or the man and the woman, the narrator who is now speaking automatically shares the perspective of the man (he does not say, 'when the human being leaves his or her father and mother'). In short, in 2.24 the narrator offers his vision of the development or the growing up of the man and presents this directly to the reader.

The narrator presents this personal message at the moment when in Gen. 2 God has shown himself to be one who creates and nurtures the human being. God exists before the human being, stands at the beginning of the human being's life and provides him with help and capabilities. Here the position of God in Gen. 2 is in a sense to be compared with the position of the father and the mother in the narrator's verse. Moreover the reader can understand the word 'leave' in 2.24 as an instruction. Just as a man leaves his father and mother to become independent, so too must human beings, man and woman, transgress God's commandment, 'leave him', to stand on their own feet. This universal truth, namely that all parents are left by their children, is made clear in 2.24 by the word 'therefore': 'therefore the man must leave his parents'. The man must take the step towards independence himself. You cannot get freedom, you can only take freedom. Perhaps one can speak of a 'necessary disobedience'. This disobedience is necessary not only from the perspective of the man or the human being, but also from the perspective of the parents and God, since both bring up the human being to be independent. The human being, too, must attain a certain independence, for what can God do with cultivators of the earth who cannot stand on their own feet, cannot take decisions themselves, but always remain dependent? The narrator says it himself in 2.24: only by leaving his parents can a man become independent and assure himself of a life with wife and children.

The moment that one begins to realize that 2.24 is an account of the man's growing up and that a similar kind of behaviour can be seen in the human being towards God, the reader can ask whether Gen. 2–3 as a whole is not a reflection of this process of growing up or becoming adult. In that case this account of the garden of Eden is a picture of a harmonious youth in which the human being is in unity with the world around him/her. The limits which God sets, the prohibition and the sanction on the transgression of the prohibition, are comparable to the position occupied by parents. The limits which they set are there to protect against pain, misery and death. The phase of the transgression of the prohibition then stands for puberty, in which the woman and the man come to years of discretion. From this perspective it is also not so odd for the woman to be the one in whom the desire to know first crops up, since, as everyone knows, her puberty begins earlier. In puberty, in the years of going beyond the limits which have been set, girls and boys acquire capacities for discernment, sexual awareness and the capacity to procreate. It is a necessary phase, since precisely by going beyond the set limits which were intended to protect them as children, they attain insight and autonomy. In this way the necessary conditions for an adult life and for the maintenance of life are fulfilled. Finally, the period of adulthood begins with the man and woman being driven out of the garden. The unity with things is lost; differences and pain take its place; continuity becomes discontinuity and simplicity complexity. And so the story of paradise can be read as a parable about the human maturation process.

The narrator gives very much of a guiding hand not only in 2.24 but also elsewhere. Not only does he make the characters speak and act, but he also adds a dimension of judgment everywhere, passing a value judgment on it all. He then guides the reader to pass a positive verdict on certain things and a negative verdict on others. Thus the narrator has given the whole garden scene such a form that the reader evaluates it positively: the extensive and lyrical description of the rivers and the lands round which they flow, the lands where gold and precious stones are to be found, have nothing to do with the story and making the garden, but they do make the reader think: 'This is an ideal situation, how splendid to live in such a resplendent garden!' Even God's prohibition against eating from the tree of knowledge does not disrupt this picture. Factors to the contrary, like the fact that God puts this tree in the midst of the garden, talks about death, forbids something, says that something is not good, makes creatures which do not completely meet human desires (2.20), all count for nothing in the description of the beauty of the garden, in the feeling that the narrator evokes that 'it is good like this'. The opposite is the case in 3.1–7 in the discussion between the snake and the woman. There the narrator puts all the emphasis on the prohibition and the transgression of the prohibition, which lead the readers to pass a negative judgment on this growth towards adulthood. The desire for insight, for understanding, for the knowledge of good and bad, is indicated here in such a way that the readers who normally regard this as a good thing pass a negative judgment on it. Although the world 'sin' does not occur anywhere in Gen. 2–3, most readers tend to supplement the text with the concept of sin. But the final result is not sheerly destructive, for the human being has come on to the earth, and that is the place where the readers are to the present day. Without the transgression that would not have been the case. Nevertheless, many of us are inclined to pass a negative verdict on the departure from the garden. You could call this the 'paradox of paradise': human beings only become adult and free by transgressing the divine commandment. Much has been lost, but more has been gained.

Readers up to the first century after Christ[3]

The narrator narrates and the readers get to work on texts. They make the texts their story. And they read them, each in his or her own time and place: they understand the text against their own background and as an answer to their own questions. Therefore the readings of texts continually change. This applies even more strongly to texts which are very important for the society in which they are read. And it applies above all to stories of the beginning, in which readers are often more influenced by the previous tradition of reading and believing than by the text itself. Something like this also emerges in the case of Gen. 2–3.

This text is constantly read anew. But in the end one interpretation, namely that of Augustine about the fall and original sin, has exercised such an influence on the Christian interpretation that now, sixteen centuries after Augustine, we are still constantly inclined to regard his interpretation as the natural one and the only good one. Thus you, the reader, may have thought now and then, 'Hey, there's something quite different in the story of paradise from what I'm reading here'. In that case you have ideas in your head which have been taken from this tradition of faith. To indicate how Gen. 2–3 has become people's own story and how these stories have functioned in successive historical periods, I shall now give a short survey of the most important interpretations of this text. Because of the limited space available, this survey can only be schematic and generalized.

Written as a creation story in the tradition of Hebrew faith, Gen. 1–3 was first of all read within the Jewish community. Three views are to be distinguished in the Jewish tradition. The first view is that the discovery of nakedness is the most important theme of Gen. 2–3. The fact that God makes clothes for the first human beings forms the climax of the story, because at this moment culture comes into being. A second view is that the story is about the growing up of human beings: we have already seen some elements of this above. The third and most widespread view is that through the sin of the first human being the harmony between God and humankind was broken, and this sin made the institution of marriage necessary in order to procreate children. Moreover, according to many people procreation is the main theme of this story. This emerges from the most important task which God gives to human beings: 'Be fruitful and multiply and fill the earth.' Thus procreation is part of creation. Perhaps it is better to put things the other way round: in the Jewish marriage law procreation has a central place, and this is supported by referring back to the creation story. So important is this precept thought to be that when a marriage remains childless the husband is obliged to divorce his woman so that he can have children by another woman. Consequently even divorce laws are formulated with a reference to Gen. 1–3.

Because procreation is thought to be very important, even polygamy is accepted as an extension of the possibility of having children. By contrast, homosexuality is forbidden because this form of sexuality does not produce any children. On the other hand, sexual intercourse with slave girls is regarded as legal, certainly if one's own wife has no children. The levirate marriage (that is, a marriage in which the brother of a dead man has to have intercourse with his widow so that the resultant child can be regarded as the child of the dead man and his name can be preserved in history) is another regulation which emerges from the need not to go on living without children. Of course it is a characteristic of this Jewish marriage legislation that the regulation has been written by and for men: polygamy gives men, but not women, more children; infertility is supposed to be above all an evil which befalls women, otherwise it does not make much sense for the man to marry again; the divorce regulations give only the husband the possibility of divorcing. In short, the main tendency in Judaism is to read Gen. 1–3 as a story which is about the origin of marriage and shows procreation as *the* task of creation.

Genesis 2–3 similarly appears in the framework of the problem of divorce in Matt. 19.1–12. Jesus is asked to give an answer to a question from Pharisees about the legal reasons for divorce. Like so many other Jewish teachers before him, here Jesus uses Gen. 2–3 to illuminate this question.

Matt. 19.3–6 And Pharisees came up to him and tested him by asking, 'Is it lawful to divorce one's wife for any cause?' He answered, 'Have you not read that he who made them from the beginning made them male and female, and said, "For this reason a man shall leave his father and mother and be joined to his wife and the two shall become one?" So they are no longer two but one. What therefore God has joined together, let no man put asunder.'

'What therefore God has joined together, let no man put asunder.' In particular this last sentence is a shock to those who ask the question. For within Jewish discussions of divorce the freedom for a man to divorce is a right and sometimes even a duty. Here, however, Jesus does not give an answer to the question about the grounds for divorce put to him, but quite simply forbids divorce. In the Jewish tradition infertile women were regarded as cursed, but Jesus does not share this view. The Jewish view is to be explained from the notion that the aim of marriage is to have children. Jesus thus differs from this: on the one hand he gives equal rights to the wife (a phenomenon hitherto unheard of) and on the other he does not correct marriage exclusively with procreation. With this view Jesus terrifies his disciples so much that they reply, 'If such is the case of a man with his wife, it is not expedient to marry.' Two things are striking here for the interpretation of Gen. 2–3. Only here in the Gospels is there a reference to Gen. 2–3, and here the only issue is one of divorce. This question is treated by means of a text from the Torah or Hebrew Bible. Here we do not have an exposition of Gen. 2–3, but only a discussion of the question of divorce. The consequence has been that for later Christian tradition, Gen. 2–3 has been exclusively connected with discussions of marriage and sexuality. The second aspect which deserves mention is that the idea of sin does not occur in connection with Gen. 2–3 in the Gospels.

Sin as an interpretation of Gen. 2–3 entered the Christian tradition through Paul's letter to the Romans (5.12–14). In it Paul describes redemption through Jesus Christ as a liberation from the sin into which we fell as a result of the first human being.

Rom. 5.12 Therefore as sin came into the world through one man and death through sin, and so death spread to all men because all men sinned . . .

Sin came into the world through one human being, the first human being that God created. This sin brought death into the world. Therefore all human beings after this first human being were to die because they were all to sin. Thus through the first fault death became a universal fact. Redemption by Jesus Christ is to be understood against this background: only through Jesus Christ can anyone be saved from sin and death.

In another letter, I Timothy, an author who is not Paul has

expressed his view on the position of men and women in the church. To give authority to his letter he has written it in the name of Paul. Here another facet of Gen. 2–3 is illuminated:

I Tim. 2.8–15 I desire then that in every place the men should pray, lifting holy hands without anger or quarrelling; also that women should adorn themselves modestly and sensibly in seemly apparel, not with braided hair or gold or pearls or costly attire but by good deeds, as befits women who profess religion. Let a woman learn to listen with all submissiveness. I permit no woman to teach or to have authority over men; she is to keep silent. For Adam was formed first, then Eve; and Adam was not deceived, but the woman was deceived and became a transgressor. Yet woman will be saved through bearing children, if she continues in faith and love and holiness, with modesty.

As in the Gospel of Matthew, here a particular notion or view is supported by connecting it with a text from the Hebrew Bible. So here Gen. 2–3 is used to demonstrate the modest and even subordinate position of the woman. Because the woman is the last to be created in Gen. 2–3 (but not in 1.26, so no reference is made to that), the author concludes that she is therefore inferior. While the authentic Paul in his letter to the Corinthians declares, 'I would that all were unmarried like myself', the 'Paul' of I Timothy insists that both men and women should marry and have families. While Paul himself in Gal. 3.28 states that 'there is neither Jew nor Greek, there is neither slave nor free, there is neither male nor female; for you are all one in Christ Jesus', another author using his name tries to impose his view that women must occupy a subordinate position. In history two elements from I Timothy had much influence on the later interpretation of Gen. 2–3, namely the ideas of the fall and of the subordinate position of the woman.

Readers in the second and third centuries after Christ[4]

In the second and third centuries after Christ the Christian movement grew. During this period Christians did not hold the view that the transgression in the paradise story was of a sexual

66

kind. On the contrary, deliberate participation in procreation was collaboration with God and continued God's work of creation. Sexual intercourse was not sinful, but part of God's original and 'good' creation. Thus these early Christians (including Clement of Alexandria) confirmed the traditional Jewish conviction that lawful procreation is a good deed. Certainly they differed from the Jews in rejecting polygamy; their view was that only monogamous marriage was instituted by God in the garden of Eden. They also rejected divorce, following Matthew 19.

Christians in this period do not so much regard sexual intercourse as the transgression which Adam and Eve began but see disobedience as a sin against God. The first human beings did not obey God's commandments, and for that they were punished with death. Certainly in these centuries, generally speaking, Christians believe that God endowed human beings with a free will. Genesis 1.26–28 indicates that God made the human being as the image of God, and that the human being is given lordship over the creation and the capacity for independent action and government. Because God has clothed the human being with 'royal' dignity, the human being is in a position to make a choice between good and bad and act accordingly. The view was added that in creating the human being God gave the gift of moral freedom. But the first human being misused this gift and as a result death came to succeeding generations.

In these centuries, in which the Christian movement was not yet an accepted religion in the Roman empire, the view that God had created the human being in his image was dangerous. On the basis of Gen. 1–3, Christians could come to the conclusion that all human beings are equal and of equal dignity before God because they are all in the same degree the image of God. They used this view as an argument in favour of their right to choose Christ freely and as an argument against emperor worship and the hierarchical social order. In so doing they presented an open challenge to the Roman system of government, which was characterized by a strictly regulated hierarchy. At the end of the second century and in the course of the third century the Christian movement spread to all corners of the Roman empire. To workers and slaves and to anyone who would hear it, the good news was preached, and with it the idea of the human being as the image of God and of free will over which they had control. Because these Christians had no respect for the Roman governors nor even for the emperor or for the Roman gods, and threatened to replace the Roman pantheon of gods and goddesses with one God, who had created all human beings equal, they were undermining the foundations of society. In a society half of which consisted of slaves – in other words, men and women who were regarded as possessions – to declare that all human beings were equal could lead to an outright revolt. Thus from the Roman perspective the persecution of Christians was very understandable. But despite all the oppression, precisely this revolutionary belief in the equality of all men and women (something that the Christian movement defended on the basis of the Jewish creation story) was very attractive to many people.

Readers in the fourth century after Christ[5]

At the beginning of the fourth century the emperor Constantine was converted to Christianity, and Christianity became the official state religion. As a result of this changed social situation, the view of the creation story also changed. It was Augustine (born 354 CE) who developed the theory of original sin in connection with Gen. 2–3. More than a thousand years after Genesis was set down in writing, Augustine was thus the first to assert that this text relates to original sin. He did not emphasize freedom of the will and the 'royal dignity' of human beings, but the slavish subjection of human beings to sin: human beings are not in a position to control themselves, certainly when it comes to the sexual drives. Therefore free will is an illusion.

Augustine characterized in negative terms what had previously been depicted with positive words: image of God, free will, freedom, self-control. The first human being got freedom as his birthright, but his desire to know and rule proved too great a temptation. This desire for freedom and self-control emerged from the tree of the knowledge of good and bad, and stands precisely for its danger. Led astray by the desire for autonomy, the first human being found himself in a situation of wretched slavery. Adam's sin is the disobedience which arose from the desire for autonomy. God punished Adam for this, and in him all human beings, who from that moment have been corrupted and changed. Augustine proves this not so much on the basis of Gen. 2–3 (which says nothing of the sort) as on the basis of Rom. 5.12. There Paul says that universal death came with the sin of the first human being, 'given the fact that all sin'. Augustine interpreted this as: universal sin (and not universal death as in Paul) came over human beings with the sin of the first human being. In fact Augustine changes one little word, *eph'hoi*, 'given the fact that', into 'in whom': 'in whom all human beings have sinned'. Thus Augustine can draw the conclusion that with the first human being, the whole human race has been irreparably damaged by sin. Augustine's exposition is in fact to a high degree determined by his christology, his view of Christ. According to Augustine, Christ came in order to free human beings from original sin. And original sin came into the world with the fall of Adam and Eve. Augustine's view is not so much an exegesis of Genesis as a reading of Genesis through the spectacles of Paul.

The world had changed considerably by the end of the fourth century. Christianity was no longer a dissident sect as before. Having been persecuted and oppressed by Rome for around three centuries, after the conversion of the emperor Constantine in 313, within a couple of generations the Christian religion had gained a firm position as a state religion. Bishops were now no longer persecuted or martyred, but given tax exemption. They got power, respect and influence at court. The churches became more powerful and richer. The traditional notions of human freedom in a politically hostile structure no longer applied. What for centuries had been the basis and motive power for free will, namely human freedom and a personal choice for Christianity against the Roman religions, now changed. Augustine formulates the new insights which fit this time better. He indicates that all human beings find themselves in the same sinful situation because of original sin. Everyone's impotence is so great that no one can any longer be nominated to power or government on the basis of their own qualities, but only on the basis of 'being appointed'. For the other, ordinary, sinful human beings that means that they have to accept the political and ecclesiastical power which is appointed over them.

Readers after that[6]

In the fourth century and afterwards Augustine's doctrine of original sin became the dominant view in the Catholic and later also in the Protestant tradition. Possibly the social circumstances in which the church increasingly entered the world and the world increasingly entered the church contributed to the spread of this view. The recognition of human sinfulness contributed to the maintenance of the *status quo* and the consolidation of the power of those who were appointed over men and women. Possibly the fact that in the Christian tradition the Hebrew Bible was read only through the spectacles of Paul also reinforced this view. Original sin had become a necessary basis for demonstrating redemption through Christ. But possibly there is another reason for the spread and general acceptance of the doctrine of original sin. Many people need logic or order in the world. They want to know the cause of their suffering. Many people have asked the question, 'Why has this disaster happened to me and not to someone else? Why me?' Feelings of guilt, punishment and sinfulness then offer the certainty that such events are not arbitrary but follow the law of cause and effect. Here the cause lies outside the sphere of any individual, outside God; it lies with the first human being. So the doctrine of original sin gives religious form to the conviction that humankind does not suffer and die completely arbitrarily, but with reason. Suffering, pain and death, evil, came through the first human being; suffering proceeds from primal human failings.

Despite all these reasons, there has always been a trend in Christianity that has been opposed to Augustine's view. There was already much opposition to Augustine's views in his own day. In his time and after it, the reading from the first centuries continued. It found its most important spokesman in the Franciscan John Duns Scotus (1266–1308), and was later continued by other Franciscans. They argued that the aim of the redemption which Christ brings is not liberation from sin but the exaltation of human beings to take part in the divine life. Moreover the human need for grace does not derive from the original situation of sin, but is given with human creatureliness, as a result of which no human being can be divine and immortal. Even without the sin of the first human being, Christ would have come on earth; in other words, sin is not necessary to make the redemption by Christ meaningful. Thus alongside the pessimistic view of the Augustinian tradition an optimistic Franciscan line arose and continued. Martin Luther, an Augustinian monk, saw to it that only the Augustinian interpretation was taken over into the Protestant tradition.

Up to the present day, in church traditions, both Catholic and Protestant, the Augustinian exposition has been elevated to a norm. It has provided the spectacles with which we are still accustomed to read, and if we then bring out the other elements in the story, it is difficult to ignore this human and sin-centred view.

Stories of the beginning

It is fascinating to see how such a story of the beginning as that given in Gen. 2–3 has been expounded, filled in or focussed in the course of history. Thus one and the same text has been used to support both polygamous marriage and divorce, monogamous marriage and opposition to divorce. Whereas at first sexuality and procreation were regarded as facts of creation, later sexuality was indissolubly bound up with human corruption. Thus a story in favour of sexuality and procreation later turned into a story against sexuality. It is intriguing that Gen. 1–3 is read both as a story of liberation and as a story about the fall. For people in the early Christian period it was a text through which they could oppose inequality, the slavery and oppression of the Roman rulers. Which of them could have supposed that some centuries later the same text would serve to keep people down under a government with a hierarchical structure, in state and church? Genesis 1–3 has been far more than just a story in all these successive historical periods. It has given people building bricks for their own view of humankind and the world the view which has served to orientate their life. On the one hand it has served to combat Galileo and Darwin, to support the status quo, to suppress women, and on the other to liberate men and women as beings who are all made as the image of God in this world.

Another striking thing about all these explanations stimulated by Gen. 1–3 is that they put the human being in so central a position. Whether it is a matter of free will or marriage, of a position for or against divorce, original sin or autonomy, in these chapters people principally look at the few verses in which human beings appear (1.26–28; 2.24; 3.1–17). As if the cosmos is not greater than this couple! From the earliest Jewish to the latest Christian interpretations everyone has always begun with the human being as the centre, the climax and the crown of creation. But the fact is that the heaven and the earth in Gen. 1, and the cultivation of the earth in Gen. 2–3, are not just incidental, but are the main point. Not only the text of Genesis itself but also another extended creation story in the Hebrew Bible, Job 38–40, indicates this. Only a few writers have compared the creation story in Job 38–40, which is presented from the perspective of God, with this story in Gen. 1–3. Anyone who makes the comparison will notice that it is wrong to regard the human being as the spearhead of creation. The mockery in God's speech in Job can clearly be felt when he says: 'The human being central in creation? Oh yes, of course, and therefore he knows precisely how everything is made; he knows where the clouds come from, when the rains fall, how the animals behave with one another?' God shows Job a creation in which human beings are a minuscule link in the whole. And are these links to regard themselves as the centre of creation? They should be glad that they appear on the periphery. Do these people want their idea of what is the cause of pain and suffering, of what is right and wrong, to be imposed on the world?

Aren't all these ideas about righteousness and justice based on causality, on the idea that everything must have a particular cause and one which human beings can understand? We have seen how feelings of guilt and sinfulness and the certainty that emerges from that furthered the spread of the doctrine of original sin. Better guilt than inexplicability: many people find it safer to apply the laws of cause and effect to the whole creation than to go around in uncertainty. The creation stories in Job and in Gen. 1–3 show us that God's view embraces the whole of the cosmos, of which the earth and human beings make up only a small part. In the relationship between human beings and earth, in the relationship between human beings and God, earth has the priority. So I shall end with a remark which is similarly bound up with my own time. In the twentieth century, in which the freedom of the individual has come to be so central, and thought and action focussed on human beings has been absolutized, the loss of the earth has become a more pressing problem than that of free will or original sin. If there can be any talk of original sin, then perhaps this is only because human beings continue to make themselves so central to their thought and action at the expense of the earth.

Genesis 4–5: The Stories of Brothers and Fathers[7]

Genesis 4.1–16: The story of Cain and Hevel

4.1   The human had intercourse with Eve his wife,
    she became pregnant,
    and she bore Cain
    and she said,
        I have produced a man with the help of YHWH.

2   Again, she bore his brother Hevel.
    Hevel was a keeper of small cattle
    and Cain was a tiller of the *earth*.

3   It happened after some time
    that Cain brought an offering of the fruits of the *earth* to YHWH.

4   Hevel also brought (an offering) of the firstborn of his small cattle and of their fat parts.
    And YHWH looked on Hevel and his offering,

5   but on Cain and his offering he did not look.
    Cain became very angry
    and his face fell.

6   YHWH said to Cain,
    Why are you angry,
    and why has your face fallen?

7   Is it not the case that if you do good
    there is raising up (of your face)?
    And if you do not do good,
    sin lies lurking at the door?
    Its desire is for you,
    but you can master it.

8   Cain said to Hevel his brother . . .
    And it happened that when they were in the field
    Cain rose up against Hevel his brother
    and killed him.

9   YHWH said to Cain,
    Where is Hevel your brother?
    He said,

I do not know.
Am I my brother's keeper?
10 He said,
What have you done?
The voice of the blood of your brother is crying out to me
from the *earth*.
11 Now you are cursed from the *earth*
which has opened its mouth
to receive the blood of your brother from your hand.
12 When you cultivate the *earth*
it shall no longer yield you its strength,
you shall be a fugitive and wanderer over the *earth*.
13 Cain said to YHWH,
My sin/punishment is greater than I can bear.
14 Look, you are driving me today from the face of the *earth*.
I shall be hidden from your sight,
and I shall be a fugitive and wanderer over the earth.
And it shall be
that anyone who finds me
will kill me.
15 YHWH said to him,
Therefore, anyone who kills Cain,
vengeance shall be taken on him sevenfold.
YHWH gave Cain a sign
to prevent anyone who found him
from killing him.
16 And Cain went away from the face of YHWH
and settled in the land of Nod east of Eden.

The story of Cain and Hevel is usually known as the story of
Cain and Abel, on the basis of the Greek translation of the
Hebrew Bible. But the Hebrew text has Hevel, a word which
has a meaning of its own and which, as we shall see, plays an
important role in the text. This story begins with the same main
characters as that of Gen. 2–3: the human being and his wife.
The last verse of the story, 4.16, shows that all this took place
close to the garden of Eden, for after all the events Cain has to
go away, and he settles in the land of Nod, east of Eden. The
name of the land, Nod, means 'land of the wanderer', or 'land
of the nomad', and is a word-play on 'I shall be a wanderer and

a nomad upon the earth'. Thus Nod is not a restful place, and others settle elsewhere. No one ever goes into the neighbourhood of Eden again. In terms of persons and place the story in Gen. 4.1–16 shows an affinity to Gen. 2–3. On the other hand, this story differs by virtue of the characters Cain and Hevel, who appear together only here, and by the naming of God, who here is no longer called YHWH God as in Gen. 2–3, but YHWH. This YHWH acts here in relation to human beings and the earth. From this we can draw the conclusion that Gen. 4.1–16 is an independent unit of text which continues the line of the preceding story of paradise.

The beginning of the story

The story begins with two people, the man and his wife. These had acquired knowledge shortly beforehand, and the first thing that they do is to put this knowledge into practice: the man has intercourse with his wife. This has an immediate effect. The wife becomes pregnant and bears a son, Cain. Soon afterwards she bears another son, Hevel. After the sons have been born, the man and his wife disappear from the story. Their only function here is to introduce new persons.

The two sons are presented in somewhat different ways. The conception, pregnancy and birth of Cain are mentioned; moreover his mother Eve also elucidates his name. In the case of Hevel we have only, 'Again, she bore his brother Hevel.' This statement is so brief that we cannot even discover from it whether he is a twin brother or a brother who was born later. There is no mention of conception or pregnancy and no explanation of the name. The explanation which the mother gives at the birth of Cain is, 'I have produced (*kaniti*) a man with the help of YHWH' (4.1) . Here there is a connection between Cain and the verb *kana*, which means create, produce or acquire, and is usually used only in for YHWH and his creative activities. On the one hand, here Eve is referring back to the knowledge that she has acquired in Gen. 3, and on the other she is indicating that in her view there is a connection between the human capacity for procreation and YHWH's capacity for creation.

YHWH makes a contribution to the birth of her son. Together they have brought forth a man. And with this exclamation Cain is welcomed to life.

Things are different with Hevel (to be pronounced with short 'e's). His name is not explained, nor is that necessary, since it means 'vapour', 'breath' – not, however, breath which gives life but breath which is fleeting. This is the word that the book called the Preacher (Qoheleth or Ecclesiastes) constantly uses to denote 'vanity and a striving after wind' or 'vanity of vanities'. Thus this second son is as empty as the wind that blows and as fleeting as breath. Hevel also means 'worthless', 'of a transitory nature' and 'worth nothing'. Who gives a child that kind of name? Since a name indicates the programme for someone's life, the naming of Hevel indicates that he comes from nothing and goes to nothing. In the case of Hevel it is not said that YHWH makes any contribution to his birth. Certainly if he should be a twin, that is shocking: to say that only the first child has been given or been made possible by YHWH and not the second is, to put it mildly, unkind. It is also striking that Hevel is at the same time born as a brother: 'Again, she bore his brother Hevel.' Thus the first lines immediately indicate the theme of the story. It is about a man and his brother. Immediately after their birth the vocations of the two men are given briefly and in a matter-of-fact way (we hear nothing about their youth or childhood years): Hevel herds small cattle and Cain cultivates the earth.

YHWH *looks (or does not look)*

After this sketch of the initial situation the story begins. The beginning is marked by the chronological note, 'it happened after some time'.

4.3 It happened after some time
that Cain brought an offering of the fruits of the earth to YHWH,
4 Hevel also brought (an offering) of the firstborn of his small cattle and of their fat parts.
And YHWH looked on Hevel and his offering,
5 but on Cain and his offering he did not look.

When we read this, we immediately ask why YHWH looks at Hevel's offering and not at that of Cain. It seem unreasonable, even unfair. Both give something; why can't YHWH look on both of them? Why does YHWH show a gracious face to one and seem not to notice the other? It is not a question of the offering, since Cain brings as a firstfruit a gift with which his occupation provides him: he cultivates the earth and so he offers the fruits of the earth. Of Hevel it is said at greater length that he brings an offering of the best parts of the firstborn of his herd, as befits a herdsman, but the word 'offering' is not used in his case. Moreover, a comparison is explicitly created by the words 'he also': 'Hevel, he also brought an offering.' In other words, they do something similar and each brings an offering that befits his occupation. Both give YHWH something; they look to him and recognize him. But YHWH looks on only one of the two. Here it said without any explanation that YHWH looks on Hevel and not on Cain. Thereupon Cain gets angry. He is insulted, hurt, disappointed and jealous. Literally, it is said that he burned with anger. Most people (above all children) who read this will identify with Cain; they find that such injustice is also done to them.

There is no indication in the text that Hevel's offering is better. What, then, is the reason why YHWH does not look on it? One clear difference between the two brothers emerges from the four previous verses: Cain gets all the attention, his birth is narrated at greater length, and the giving of his name, Cain, is described explicitly. The content of this explanation is also high praise for Cain: both YHWH and the first human beings have contributed to the birth of this first man to be born from human beings. The birth of Hevel indicates that he just tagged along; neither the narrator nor his mother pay much attention to it. His name, Hevel, is not explained, but this name needs little explanation, since it speaks for itself. It indicates that he is transient, fleeting, worthless. He is not worth much in people's eyes. And YHWH looks on Hevel, the one who is not thought to be worth anything, and not on Cain, who so far has had all the attention. Therefore it is more probable that Cain is jealous, not because Hevel is more successful than he is, but because YHWH looks at a blunderer like Hevel, while ignoring him, Cain.

Immediately after the verse in which YHWH looks on Hevel and not on Cain, there follows a conversation between YHWH and Cain. He reproaches Cain for his anger and asks why he does not lift up his face, why he looks at no one. No one? No, with his offering Cain at any rate looks at YHWH. With his sacrifice he looks up to YHWH, but not around at Hevel, his worthless brother. YHWH criticizes Cain twice:

4.6 Why are you angry,
and why has your face fallen?
7 If you do good
will you not be raised up (your face)?
And if you do not do good,
sin lies lurking at the door.
Its desire is for you,
but you can master it.

And just before this it says that Cain gets cross and 'that his face fell'. Now this is often translated as 'his face clouded over', but here it is meant literally: Cain hangs his head and does not look at anyone. Thereupon YHWH asks why Cain's face has fallen: 'Is it not the case that if you do good, you raise up your face?' The sentence which follows is difficult: 'And if you do not do good, sin lies lurking at the door, namely the sin of *robets*.' This word *robets* is used of wild animals which lie asleep but emanate a certain threat, of tame animals which lie quietly asleep, or of wild animals which lie lurking in an ambush for their prey. In a transferred sense it is also used of disasters (a flood or a curse) which can strike at any moment. Cain is not a wild animal or a tame one, but his behaviour is compared to them. The sin which lies at the door is that Cain begins to lurk and assumes a threatening attitude towards his brother. This attitude seems like that of a wild animal lying in ambush to strike. YHWH calls this attitude a sin, and describes how Cain's desire lurks to ambush Hevel. But by the last part of his question YHWH makes it clear that it is not too late: Cain can still master this desire.

This conversation between YHWH and Cain is very important

for explaining why YHWH looks on one offering and not on the other. The first parts of YHWH's questions are all about ethical categories: being angry, doing good, not doing good; the second parts connect these with forms of looking: letting one's face fall, raising up one's face and lying in wait. In this text, looking is the highest form of a good relationship, and not looking (with face fallen) or watching in a threatening way is precisely the opposite. Looking at is looking someone in the face, in the eye. Lying in wait is not looking at someone but trying to catch them. YHWH accuses Cain of not looking directly at his brother but watching him with a fallen face in order to see that he doesn't get anything more. YHWH's rhetorical questions expose Cain's bad intentions, and he tries to compel him by his questions to do good, to raise his head and look at his brother.

The second time that YHWH speaks, he asks Cain quite directly, 'Where is Hevel, your brother?' (4.9). In vv. 10–12 YHWH speaks for the third time and accuses Cain of having murdered his brother. Only after a kind of confession by Cain does YHWH end the conversation in 4.15 and give Cain a sign to protect him. Each time that YHWH says anything, it is on one and the same theme: the relationship between Cain and his brother. This is YHWH's great concern and the continual orientation of his actions: he confronts Cain with the fact that he has not behaved as a brother. This also emerges from the fact that Hevel is always called Cain's brother, but Cain is never called Hevel's brother. Cain *has* a brother but is not himself a brother. The possessive pronouns with the word 'brother' reinforce this picture. Whenever YHWH speaks to Cain, four times we have 'his' brother and three times 'your brother'; the only time that Cain speaks about 'my' brother is in a negative sense. In this last case the emphatic word 'I' indicates that Cain puts all the emphasis on himself. Cain is not a brother, nor does he live as if he has a brother. In the way he speaks and looks, YHWH forces Cain to accept Hevel as his brother, as someone who is worth looking at and is not simply 'air', and in so doing compels him to be a brother . . . but it does not happen like that.

Cain looks and speaks

From the beginning Cain is bound up with the earth, the *adama*. After the human being has been tied to the earth for good at the end of the story of paradise, Cain is the first human being to cultivate the earth outside the garden. And the earth produces fruits, so that Cain can bring an offering of the fruits of the earth to YHWH. In so doing he recognizes the bond between YHWH, human beings and the earth. Here on the basis of Gen. 2–3 one might think that everything would be in order. Everything that is stated in Gen. 2–3 as a necessary relationship is developed here. But there seems to be one more essential relationship, namely that between the human being and his fellow human being, between the man and his brother (no attention is paid to the woman and the sister).

Cain is not so aware of this bond with his brother. It is YHWH above all who draws his attention to it. Cain is more concerned with the land and with offering the products of the earth. He reacts furiously when YHWH looks on his inept brother. He hangs his head. When YHWH tells him to raise his head, Cain reacts with silence.

Immediately afterwards Cain addresses his brother, Hevel.

> 4.8 Cain said to Hevel his brother . . .
> And it happened when they were in the field
> that Cain rose up against Hevel his brother
> and killed him.

In the Hebrew text what Cain says to Hevel has no content, although the translations often wrongly supply something like 'let us go into the field'. This speaking without anything to follow is very striking, since on the other six occasions on which something is said in the story, there is some content. This suggests that the very fact that the content is not mentioned is significant. It indicates the emptiness or lack of content in the contact between Cain and Hevel. Moreover this speaking is 'speaking with an eye to', just as Cain's looking is 'lying in wait with an eye to'. Just as the lying is no ordinary lying, but lying in wait in order to kill, so here the speaking is no ordinary speaking, but speaking which aims at liquidating his brother. Nowhere is it said that Cain looks at his brother; he is simply angry when YHWH looks at his brother. His face falls and YHWH asks him to look at his brother. When Cain reacts, his speaking without content, like his failure to look at his brother, anticipates what is to come.

The result of all this is that Cain rises up against his brother and kills him. This is described dryly and extremely briefly. The process which precedes this is given more attention than the murder itself. 'He rose up and killed him.' One could hardly put it more briefly than that. The word 'rise up' seems to be a reaction to everything that YHWH had said previously. The comparison with the wild animal is continued: Cain does not raise his head to look at Hevel, but raises his body on its hind legs and leaps on his prey like a wild animal . . . and murders him. His previous anger, his refusal to look at his brother, what he says with its lack of content, and the murder in the field, where there are no witnesses, make it clear that this is a premeditated murder.

After the murder, in his second conversation with YHWH in 4.9, Cain shows that he has not changed. The first part of Cain's answer to YHWH's question, 'Where is Hevel your brother?', is a lie: 'I do not know.' The second part is the rejection of the most important question there is: 'Am I my brother's keeper?' Cain suggests that the answer is, 'No, I am not.' The text shows that this is the core of the story: Cain disowns his brother and in so doing denies that he himself is a brother.

As a result of all this, there is also a break in the relationship which Cain has with the earth and with YHWH. He is accused by the earth, and an extended conversation with YHWH follows. After the question 'What have you done?' follow the accusation, the cursing and the punishment. Only after he has been punished with banishment from the earth does Cain react at greater length:

13 My sin/punishment is greater than I can bear.
14 Look, you are driving me today from the face of the earth.
I shall be hidden from your sight,

and I shall be a fugitive and wanderer over the earth.
And it shall be
that anyone who finds me
will kill me.

Here Cain uses the word *awon*, which means both sin and punishment. This shows that Cain recognizes that the transgression is too great and that its consequences are intolerable. Perhaps Cain now feels for the first time the position Hevel found himself in: he is now the one who can be killed. And at the precise moment that Cain finds himself in this position, YHWH protects him also. He gives Cain a sign, so that he is not killed by anyone who finds him. YHWH always stands up for the weaker brother, whoever he is. The moment that Hevel is in that position, YHWH looks on Hevel and his sacrifice, and not on the one for whom everything is going well. He accuses the stronger brother of not looking to the weaker brother, of not noticing that things are not going well with him, the weaker one; he is hostile and jealous and grudges him his happiness. Although he is warned by YHWH, Cain does not lift up his head, but rises up and kills his brother. Even after his brother's death he tries to disown his responsibility. Only when he has been punished and is himself in a vulnerable position does he seem to have some sense of what he has done. And then YHWH gives him a sign to protect him. We do not know what sort of a sign this is. Nor does that in fact matter, since for this story the only thing that matters is that YHWH protects those who run the risk of being swept away by others.

The face of the earth

Up to now it looks as if the story of Cain and Hevel is only about what the Jewish philosopher Levinas was to call 'the face of the other'. The criterion of action for a human being is not defined by his or her own autonomy but by the face of the other, which shows what is to be done and allowed to be done. That is why Cain's failure to look at Hevel is so significant: he does not look into the face of the one who is his brother. Here the focus is on the face of the one who in the eyes of his brother is 'worthless'. At the same time Gen. 4.1–16 shows what Levinas and many with him overlook, namely that the earth also has a face.

4.10 He said,
        What have you done?
        The voice of the blood of your brother is crying out to me
            from the *earth*.
11   Now you are cursed from the *earth*
        which has opened its mouth
        to receive the blood of your brother from your hand.
12   When you cultivate the *earth*
        it shall no longer yield you its strength,
        you shall be a fugitive and wanderer over the earth.
13   Cain said to YHWH,
        My sin/punishment is greater than I can bear.
14   Look, you are driving me today from the face of the *earth*.
        I shall be hidden from your sight,
        and I shall be a fugitive and wanderer over the earth.

The earth cries out. It opens its mouth to swallow the blood that drips from Cain's hands and it curses the one who shed the blood. This is the breaking-point for Cain: from now on his bonds with the earth are broken. *ata arur ata min ha-adama*, 'Now you are cursed from the earth'. The metre and the rhythm of this curse is strong (*atá arur atá min ha-adamá*), and with every group of letters emphasizes the severe blow that is dealt to Cain. Cain will receive no more fruits. He can no longer cultivate the earth and can no longer settle, but has to wander around. From now on the earth has become a labyrinth for Cain. In the previous chapter of Genesis the earth is cursed because of human beings (3.17); now the human being is cursed because of the shedding of blood by a fellow human being. The Hebrew words demonstrate the indissoluble bond between *dam*, *adam* and *adama*: blood, human being, earth. Here the earth lets its own power be seen and shows its own face.

The story shows a clear connection between the 'face' of the human being, the earth and YHWH. By Cain's face falling and blood coming into the mouth of the earth, Cain is cursed by the earth and driven from the face of the earth, and has to hide from YHWH's face. Thus the broken bond with the brother results in a broken bond with the earth and with YHWH; this break is expressed by departure from the face of the earth and the face of YHWH. So as well as a human face there also seems to be a face of the earth.

Conclusion and personal evaluation

In the twentieth century, too, it seems that human beings can give the impression that others are worthless. This happened in the Second World War, when Jews were not treated as human beings but slaughtered; or when in the colonies or in South Africa negroes were treated as cattle; or when Indians were so oppressed in the exploitation of the forests of the Amazon and were therefore simply brushed aside; or when Muslims were no longer regarded as human by Serbs nor Serbs by Muslims or Croats, or Tutses by Hutus or Hutus by Tutses. These all stand for people who have been regarded as worthless by others. It is evidently possible to give someone the impression that someone else is worthless, not a real human being like himself or herself. One only has to read the accounts. The images are blood-curdling and cry out to heaven. But in the eyes of the perpetrators one can read: 'What are you making a fuss about? These people don't count, they aren't worth so much compassion and concern.' That is what *hevel* stands for here, for those who do not count in the eyes of others. In my view the crime which is most committed is not murder or hatred, but the vacuity with which people make light of others: not anger but a boundless emptiness and indifference. It doesn't matter, the other doesn't count. Do I have anything to do with these others? Am I their keeper?

A cry is resounding through the world; blood that is shed is crying from the earth. It seems that God sometimes hears it and sometimes doesn't. God also hears the accusations against him: 'Why, God?' Moreover that is the function of these Bible stories, to show that this is the heart of the matter: being the guardian of your weaker sister or brother. The whole Bible shows that God is always on the side of the victim. It is not just a matter of a covenant with the elect people: everyone is chosen who belongs to the weaker group, the group which is denied. Together they form the people of the *hevel*s. God makes a covenant with them. God looks on them, since they urgently need it. Alas, only a few people look with him.

A creed

If I believe,
then I experience that I am here to be a sign of God
in a world in which so little godliness is present.
If I know that God keeps choosing the *hevel*s among us,
for the earth which cannot defend itself against us,
then I know how I can be the image of God:
by making God present on the earth
and looking at the vulnerable among us.

If I doubt,
I sometimes discover pointers to God in other people,
especially by looking at those who in a world of self-interest
do not attach importance to themselves,
who despite all the killing forgive one another,
who do not make evil central in their thoughts and lives
but live by particular ideals.

If I believe,
then it is that I am not only here for myself
to defend my right to exist, to survive,
to hand on my genes, to assert myself, to draw attention to
    myself,
but to look others in the eye
and to look at the face of the earth.

What I do not want to forget
is the experience of being supported by God
in whose eyes all human beings are equal,
to know that I am challenged by God
who has given life to the earth and to all these people.

Genesis 4.17–5.32: *the genealogies of the fathers*

4.17   Cain had intercourse with his wife
and she became pregnant
and she bore Enoch.
He was the builder of a city.
He called the name of the city by the name of his son, Enoch.

18   To Enoch was born Irad;
and Irad fathered Mehujael.
Mehujael fathered Methushael,
Methushael fathered Lamech.

19   Lamech took two wives,
the name of the first was Adah
and the name of the second was Zillah.

20   Adah bore Jabal;
he was the father of those who dwell in tents and have cattle.

21   The name of his brother was Jubal,
he was the father of all those who play the lyre and pipe.

22   And Zillah also gave birth, to Tubal-cain;
(the father of) all smiths, who work copper and iron.
The sister of Tubal-cain was Naamah.

23   Lamech said to his wives,
Adah and Zillah, hear my voice;
you wives of Lamech, listen to what I say.
Truly, I killed a man for wounding me,
a young man (I killed) for striking me.

24   Truly Cain is avenged sevenfold,
and Lamech seventy-sevenfold.

25   The human being/Adam had intercourse again with his wife
and she gave birth to a son,
and she called his name Seth (saying),
Truly God has given me other seed in place of Hevel,
for Cain has killed him.

26   To Seth also a son was born
and he called his name Enosh.
At that time people began to call on YHWH by name.

88

5.1 This is the book of the history of the human being/Adam.
On the day that God created the human being/Adam,
he made him in the likeness of God,

2 male and female created he them
and he blessed them,
and he named them 'human being'
on the day that they were created.

3 Adam lived for one hundred and thirty years
and he fathered (a son) in his own likeness, as his image,
and he named him Seth.

4 The days of Adam, after he fathered Seth, were eight hundred
years
and he fathered sons and daughters.

5 All the days that Adam lived were nine hundred and thirty years
and he died.

6 Seth lived for a hundred and five years
and he fathered Enosh.

7 Seth lived after he had fathered Enosh for eight hundred and
seven years
and he fathered sons and daughters.

8 All the days of Seth were nine hundred and twelve years
and he died.

9 Enoch lived for ninety years
and he fathered Kenan.

10 Enosh lived after he fathered Kenan eight hundred and fifteen
years,
and he fathered sons and daughters.

11 All the days of Enoch were nine hundred and five years
and he died.

12 Kenan lived for seventy years
and he fathered Mahalalel.

13 Kenan lived after he had fathered Mahalel for eight hundred
and forty years
and he fathered sons and daughters.

14 All the days of Kenan were nine hundred and ten years
and he died.

15 Mahalel lived for sixty-five years
and he fathered Jared.

16 Mahalel lived after he had fathered Jared for eight hundred and
thirty years
and he fathered sons and daughters.

17 All the days of Mahalel were eight hundred and ninety-five
   and he died.
18 Jared lived for a hundred and sixty-two years
   and he fathered Enoch.
19 Jared lived after he fathered Enoch eight hundred years
   and he fathered sons and daughters.
20 All the days of Jared were nine hundred and sixty-two years
   and he died.
21 Enoch lived for sixty-five years
   and he fathered Methuselah.
22 Enoch walked with God after he fathered Methuselah three
      hundred years
   and he fathered sons and daughters.
23 All the days of Enoch were three hundred and sixty-five years.
24 Enoch walked with God
   and he was not (any longer),
   for God had taken him.
25 Methuselah lived for one hundred and eighty-seven years
   and fathered Lamech.
26 Methuselah lived after he fathered Lamech for seven hundred
      and eighty-two years
   and he fathered sons and daughters.
27 All the days of Methuselah were nine hundred and sixty-nine
      years
   and he died.
28 Lamech lived for eighty-two years
   and he fathered a son.
29 He called his name Noah, saying:
      This shall comfort us in our work and the toil of our hands
         on the *earth*,
      which YHWH has cursed.
30 After he had fathered Noah Lamech lived for five hundred and
      ninety-five years
   and he fathered sons and daughters.
31 All the days of Lamech were seven hundred and seventy-seven
      years
   and he died.
32 Noah was five hundred years old
   and Noah fathered Shem, Ham and Japhet.

The line of the previous story is continued. Gen. 4.17 begins with the same main character, Cain: 'Cain had intercourse with his wife.' We do not know what his wife was called, and where she came from is a riddle. Up till now there have only been four human beings, one of whom is dead; so now there are only three. Sometimes it is assumed that this woman is one of the daughters that the first human being fathered after the birth of Seth (see 5.4), which would be an arithmetical wonder. Moreover Cain's wife would then at the same time be his sister: that does not seem to me to be any improvement either. The aim of these genealogies is to show that all the human beings throughout the world go back to one pair of parents. That is the aim of the composition, and therefore in 4.17–26 and in ch. 5 the *toledot*, the genealogies of the sons of the first human being, are repeated as closing lines. Elements which fit in less well, like Cain's wife, are left vague. The reason why there are two lists is because with the birth of Seth a new line is begun alongside that of Cain. Both lines have three own characteristics and functions, and so the text falls into two parts, 4.17–26 and 5.1–32.

Genealogies

Genealogies are always written from the perspective of a later time; those in them first have to have died. They are written in retrospect from a later period. This is also an explanation of the great ages. When people put this text here, they had in mind both a date for the creation and a number of names of people who had lived in the generations before them. The known names were divided over this whole period (consisting of a period before and a period after the great flood), with the result that the ages were very great. So anyone who reads this need not be surprised at the ages of these people, for these are artificial ages which have come about subsequently by a distribution over the period. Here particular principles of calculation were also used: the person who occupies seventh place in a genealogy is a special figure. Also figures like a lifetime of one hundred, five hundred, seven hundred and seventy-seven years indicate the special position of the person in question. So there are general principles of distribution, the most important of which is that the known persons together have to fill the period (which is presupposed) between the creation and the flood. As well as this, there are some lesser criteria for distinction, like numerical value and the like, which explain the great difference in ages. Moreover it is extremely important that the structure of these lists shows great similarities to the ancient king lists from Mesopotamia. In an ancient Sumerian list eight kings are mentioned before the flood who together reign for 241,000 years. The average age of a king on this list is around 30,000 years, compared with which Methuselah at 969 is a young stripling. Here too we have a retrospective construction.

One of the insoluble problems in ch. 5 is that there are notable differences in the ages as given in the three ancient textual traditions, namely the Massoretic text (MT), the Samaritan Pentateuch (SP) and the Septuagint (LXX). The Massoretic text is the edition from which present-day scholarly exegesis begins and on which the most important biblical translations are based. It is also the starting point for this book. This text goes back to the edition of the text prepared by rabbis (the so-called Massoretes) from the eighth century CE which was regarded by Jews and later also by Christians as the text of the Hebrew Bible. The Samaritan Pentateuch has a very old tradition and comes from the fourth century BCE, but it was recognized only by the Samaritans and was rejected by the Jews. The Septuagint is the Greek translation of the Hebrew Bible from the third century BCE which in the first instance was made by and for the Jews, and was very authoritative for them. Because this Greek text was later taken over by the Christians and recognized as authoritative, it was later no longer recognized as authoritative or holy by the Jews (from the first century CE). Now these three ancient textual witnesses give ages which diverge from the genealogy of Gen. 5. In the table below, the first column of each version of the text gives the age of the person at the birth of his first son, and the second the age at his death.

age at	MT birth of first son	death	SP birth of first son	death	LXX birth of first son	death
Adam	130	930	130	930	230	930
Seth	105	912	105	912	205	912
Enosh	90	905	90	905	190	905
Kenan	70	910	70	910	170	910
Mahalalel	65	895	65	895	165	895
Jared	162	962	62	847	162	962
Enoch	65	365	65	365	165	365
Methusaleh	187	969	67	720	167	969
Lamech	182	777	5	653	188	753
Noah	500	950	500	950	500	950
Time to flood	100		100		100	

| Time between Adam and flood | 1656 | | 1307 | | 2262 | |

In this table we see that the differences even increase. According to the Masoretic Text there are said to be 1656 years between Adam and the flood; according to the Samaritan Pentateuch there are 1307 years, and according to the Septuagint 2262. From this it again emerges that we must not regard the figures as hard historical facts but as literary arrangements of the past.

The beginning of the genealogy of Cain

'Cain had intercourse with his wife and she became pregnant and she bore Enoch' is almost like 'the human being had intercourse with Eve his wife, she became pregnant and she bore Cain' (4.1). Only the name of Cain's wife is missing. Both texts continue with the mention of the son's occupation: 'He was the builder of a city', 'Hevel was a keeper of small cattle, and Cain was a cultivator of the earth'. Because the formula is exactly the same, we can deduce that here the occupation of the son is described and not that of the father: Enoch is the builder of a city, Cain is not. That is supported by two other arguments: Cain is a wanderer; he wanders over the earth and finds it difficult to settle. The term 'builder of a city' indicates that the son of this wanderer settles in one place for the first time. The second argument is that the father names the city after his son Enoch. The word-play in Hebrew between 'his son' (*beno*) and 'builder' (*bone*) indicates how strong the relationship is between the son and the city, Enochville. But it is unthinkable that Enoch built the city all by himself. Had that in fact been the case, he would not have needed a complete city to live in. These verses implicitly indicate that there were already more human beings and that the history of settled people has begun.

It is striking that the wives are mentioned in the genealogy in 4.17–26 and not in Gen. 5. In 4.17–26 we do not have 'he fathered', but 'she became pregnant, she bore' and 'Irad was born to Enoch', 'Adah bore Jabal', 'Zillah also bore', and 'she (= Eve) bore'. Why do the women have a role in Gen. 4? In general, in a genealogy there is a concern to arrange individuals or groups in a network of relationships and affinities, and women form part of these networks. Here of course from a biological perspective both sexes, male and female, are needed for subsequent generations. But because of a particular cultural feature women may be indispensable for a genealogy. At a time when a man can have more than one wife, the mention of these wives is necessary to define the hierarchy or affinity between the different sons. Thus in the case of Lamech's two wives we are told whom Adah bears and whom Zillah bears, though the relationship between them is not made clear. Since Gen. 4.17–26 gives a lateral indication of the relationships between the kinsfolk, it is necessary for wives to be mentioned. Genesis 5 is principally occupied with the line in depth and therefore does not need wives: the hierarchy between the children after the first son is not thought to be important. Therefore we can often also have, 'and he fathered sons and daughters'. The relationships of affinity between these children (which are to be determined by the women who give birth to them) are not thought relevant, since Gen. 5 is solely concerned with the uninterrupted linear relationship between creation and flood. Something else is striking against the background of the book of Genesis as a whole. In patriarchal societies, as in the ancient Near East, the genealogies usually give only men's names. But now and then in Genesis women are also mentioned, like Sarah,

Rebecca, Rachel, Leah, Tamar. Perhaps one could say that women appear on the stage when something special is about to happen. They form a kind of crossroads on the otherwise straight highways of the male genealogies.

The middle of the genealogy of Cain

The seventh son in the generations from Adam (Adam, Cain, Enoch, Irad, Mehujael, Methuselah and Lamech) is married to two wives, Adah and Zillah. Together they have four children, three boys and a girl. The girl is called Naamah, the lovely, a name which is the same as Naomi. The three boys have names which phonetically resemble one another: Jabal, Jubal and Tubal. Each of them is described as the forefather of a cultural achievement: Jabal of rearing cattle, Jubal of music and Tubal of metal-working. Here they represent important phases in the cultural development of the city. They and their families possibly stand for the population of the city: the cattle-rearers live in the suburbs of the city, the smiths or metal-workers make carts and equipment, and the musicians represent the artistic side of city life. From this one can infer that Gen. 4.17–26 gives the line of development of those who are sedentary or semi-sedentary, in other words the inhabitants of the villages and towns and those who are economically dependent on them. By contrast, Gen. 5 sketches out the non-sedentary line: here we have the generations of nomads and semi-nomads from which Noah, Shem, Abraham, Isaac and Jacob are later to come.

Here the text hands down a song or poem of Lamech which is assumed to be very old. It is not only old but cryptic in content.

4.23 Adah and Zillah, hear my voice;
     you wives of Lamech, listen to what I say.
     Truly, I killed a man for wounding me,
     a young man (I killed) for striking me.
24 Truly Cain is avenged sevenfold,
     and Lamech seventy-sevenfold.

Lamech's song is not notable for its jollity. In the first two lines he summons his wives to listen. In so doing he wants to give the impression that what is coming is very important. After this summons comes the actual content, but the following lines can be translated in so many different ways that it is not immediately evident what they mean. Here is a series of possibilities. The verbal form of 'kill' can be translated 'I have killed', 'I kill' or 'I shall kill'. In the first instance ('I have killed') he has already in fact killed, and the reason for this murder was that another man had wounded him first. In the last case ('I shall kill') he is speaking about a possibility: if anyone does anything to me, I shall smite him dead. In the translation 'I kill', finally, both possibilities are left open. Lamech can already have killed someone or will be able to do so in the future. In addition to the problem of the verb there is the question of the meaning of the word *yeled*, which can stand for a powerful young man but also for a (weak) child. If the reference here is to a young man, then Lamech is speaking in two parallel verses, which say the same thing twice, like the first lines ('listen' and 'hear'): anyone who does anything to Lamech, any strong man who strikes him, he will kill. This interpretation is supported by the fact that the two words 'wound' and 'strike' often occur together and form a single whole. But the term *yeled* might also refer, not to a man but to a child: Lamech will kill a man who does anything to him; and, to go a step further, he will kill even a child who does anything to him. In that case these two verses are more like the following two lines, which speak of an escalation: 'Truly Cain is avenged sevenfold, and Lamech seventy-sevenfold.' Here we have disproportionality, since there is just no relationship between the two: to kill someone for inflicting a wound is beyond any reasonable measure of retribution, certainly if that person should be a child. The third and perhaps the greatest problem is the tiny little word *le* (literally 'for'), which can change the whole meaning of the text. That calls for more elucidation.

In Jewish tradition in the first centuries after Christ the song of Lamech was given a different meaning on the basis of the terms *ish*, 'man', and *le*, 'for', and on the basis of the fact that nowhere in Gen. 4 is it stated that Cain dies. The only person who so far has been called 'man', *ish*, is Cain (4.1). Lamech has killed a man, his ancestor Cain. Lamech did this by accident, because he was blind (this tradition is fond of forming legends). Lamech was a good but blind hunter and a young man always accompanied him on the hunt. By accident he killed Cain and the young man. When he discovers this, he exclaims: 'Have I killed a man because of my wounding (= for wounding me) and a young man because of my blow (= for striking me)?' The wounding and blow stand for Lamech's blindness and form the cause of his action. That is expressed by the little word *le*, 'for, because of''. In contrast to the modern interpretation of the text, in which Lamech's song is always seen as a text in which he is boasting about his great strength, in antiquity it was seen by Jewish exegetes as a confession and expression of regret. In their view the sentence which follows also indicates this. If vengeance was taken sevenfold on Cain, and thus in 4.15 YHWH expressed his great sense of justice, then vengeance will be taken seventy-seven fold on Lamech (with his blindness) because he will be treated even more justly by YHWH. For Cain had killed deliberately, whereas Lamech killed merely by accident because he had been wounded.

Thus again it becomes clear (as in the exposition of Gen. 2–3) how differently people can interpret a text. And this exegesis of one sentence has consequences for understanding the text as a whole. Modern exegetes are almost unanimous in seeing Gen. 4 as a story about the fall 'from bad to worse': Cain murders his brother out of jealousy, Lamech kills a man and even a child without any reason. Therefore YHWH punishes Cain seven times and Lamech seventy-seven times. Various modern exegetes even draw from this the conclusion that this rebounds on Cain's whole generation. And because the cultural development has begun from this generation, here at the same time culture, the city, cattle-rearing, metal-working and art are cursed. According to the same exegetes, only with Seth's line does an improvement come. But first this line of Cain's must be written off for good.

However, the question is whether this is the content of the text. The Jewish tradition can draw our attention to the fact that the content of the sentence 'seven times . . . seventy-seven times' in 4.15 is not an expression of an unreasonable revenge, but of justice; not something negative but something positive. Murder or killing is a serious crime, but here all the attention is focussed on the degree of retribution which is thought just. This does not make Lamech's song, seen as a boast or a confession, any less serious. But it does seem to me somewhat of an exaggeration to make this song the criterion for a whole generation: one cannot write off a whole line as a result of one braggart or penitent. Moreover, nowhere are any negative elements mentioned in 4.17–26. It is not said that Cain is killed or that Enoch dies, or that the generation of Cain passes away after them, whereas death runs like a scarlet thread through the genealogy of Seth: 'He fathered, he lived and he died.' One has only to read through Gen. 5 once to find the genealogy of Seth more a list of the dead than a genealogy.

Could it not be that the Christian tradition has assessed Gen. 4.17–26 in too negative a way? Perhaps even slogans like 'nature is good' and 'culture is a mistake' play a role here, whereas cultural achievements are being described here in a positive way. Another element that is usually overlooked is that 4.25 says that the first human beings again have a son 'in place of Hevel'. It does not say 'in place of Cain'. Cain is not written off, although most people automatically assume this. However much Cain, too, has committed a crime, he is punished and protected by YHWH. The break which is often presupposed between 4.16 and 4.17, as if the Cain of 4.1–16 is different from the father of the builder of a city, has often been necessary because people have not been able to imagine how history can still go on for someone like this. The readers are stricter on Cain than the text, stricter than YHWH. They are therefore also stricter on Lamech, who here recognizes the ability to commit a crime because he has been wounded, and who here (in anticipation) calls for even greater forgiveness. But we have already punished him and banished him to a dead end in history. However, no human lines seem to be dead ends; no one is written out of history or written off in it, except by readers.

The end of the genealogy of Cain

With the birth of a new son from the first human being and his wife, a new generation begins alongside that of Cain. 4.25–26 provides a smooth transition between Gen. 4 and Gen. 5.

4.25 The human being/Adam had intercourse again with his wife
and she gave birth to a son,
and she called his name Seth (saying),
Truly God has given me other seed in place of Hevel,
for Cain has killed him.
26 To Seth also a son was born.

This is the only place where the names of the three sons, Cain, Hevel and Seth appear side by side, so it becomes evident that the line of Cain and Hevel is now being continued. Here Seth takes the place of Hevel and we read about his descendants in ch. 5. The way is also prepared for Gen. 5 by the use of the word *adam*. The word *adam* appears without the definite article for the first time in 4.25, so that it can function as a proper name, Adam. This word then points forward to 5.1–6, in which Adam is also mentioned. At the same time it is also said of this *adam* in 5.1–2 that *adam* is like God, and is male and female. We therefore have to conclude that the word also refers to human beings in general. In other words, 4.25–26 and 5.1–2 serve as a hinge between Gen. 4 and 5, with word *adam* functioning as a pivot: Adam/human being (4.25), human being (5.1), human being (5.1), human being (5.1), Adam (5.3). Here the transition is made from 'the human being' to the individual, Adam. Here the human being becomes an individual.

While the human being (undifferentiated) may name the animals, the woman is always the one who names the newborn children: first she gave Cain his name, now Seth. In the naming of Cain she emphasizes that she has brought forth a man with the help of YHWH; now she similarly emphasizes God's contribution. She connects the word Seth with the verb 'set, place, give': God has given her seed in the form of a descendant. The word seed refers back to Gen. 3.15, where there is mention of the woman 'her seed', only in 4.25 'seed' has no possessive pronoun. But it remains remarkable that the woman is the one connected with procreation. It is equally striking that it is the woman who recognizes God's contribution to her childbirth. In the list of fatherings in Gen. 5, by contrast, only the male capacity for procreation is mentioned. None of these men recognizes God's contribution to their fertility in so many words. Perhaps the one who is pregnant and gives birth is more aware of the 'receptive' character of procreation than the narrator who in Gen. 5 acts as if descendants are secured by the male act of impregnating.

The newborn Seth grows up quickly, since in the next verse he already becomes a father. He gives his son the name Enosh. This name is striking, since *enosh* means 'human being'. It is a general term which occurs very frequently and is synonymous with *adam*. Just as the generic name *adam* is used as a proper name, so here too the generic name *enosh* is also used as a proper name. This generic name seems to fulfil a specific function in this context.

4.26 (Seth) called his name Enosh.
    At that time people began to call on YHWH by name.

This is what it is about: the human being with the name *enosh* calls on God by the name YHWH. It is often thought that YHWH first revealed the divine name to Moses in the burning bush and that this YHWH is only the covenant God of Israel. But from the fact that the first human beings, Cain and Hevel, Enosh and Noah, call upon YHWH or sacrifice to him, it emerges that this is not the case. This is confirmed by the fact that the patriarchs Abraham and Isaac also build altars to YHWH and sacrifice to him. There precisely the same words are used as here in 4.26: 'He called there on YHWH by name' (Gen. 12.8; 13.4; 21.33; 26.25).

Genesis 1–11 thus shows a more universal picture of God than some later parts of the Hebrew Bible. There is a relationship between YHWH and all human beings, whereas in books like Exodus and Deuteronomy only the covenant side of YHWH with Israel is made visible. The stories in Gen. 1–11 are focussed on universal relationships: on the relationships between heaven and earth, human beings and earth, man and woman, human beings and fellow human beings, human beings and posterity. Here for the first time the reciprocal relationship between human beings and God is put into words: they worship him as YHWH; it is their response to the relational side of God. Human beings address God under the name YHWH and in so doing indicate that for them he is a God who 'is with them'. Of course that does not mean that God coincides with this name; he is known among human beings under this name and by calling on him in this way they enter into contact with him. In other words, there are always specific perspectives from which human beings approach God and express their relation with God. Genesis 1 shows God as the creator of heaven and earth and names him *elohim*, Gen. 2–3 indicates above all the bond between God the creator and the relational God who comes into contact with creatures and expresses that by the name *yhwh elohim*; Gen. 4 presents God in relation to weaker human beings and for that uses the name *yhwh*. At the end of Gen. 4 the human response is made explicit for the first time, and it is shown that human beings call on or address God under the name *yhwh*. So the reader always sees God illuminated from a particular perspective.

The genealogy of Adam and Seth

The genealogy of Seth is preceded by the announcement, 'This is the book or the list of the *toledot*, the history or the fatherings of the human being.' And then the generations of humankind are neatly summed up in order: he lived so many years, he fathered a son, he lived after his fathering, and he died. In each segment of the list a father is central. Therefore we do not have 'after the birth of' but 'after his fathering'. After the fathering of the firstborn (here it is always assumed that the firstborn was a son), there follow an indeterminate number of sons and daughters, which further the progress of the human race. Without mothers, survival is already difficult enough, but it would become doubly impossible without daughters.

In the genealogy of Cain the mother mentioned the contribution of YHWH to the birth of her child. In the list of Seth the relationship with God is established in another way. At the beginning of the genealogy the creation of the human being by God from Gen. 1.26–28 is recalled:

5.1 On the day that God created the human being/Adam,
he made him in the likeness of God,
· 2 male and female created he them
and he blessed them,
and he named them 'human being'
on the day that they were created.

Here we twice have the word *adam* without the article, but the text must refer to the human being, since the individual Adam cannot at the same time be both male and female. This human being is created in God's likeness and so the individual human being Adam can father a son in his own likeness. Thus what is handed on in the fathering is given an ultimate value: it is the likeness with God which continues in history.

Human beings are born and human beings die, but the seventh person in the series differs from the one who precedes and the one who follows. It is Enoch, an important person, since he 'walked with God'. That is said not once, but twice. It is the expression of the ideal relationship with God, and later it will be said again only of Noah. Moreover Enoch is the only person in this list who does not die, but is taken up by God. Enoch shares this privilege in the Hebrew Bible with Elijah. It is also said of Enoch that he lived 365 years (on earth), and this number corresponds to the number of days of a solar year. So from antiquity Enoch has been associated with the sun: his being taken up by God is then connected with the rising and setting of the sun in heaven.

The son of Enoch is the person who lives longest before the flood. He is called Methuselah. Methuselah's son is Lamech. He is a different Lamech from the one in Cain's list: in families it often happens that names occur several times. It is striking that in this genealogy Lamech is given space to say something:

29 He called his name Noah, saying,
  This shall comfort us in our work and the toil of our hands
    on the earth,
  which YHWH has cursed.

The name Noah (in Hebrew written in consonants as *n.ch*)
literally means 'rest' . But his father Lamech makes a connection
between the name Noah and the verb for 'console' (*n.ch.m*):
Noah is to offer people consolation in their toil on the earth
which YHWH has cursed. It seems intended as a kind of programme for the life of the newly-born Noah. And with this
Noah and his three sons Shem, Ham and Japhet the genealogy
ends. Noah does not die, and we shall be hearing more of him.

Conclusion

Although in our time there is a great deal of interest in personal
family trees, the genealogies in Genesis usually do not attract
many admirers. Most people prefer to pass over them and
simply read the stories. For stories are lively and attractive, and
the genealogies are dry and not very exciting. I do not believe
that anyone has ever asked how a genealogy ends. The end is
already known: the last one dies. That makes such a list pre-
dictable: he (she) lived, had a child and died. A varied life
sounds different. For depth, psychological development, sense
and meaning you have to go to stories.

But this must to some degree be qualified. Genealogies also
'relate' their view; they reconstruct the past and order history.
What genealogies show is the unproblematical succession of
generations, a succession the success of which is guaranteed.
They are the expression of a deep regularity, of a fundamental
certainty in existence: birth, conception, children who continue
the line, death. Despite all variations in life, they show its under-
lying uniform rhythm. Therefore the genealogies are the most
convincing reflection of the continuity in life and death. Thus
they bear witness to a certain determinism: they put the past in
an irrevocable order.

In this sense the genealogies show agreements with the

creation story in the first chapter of Genesis. The ordered account in Gen. 1 which presents the beginning and the order of creation corresponds to the genealogy of Gen. 5 which expresses the regularity of the coming into being of creation. Thus the order of creation in Gen. 1 finds its natural continuation in Gen. 5. At their creation, in Gen. 1, human beings are given the task of multiplying, filling the earth and cultivating it. The genealogy shows that they fulfil this task. Moreover in this way it becomes evident that the order presented is not just that of the human being but similarly that of the earth. It is an order which transcends human beings and in a sense is independent of them. Looked at closely, a genealogy does not give 'meaning' to the life and death of human beings, to generations which follow one another in continuity. By contrast, human beings derive their own meaning and significance from their spread over the earth and their cultivation of it.

The combination of stories and genealogies produces a subtle tension in Genesis between the order and determinism of the lists and the ambiguity in the stories. The stories give meaning to the ways of real life, the problems, the uncertainties. They are a kind of exercise in giving form to ambiguity. The genealogies indicate the stability which underlies this ambiguity. It is even probable that the two aspects of God which we encounter in Genesis 1–11 correspond to this subtle relationship. *Elohim* is then the side of God which represents creation and the genealogy, or the stability and the necessary continuation. *Yhwh* shows the side of God which the stories also present: the God who comes into existence in actuality. *Yhwh* and *Elohim* present God in two ways, just as the stories and the genealogies represent reality in two ways.

Genesis 6–9: The Story of the Flood[8]

6.1   The human beings began to become numerous upon the face of
        the *earth*
        and daughters were born to them.

2   The sons of god saw the daughters of men
        that they were good,
        and they took for themselves wives
        which they chose.

3   YHWH said,
        My spirit shall not abide in the human being for ever,
        because he is also flesh,
        his lifetime shall be a hundred and twenty years.

4   The giants were on the earth at that time, and also later,
        then the sons of god came to the daughters of men
        and they bore their children.
        They were the giants, the men of name of the before time.

6.5   YHWH saw that the wickedness of the human being had become
        great on the earth,
        and that all the thoughts which he formed in his heart were
        sheer evil,
        all the days (of his life).

6   YHWH was sorry that he had made the human being on the earth
        and it gave him pain in his heart.

7   YHWH said,
        I shall sweep away the human being
        whom I have made
        from the face of the earth,
        from human being to animal, from creeping beast to birds of
        the air.
        For I am sorry that I have made them.

8   Only Noah found grace in the eyes of YHWH.

9   This is the history of Noah:
        Noah was a righteous man,
        he was blameless among his contemporaries,
        Noah walked with God.

10   Noah fathered three sons, Shem, Ham and Japhet.

11   The earth was destroyed before God's face
     and the earth was filled with violence.

12   God saw the earth
     and look, it was destroyed,
     truly, all living beings destroyed their way on the earth.

13   And God said to Noah,
       The end of all living beings stands before my eyes
       for the earth is filled with violence through them.
       Look, I shall destroy them from the earth.

14   But make for yourself an ark of gopher wood,
     you must make rooms in the ark
     and you must smear it inside and outside with pitch.

15   Thus you must make it:
     the length of the ark shall be three hundred ells,
     its breadth fifty and its height thirty;

16   you must make a roof for the ark,
     up to one ell high you must make it;
     you must put the entrance to the ark on the side,
     you must make it with a first, second and third deck.

17   For my part,
     I shall bring a flood upon the earth on all living beings,
     to destroy everything
     in which there is the breath of life under the heaven.
     Everything on earth will perish.

18   I shall make my covenant with you
     and you shall come into the ark,
     you, your sons, your wife and the wives of your sons with
       you;

19   and of all the life, of all living beings, you shall bring two
     into the ark
     in order to survive with you,
     they must be male and female.

20   Of the birds after their kind and of the cattle after its kind
     and of all that creeps upon the *earth* after its kind,
     one pair must come to you to survive.

21   For your part,
     take all the food that is eaten,
     store it with you
     and it shall be food for you and them.

22   Noah did it,
     all as God had commanded him

he did.

7. 1   YHWH said to Noah,
      Come, you and your whole house into the ark,
      for I have seen that you are righteous before me in this
          generation.

2   Of all clean animals take seven pairs,
      seven males and females,
      and of all animals which are not clean one pair,
      a male and a female.

3   Also of the birds of the air seven pairs,
      seven males and females,
      to keep their kind alive over the whole earth.

4   For in seven days I shall make it rain upon the earth,
      forty days and forty nights.
      I shall sweep away from the face of the *earth*
      all the living things
      that I have made.

5   Noah did all
      that YHWH had commanded.

6   Noah was six hundred years
      when the flood came over the earth.

7   Noah went into the ark
      – and his sons, his wife and the wives of his sons with him –
      because of the flood.

8.   Of the clean animals, of the unclean animals,
      of the birds and all that creeps upon the *earth*,
      two by two they came to Noah in the ark, male and female,
      as God had commanded Noah.

10   It happened after seven days
      that the waters of the flood came over the earth.

11   In the six hundredth year of Noah's life, in the second month,
      on the seventeenth day of the month,
      on that day all the foundations of the great deep burst open
      and the sluice gates of the heaven were opened.

12   Rain fell upon the earth for forty days and forty nights.

13   On that same day Noah
      – and Shem, Ham and Japhet, the sons of Noah, and Noah's
        wife and the three wives of his sons with them –
      went into the ark.

14   They and all life after its kind, all the cattle after its kind,
      everything that creeps upon the earth after its kind,

all birds after their kind, and every kind of winged creature.

15 They came to Noah to the ark,
two by two of every living being in which there is the breath of
life.

16 Those that came were the males and females of all living beings,
as God had commanded him.
And YHWH shut the door after him.

17 The flood was forty days upon the earth
and the waters rose
and lifted up the ark
and it rose above the earth.

18 The waters became more powerful,
and increased greatly upon the earth,
and the ark floated on the face of the water.

19 The waters became even more powerful upon the earth
and all the high mountains under the whole heaven were
covered.

20 Fifteen ells above them the waters rose
and the mountains were covered.

21 All living beings that creep upon the earth,
the birds, the cattle, all life,
all the teeming creatures that teem upon the earth
and all human beings perished.

22 Everything with the breath of life in its nostrils, everything on
the dry land, died.

23 He swept everything that exists from the face of the *earth*,
from human being to animal,
from creeping beast to birds of the heaven,
they were swept away from the earth.
Only Noah survived,
and what was with him in the ark.

24 The waters became more powerful upon the earth,
for one hundred and fifty days.

8.1 God remembered Noah and all the life and all the cattle
that were with him in the ark.
And God made a wind blow over the earth
and the waters came to a standstill.

2 The fountains of the deep and the sluice gates of heaven were
closed,
the rain from the heaven stopped,

3 The waters gradually retreated from the earth,

the waters decreased after one hundred and fifty days.

4 And in the seventh month, on the seventieth day of the month,
the ark came to rest on the mountains of Ararat.

5 The waters dropped gradually until the tenth month
and in the tenth month, on the first of the month,
the tops of the mountains became visible.

6 It happened after forty days
that Noah opened the window of the ark
which he had made.

7 He let out the raven
and this flew to and fro
until the waters upon the earth had dried up.

8 He let out the dove
to see whether the waters were less upon the face of the *earth*.

9 But the dove found no place to rest her feet.
And she returned to him and the ark,
because there were still waters upon the whole face of the earth.
He stuck his hand out
and took her
and brought her to him in the ark.

10 He waited another seven days,
and again he let the dove out of the ark.

11 The dove came back to him in the evening,
and look, a plucked olive leaf was in her beak.
And Noah knew that the waters on the earth had subsided.

12 He waited yet another seven days
and he let the dove out,
but she did not return to him again.

13 And it happened in the six hundredth year on the first day of the
first month
that the waters of the earth dried up,
and Noah opened the roof of the ark
and he looked out
and behold, the face of *the earth* had dried up.

14 In the second month on the twenty-seventh day of the month,
the earth was dry.

15 God spoke to Noah, saying,

16 Go out of the ark,
you, your wife, your sons and the wives of your sons with
you.

17 Let all the life that is with you,

all living beings, the birds, the cattle and the animals that
   creep upon the earth,
go out with you,
let them swarm all over the earth,
so that they are fruitful
and become numerous upon the earth.

18   Noah went out and his sons, his wife and the wives of his sons
   with him.

19   And all life, everything that creeps, all birds, everything that
   creeps on the earth,
kind by kind, went out of the ark.

20   Noah built an altar to YHWH
and he took of every clean animal and every clean bird
and he burnt a burnt offering on the altar.

21   YHWH smelt the restful sacrifice
and YHWH said to his heart,
   I shall never again regard the *earth* as cursed because of the
      human being,
   although what is formed in the human heart
   is bad from youth up.
   I shall never again destroy everything that lives
   as I have done.

22   From now on all the days of the earth,
   seed-time and harvest,
   cold and heat,
   summer and winter,
   day and night,
   shall not cease to exist.

9.1   God blessed Noah and his sons
and he said to them,
   Be fruitful,
   become numerous
   and fill the earth.

2   Respect for you and fear of you shall there be among all life
   on the earth, among all the birds of heaven, among everything that creeps upon the *earth* and among all the fishes of
   the sea.
Into your hand they are given.

3   Everything that moves and lives shall be your food,
likewise the green plants.
I give you everything.

4   Truly, flesh with its life or its blood in it you may not eat.
5   Truly, I shall require a reckoning of your blood and life.
    From the hand of every living being I shall ask it.
    From the hand of the human being,
    from the hand of the man and his brother
    shall I require a reckoning for the life of a human being.
6   Whoever sheds human blood
    his blood shall be shed by the human being,
    for in the image of God he made the human being.
7   And you, be fruitful,
    become numerous,
    teem upon the earth
    and be numerous there.
8   God spoke to Noah and his sons with him, saying,
9   For my part,
    look, I make my covenant with you and with your seed after
        you,
10 with all living beings who were with you, with the birds,
    the animals and all life on earth with you, from all those who
        came out of the ark to all the life on earth.
11 I establish my covenant with you
    that all living beings shall never be cut off by the waters of the
        flood.
    No flood shall come to destroy the earth again.
12 God said,
    This is the sign of the covenant which I make between me and
        you,
    between all that lives which is with you,
    for all following generations.
13 I have placed my bow in the clouds
    and this shall be a sign of the covenant between me and the
        earth.
14 It shall be that whenever I bring clouds over the earth,
    the bow will become visible in the clouds.
15 Then I will remember my covenant between me and you and
        all living beings,
    and never again shall the waters of the flood destroy every-
        thing that lives.
16 When the bow is in the clouds,
    then I shall see it
    to recall the everlasting covenant between God

and all living beings which are upon the earth.

17 God said to Noah,
This is the sign of the covenant
that I have made between me and all living beings
that are upon the earth.

Sons of god and daughters of men

Genesis 6.1–4 is a strange piece of text. It is a mythological miniature in which sons of gods pair up with daughters of men. What can the significance of such a piece of text in the Bible and in Genesis be?

The background against which this story must be read is that of a pluriform image of God. The sons of god who appear in Gen. 6.1–4 belong to the class of gods and differ from human beings. Just as 'sons of men' denotes human beings generally and 'the sons of Israel' represents all Israelites, so the 'sons of god' stand for the gods in general. They appear, for example, in Ps. 89.7, where we read: 'Who in the heaven can be compared with YHWH? Who of the sons of god is like YHWH?' And in Job 1.6 and 2.1: 'On a certain day the sons of god came to present themselves before YHWH.' The pluriformity and plurality of the world of the gods is presented in these texts as a matter of course. Only in Gen. 6.1–4 these divine male beings enter into a relationship with human female beings.

Later generations of believers, Jews and Christians, have had difficulty with this polytheism and this mythology. They cannot accept a pluriform image of God and therefore translate the term 'sons of god' in Gen. 6.1–4 as 'angels'. But angels are the product of a much later historical period. To speak of angels here would be an anachronism, a projection from a later time to an earlier one. It would be just like having Noah survive in a space ship, or seeing Abraham leave Haran in a Mercedes, or having Solomon walk around in an Armani suit. In short, to speak of angels here shows little historical sense. Let's recognize the mythological character of this text and regard myths, too, as one of the narrative forms in which people tell of the beginning. So let's look at the text sentence by sentence and judge it on its own merits.

Genesis 6.1–4 opens with the statement, 'the human beings began to become numerous upon the earth and daughters were born to them'. The reader knows that directly before this is the genealogy of human beings with the fatherings by Adam, Seth, Enosh, Kenan, Mahalel, Jared, Enoch, Methuselah, Lamech and Noah, each time concluded with the statement 'and they fathered sons and daughters'. These anonymous daughters are now brought to the forefront in this mini-story. Having hitherto been the anonymous collaborators in history who have not been given any name in the genealogies, now for the first time they are noticed by the sons of god. This must be a folk tale. They are said to be 'good'. Here in the Hebrew we have *tov*, which usually means 'good'. The word occurs hundreds of times in the Bible. But it is striking that while every time the word occurs in connection with men it is translated 'good', in the case of women it is always translated 'attractive'. Thus there is not a single translation into a modern language which says in Gen. 6.2 that the sons of god saw that the women were 'good'. One translation has 'fair', another 'beautiful' and yet another recognizes that what the text really says is 'good' but concludes from it that here the term must mean 'well suited to be a husband or housewife'. I shall just translate it 'good'.

In Gen. 1.26–28 God has instructed human beings to be fruitful, to multiply and to fill the earth. 6.1 shows that here these instructions have been obeyed: human beings are beginning to become numerous upon the face of the earth. For the first time now daughters are also mentioned. This seems to me to be a good thing for procreation on earth. The sons of god see that the daughters of men are good and they choose a wife. On the basis of three elements, people have often decided on a negative interpretation of 6.2. The first is the plural 'wives', from which it is assumed that here we have polygamy. Above all Christian exegesis gives a negative evaluation of this: by contrast, in the Jewish tradition polygamy is (was) allowed and sometimes is even thought worth commending, because polygamy furthers procreation. However, it is not completely clear whether 6.2 speaks of having 'many wives'. It is said that the sons of god take wives, which can mean that each of them takes one. Had it been said that they took 'one wife', again people could have said that it was a scandal that many men together took one wife. In short, it is not clear whether the word 'wives' refers to more than one wife per person (= son of god), but the text mentions it in a matter-of-fact way and does not say anything positive or negative. The second element which has prompted questions is the word 'take'. No marriage is concluded and they all 'take' one another. However, in Gen. 1–5 nothing different has been done up to that point: with the 'taking', the relationship between man and woman is a fact. That is not so strange, since the institution of marriage developed only much later and cannot appear in the text here, far less be projected back on to it. In the Hebrew Bible, 'take a wife' is the usual expression for describing the new relationship between man and woman. The third element, 'from all whom they chose', has also given rise to doubt. 'The sons of god took whoever they wanted and brought them back into their harem.' But 6.2 simply says that the sons of god took whoever they wanted, whoever they chose: they took the daughters to wife. What then do people want, for them to have taken wives they didnt want? In other words, here there is no question of a positive or negative judgment; we have a neutral description: the sons of god took a wife from the daughters of men because they found these good. And they sought out those whom they appreciated.

YHWH reacts to this with the following words:

6.3 My spirit shall not abide in the human being for ever,
     because he is also flesh, his lifetime shall be a hundred and
     twenty years.

In the negative interpretations of this story this verse is interpreted as a punishment: the human being is flesh, and from antiquity flesh has had a bad connotation: it is 'bad' ,'weak', 'vulnerable'. In this conception flesh represents the bad, untrustworthy side of human beings. However, there is nothing of that here in the text of 6.3. Flesh stands for a living being or a human being (thus also in Gen. 6.5–9. 17) and here is associated only with a limited lifetime. So we see here that the sons of gods who were characterized by eternal life had intercourse with daughters of men who were characterized by mortal life. The moment that they have children together, the question is whether these will resemble their father or their mother in the matter of (im)mortality. Here YHWH takes a decision: because they are also flesh (human) they shall also be mortal: 'My spirit or breath of life shall not remain in human beings for ever or for an unlimited time, the maximum number of years of life shall be 120.' (That this maximum is later also viewed as an optimum emerges, among other things, from the fact that Moses dies at the age of 120.) The threat of overpopulation, of both pro-creation *and* eternal life is averted here: as already happened (in Gen. 3) in the case of relations between ordinary human beings, YHWH's appearance in 6.3 also takes this threat away from relations between sons of god and daughters of men. In other words, the main theme of Gen. 6.1–4 is mortality, not questions of good and evil, i.e. morality. The involvement of YHWH here is with human beings and gods, but above all with the earth. It is not for nothing that the opening sentence of the story mentions that human beings become numerous 'on the face of the earth'. It is the earth that is getting overpopulated, and damaged as a result. A limited lifetime for human beings is in the first place a favour for the earth, not for human beings.

In the last verse, the narrator puts the event in a distant past, the before time. He relates that the children who resulted from the intercourse of sons of god with daughters of men were giants. He himself calls them 'men of name', and in the Bible these are prominent men, men of renown. Thus nothing negative emerges from the evaluation of the narrator. However, he does make something else clear by a word-play: the human beings who seemed to live *le-olam* , 'for all time' or 'for unlimited time', now in the end seem to be people who lived *me-olam*, 'for some time' or 'in the before time'. Those who seemed to have the eternal future prove to be definitively *passé*. Here the narrator addresses the reader directly and shows that the question of immortality has gone for good.

In short, this mini-story concentrates on the time of human life on earth. As an independent class, human beings are different from the class of the gods, and therefore they and their hybrid children are not immortal but kept to a limited life-span. Just as human beings are bound to a particular place, namely the earth, so they are also bound to a particular time: the maximum number of years on earth is limited. This limitation on the time of human beings is reflected in the limitation of the time of the story: in the first line the story began with the beginning (6.1); in v. 3 it goes via eternity to the limited lifetime (6.3); and in v. 4 puts the whole thing in the past.

Text in context

The context in which Gen. 6.1–4 functions can provide yet more clarification. In the first place this is formed by the story of the flood which immediately follows Gen. 6.1–4. This story of the flood opens in 6.5 with 'YHWH saw that the wickedness of the human being had become great/numerous on the earth'. Thus over against the beginning in 6. 1–4, which describes how human beings have become numerous on the earth, we have the opening of Gen. 6.5–9.17 (= Gen. 6–9), which is about evil deeds becoming numerous on the earth. Whereas the story of the sons of god and daughters of human beings addresses the problem of the time of human beings on earth and especially immortality, the story of the flood focusses on the place of human beings on earth and their unethical behaviour, immorality.

As well, this story in Gen. 6 functions as an introduction to the story of the flood within the context of other flood stories which were in circulation in the ancient Near East. Two of these stories which come from Mesopotamia are known to us, the Atrahasis epic and the Gilgamesh epic. The flood story in the Neo-Assyrian Gilgamesh epic seems to be a reworking of the (older) Old Babylonian Atrahasis epic. These Mesopotamian stories of the flood show a strong similarity to the flood story in Gen. 6–9 at particular points. In these three stories God or the gods play an important role in the decision to allow a flood to come upon the earth: there is a hero (Atrahasis, Utnapishtim and Noah respectively) who saves all the animals and his family by means of a boat, who sends out birds (in Genesis a raven, a dove and a dove; in the Atrahasis and Gilgamesh stories a dove, a swallow and a raven), and at the end of the flood offers a sacrifice to God or the gods; and finally the situation which existed before the flood is restored.

On the other hand there are also great differences: in Gen. 6–9 the only God is called YHWH and Elohim, whereas many gods with Old Babylonian or Neo-Assyrian names are mentioned in the Atrahasis and Gilgamesh epics. In these Mesopotamian stories the gods resolve on a great flood because there are too many people who are making too much noise, so that the gods cannot sleep. They bring a flood upon the earth which sweeps everything away. Later the gods go back on their decision because they begin to miss the sacrifices from the human beings. In the Atrahasis story they leave some people alive and solve the problem of the noise and the over-population that could happen again in the future by putting limits on pro-creation. To this end the gods make more women infertile, allow more children to die and limit the number of available women by requiring virginity of women dedicated to a deity (a kind of Vestal Virgin).

In the Gilgamesh epic the flood story functions in the frame-work of Gilgamesh's journey in search of immortality, On this journey Gilgamesh encounters Utnapishtim, who tells him the story of the flood. Utnapishtim describes how before the flood human beings were immortal and made more and more noise as a result of their growing numbers. By means of the great flood the gods were able to limit the number of people and the noise. In order to prevent the noise starting up again, the gods made people, apart from Utnapishtim, mortal. Thus both stories from Mesopotamia are about the over-population of the earth; in the Atrahasis myth this is limited by the gods allowing fewer people to be born, and in the Gilgamesh epic by the institution of death and the abolition of immortality. Genesis differs in its flood story from these two Mesopotamian stories by making the theme not immortality, but the bad behaviour of human beings. The regulations which YHWH issues after the flood are aimed at an improvement in human behaviour. Gen. 6–9 need not be occupied with the question of overpopulation and immortality, because Gen. 6.1–4 has already solved that problem.

Anyone who notices all this will discover the bridging function that the mini-myth of Gen. 6.1–4 fulfils between the creation story in Gen. 1–5 and the flood story in Gen. 6.9. Genesis 1 is about the creation of the cosmos, the population on earth and the position of the human being on earth. Genesis 2–3 develops only the last sub-division, the relationship between human being and the earth. These chapters show that there is a connection between the relationship between man and woman on the one hand and between human being and the earth on the other. Moreover Genesis 2–3 shows the connection which exists between the acquisition of the capacity for procreation and the introduction of death, or in terms of Gen. 2–3 itself, the impossibility of eating from the tree of the knowledge of good and bad and from the tree of life at the same time. Now that the man and the woman are in a position to produce children, YHWH puts an end to their immortality and introduces death as the limit of their life. Genesis 4.1–16 continues this line and shows that the relationship between human beings and the earth is also dependent on that between the man and his brother, between the human being and his (weak) fellow human being. So a network of relationships has grown in Gen. 1–4 which is concluded in 4.26 by the relationship between human being and YHWH: the relationship of YHWH-earth-human being, man-woman, and human being-fellow human being thus becomes a totality of reciprocal relationships. Next the genealogies in Gen. 4.17–5.32 present the success of human procreation: the network continues and the earth is populated. Then Gen. 6.1–4 begins, with the report in the first verse that human beings have become numerous on the earth. Stories from neighbouring lands had shown that the danger of over-population and too much noise was regarded as the cause of a flood. In these stories the limitation of fertility or the introduction of death were the solutions for avoiding overpopulation. Genesis 6.1–4 starts from this same fact that there are too many people on earth, but goes on to show that this is not the occasion for a great flood. The possibility of too many people is avoided by the limitation of human life-spans, which are tied to a maximum of 120 years. Then the flood story shows that it is not the large number of human beings but the large number of crimes that they commit which is the cause of YHWH's decision to cause a flood. Thus Gen. 6.1–4 continues the central theme of Gen. 1–5, i.e. the creation and propagation of human beings over the face of the earth, but avoids any possibility that the flood story in Gen. 6–9 might be regarded as a story about human over-population. Thus a mythological story, too, performs a function in the totality of the stories of the beginning.

The cause of the flood

6.5   YHWH saw that the wickedness of the human being had become
      great *on the earth*,
      and that all the thoughts which he formed in his heart were
        sheer evil,
      all the days (of his life).
6   YHWH was sorry that he had made the human being *on the earth*
      and it gave him pain in his heart.
7   YHWH said,
      I shall sweep away the human being
      whom I have made
      from the face of the earth,
      from human being to animal, from creeping beast to birds of
        the air.
      For I am sorry that I have made them.
8   Only Noah found grace in the eyes of YHWH.
9   This is the history of Noah:
      Noah was a righteous man,
      he was blameless among his contemporaries,
      Noah walked with God.
10   Noah fathered three sons, Shem, Ham and Japhet.
11   *The earth* was destroyed before God's face
      and *the earth* was filled with violence.
12   God saw the *earth*
      and look, it was destroyed,
      truly, all living beings destroyed their way *on the earth*.
13   And God said to Noah,
      The end of all living beings stands before my eyes

for *the earth* is filled with violence through them.
Look, I shall destroy them from *the earth*.

God has just had enough. Human beings have ruined things. They have not only become numerous on the earth but wickedness has increased proportionately. And then people ask where the evil comes from! Here it says clearly: from human beings! Human actions and thoughts are impressively bad: selfishness, injustice towards other people and defaulting over the earth characterize human behaviour. But the text is more interested in the consequences of human wickedness for the earth than in the nature and cause of evil. God regrets having made human beings on the earth. He is sorry that he did not provide the earth with other inhabitants. Even the animals have to suffer at human hands. They are not to blame for the wretchedness on earth, but they share in the consequences. God is involved in the earth and its population, and so it is close to his heart. He feels pain in his heart, and it is the same pain (and the same word) as the pain and difficulty which human beings experience when they cultivate the earth. God wanted things otherwise. In the meantime he has seen enough and fears that the earth is being destroyed. He has to make up his mind, and with the slogan 'save the earth, remove human beings', he sets to work.

All the details of the first verses of the flood story support this. The word for 'earth' (*erets*) occurs eight times, which shows that the earth is central in God's concern. The creator who has made the earth is now confronted with people who are destroying the earth. A feeling of desolation comes over God. He feels revulsion at these people whom he himself has created. Human beings, who are usually inclined to blame God for all their misery, now seem to be causing pain and sorrow in God's heart. Although God had already entrusted the earth to human beings, no one was aware that God's concern for the earth would be so great that he himself would intervene when they threatened the earth. If we look with God's eyes on the earth, God's resolve to destroy human beings becomes more understandable. Moreover God himself shows the connection between his resolve and human behaviour by using the same word, *shachat*, destroy or ruin, for both: 'The earth was destroyed before God's face' (v. 11), and 'I shall destroy them from the earth' (v. 13). What God will do corresponds to what human beings have done to the earth.

An anti-creation story

God is not only the one who devises and directs creation, but also seems to be the one who devises and carries out a flood which destroys the whole of creation. Here God works in accordance with an anti-creation scenario which is developed as an opposite to the creation scenario in Gen. 1. This emerges right at the beginning. Whereas Gen. 1 is concluded with, 'And God saw everything that he had made and look, it was very good' (1.31), Gen. 6.12 begins with, 'And God saw the earth, and look, it was destroyed'. In formulating his plan and announcing the destruction, God also at the same time refers back to his creation. 'I shall blot out the human being *whom I have made* from the face of the earth, from human being to animal, from creeping beast to birds of the air. For I am sorry *that I have made them*' (6.7). And he communicates this annihilation to Noah like this: 'I shall sweep away from the face of the earth all the living things *that I have made*' (7.4). And at the end of the flood he says to himself, 'I shall never again destroy everything that lives' (8.21). God puts an end to what he himself has begun and thus explicitly relates his creation and destruction to each other. Here the comprehensive phrases 'all living beings' or 'human beings and all animals', and the verbs 'sweep away' and 'destroy', indicate the total destruction of creation that is involved here. The actual implementation of this destruction of creatures is described both simply and absolutely:

7.21 All living beings that creep upon the earth, the birds, the cattle, all life, all the teeming creatures that teem over the earth and all human beings *perished*.

22 Everything with the breath of life in its nostrils, everything on the dry land, *died*.

23 He *swept* everything that exists from the face of the earth, from

human being to animal, from creeping beast to birds of the heaven, they were *swept away* from the earth.

Genesis 6–9 is also the anti-story to Genesis 1 in another respect. In Gen. 1 the initial state was a boundless surface of water, both vertically and horizontally. In it, the heaven is distinguished as a vault between the vertical waters, and the earth is distinguished as the dry land which appeared between the waters under the heaven. In Gen. 6–9 these distinctions are done away with again. God opens the fountains of the deep and the sluice gates of heaven and the waters come to submerge the earth both from below and from above. Everything disappears under a boundless mass of water. It is a kind of return to the primal state. Although the heaven and the earth seem to continue to exist, all creatures (except for the fish) perish. Against this background one can explain why God takes the rigorous decision to destroy all living beings and not only human beings. The animals must suffer along with the human beings, because here we have anti-creation: all created things disappear because of the excessive wickedness of human beings. So the animals are not punished for their own actions, but because of the extreme wickedness of human beings. Human beings involve the whole of creation in their wickedness, and it has to perish.

Finally, Gen. 6–9 corresponds to Gen. 1 in its attention to days and dates. In the creation story we see how God achieves the creation in six days, and how every day ends with the note 'it became evening and morning, the first, second . . . sixth day'. The anti-creation story in Gen. 6–9 shows something of this sort. Above all the beginning and end of the story illustrate this:

6.5 (YHWH saw that)
    all the thoughts which he formed in his heart were sheer evil, *all the days* (of his life).

8.22 (YHWH said,)
    From now on *all the days of the earth*,
    seed-time and harvest,
    cold and heat,
    summer and winter,
    day and night,
    shall not cease to exist.

No longer shall 'the days of human beings' be determinative for God', but 'the days of the earth'. This is the change that the story shows. Although the human being is prone to evil all the days from his youth, the continuation of all the days of the earth after the flood will be guaranteed. The episode between this beginning and end does not relate to 'all the days', but concentrates on specific days. These indications of time seem to have been arranged precisely:

7 days: the flood begins 7 days after God sends Noah into the ark
40 days: the rain falls on the earth for 40 days
150 days: the waters are on the earth for 150 days
40 days: Noah opens the window of the ark after 40 days
7 days: Noah disembarks after 7 days

Seven days and nights mark the beginning and the end of the flood. The number 'seven' for the days confirms the impression that the text refers back to the seven days in Gen. 1. The seven days of the destructive power of God in Gen. 6–9 thus correspond to the seven days of the creative power of God in Gen. 1. From all this, Gen. 6–9 emerges as a precisely developed anti-creation story in which what was built up in the creation story in Gen. 1 is broken down.

The rescue plan

God's plans are shattering. However, fortunately we see that he is not only following a scenario of destruction but also a rescue plan. The wickedness of human beings would justify a total devastation, but nevertheless God decides on a rescue programme as well as a programme of destruction. God's rescue scenario is based on 'grace', on something which is not merited and yet is obtained. It is an example of disproportionality, since the preservation of creatures bears no relation to the wickedness which is emphasized. In the destruction scenario God acts in accordance with the human idea of justice and causality. It is as if God were saying, 'This is what human beings would call *quid pro quo*. Human beings administer justice in accordance with the principle of causality, a proportional distribution of punishment and reward. In accordance with that idea of justice I would have to destroy everything, since the destructive evil of human beings has to be met by my destruction of them. But I want to show that there is more than this kind of justice. What would creation look like if there were no grace, if nothing were given "free"?' According to the rescue scenario, God therefore gives grace to Noah and through him to other human beings. The fact that Noah is chosen is understandable from the perspective of the Hebrew, since the text shows that there is a relationship between the word Noah (*n.ch*) and the word grace (*ch.n*). Noah is an example of those who will be saved. With him God wants to begin a new history of human beings and animals on earth.

So here we see two sides of a single coin. The first verses visualize this in a notable way. On the one hand God 'sees' the wickedness of human beings and is sorry (in Hebrew *n.ch.m*); on the other hand Noah (*n.ch*) finds grace (*ch.n*) 'in the eyes of God'; the first seeing causes regret and sorrow, the second (7.1) brings grace. So devastation and rescue go hand in hand: the destruction of the earth by human beings brings destruction in its train; grace brings preservation or rescue. By means of a plan involving a boat, Noah can mediate between the human beings whom God regrets and the human beings who find grace in God's eyes. With the help of this Noah and his ark God will rescue the creatures on earth. So we need to say something more about him.

Noah is a righteous man who walks with God (just like Enoch in 5.22). He is the hero of the flood story. However, he is not very heroic. When God tells him that everything will be destroyed, not a word of amazement, protest or anger passes his lips. At least Abraham protests when God tells him that he is going to raze Sodom and Gomorrah to the ground; he negotiates with God over the rescue of some good souls. Not Noah. Noah is silent and assents to the destruction to everything. When God tells him that he himself and his family will be saved, he does not cry out in joy and fall on his wife's neck with happiness. He simply carries out the orders which God gives him. God says, 'Make an ark.' And Noah makes an ark. God does not put the hammer and nails in his hand, but in other respects he specifies everything down to the smallest detail: how big the ark must be, where and how the roof must be fitted, that it must be smeared with pitch, how many decks there must be in it, precisely what human beings and animals there must be in it. When it comes to numbers God is not so precise: on one occasion he says that Noah must take one pair of every kind of animal with him into the ark, and then on another occasion he mentions seven pairs of clean animals. Of course God is to be forgiven for this inconsistency, since we understand that *clean* animals are necessary for a sacrifice. Moreover it is useful to have seven pairs, since if Noah had only one pair, he would exterminate a whole species of animal with one sacrifice. Noah does all this precisely as God commands him. He does nothing on his own initiative. And he does not speak at all. It is certainly remarkable that the only two times that the word *teba*, ark, appears in the Old Testament it is associated with two persons who have not come of age, namely for the 'rush basket' of baby Moses (Exodus 1–2) and for the boat which rescues Noah. (In English we also speak of the 'ark of the covenant', but that is a different word from *teba* in Hebrew.) Noah and Moses rescue humankind and a people by means of a primitive vessel in the water; these little boats and their not very enterprising but righteous passengers are to be decisive for the progress of history.

Later, Noah's contribution to the rescue of human beings becomes notably greater. In order to be able to understand this we have to go back to Gen. 5.29. There Lamech, the father of Noah, was present at the birth of his son and gave him the name Noah. Because *n.ch* pronounced normally simply means 'rest', the name indicates that this son will give rest. Nevertheless father Lamech explicitly makes a connection between the name Noah and the verb *nacham* (*n.ch.m*), a word which occurs often in the Hebrew Bible and has many different meanings. Usually the assumption is that its basic meaning is to 'change thoughts, feelings or behaviour'. Depending on the context, *nacham* can then mean 'comfort' or 'regret', 'suffer pain' or 'exact vengeance'. Sometimes here it relates to a change in emotion, behaviour or thinking. In 5.29 it is generally assumed that it has the meaning 'bring comfort'; there father Lamech says, 'Noah shall comfort (*n.ch.m*) us for the work of our hands on the earth which God has cursed'. When the story of the flood begins, the reader has this relationship between Noah and *n.ch.m* (change, in the sense of comfort) in mind. Then the story of the flood begins with God, who in vv. 6 and 7 twice expresses his regret. This is indicated by precisely the same word, *nacham* (*n.ch.m*). God regrets that he has made human beings on earth, and Noah (*n.ch*) is the only one who finds grace (*ch.n*) in God's eyes. The similarity between the three words *n.ch.m*, *n.ch* and *ch.n* is too striking to be fortuitous, all the more so as Lamech had also already associated Noah's name with *nacham*. At the beginning of the story of the flood Noah thus functions in a context of God's regret over human beings, and here only a personal grace colours his unique position.

The end of the story of the flood is similarly instructive in this respect. The flood is over and the rescue complete, and Noah and his people have come out of the boat. But then something special happens: Noah does something on his own initiative for the first time (8.20). He builds an altar and makes a sacrifice of clean animals to God. The smell rises above the altar. God smells the savour of the sacrifice and immediately changes his mind and says: 'I shall never again regard the earth as cursed because of the human being, although what is formed in the human heart is bad from youth up' (8.21). The sacrifice brings about a good deal. Moreover it is not just a sacrifice, but a *nichoach* (*n.ch.ch*) sacrifice. This Hebrew word is a form of the same verb *n.ch*, rest or bring to rest, which is contained in the name Noah: it is a rest-giving sacrifice. (Unfortunately most biblical translations have rendered *nichoach* 'fragrant', on the basis of the Septuagint translation.) Through his sacrifice Noah is true to his own name: he gives God rest. At the same time Noah fulfils the life's task which his father had given him at his birth, namely that he was to be a consolation, *nacham*, to human beings and take away the curse from the earth. Noah's sacrifice brings God rest and means that God is no longer associated with *nacham* in the sense of regret but with *nacham* in the sense of consolation. This sacrifice which brings rest makes God remove the curse from the ground. So Noah seems to be of greater importance than we first thought. He is distinguished from the other human beings by his righteousness, his building of a boat and his sacrifice.

After everything that has happened, God gives Noah the promise that the earth will continue to exist despite the bad behaviour of human beings. Human beings have not changed; their preference for and proneness to the bad has not changed. Nevertheless God promises never again to do what he has done and guarantees the ongoing existence of the earth. Seed-time and harvest, summer and winter, cold and heat, day and night will continue to exist, all the days of the earth. At the end of the paradise story in Gen. 3.17 the earth is cursed because of human beings. Lamech hoped that his son would remove the curse. And now it seems that Noah has in fact removed the curse from the earth. Contrary to what Lamech thought, here it is not so much human beings who are helped, but the earth. The earth continues to be dependent on human beings for its cultivation, but the ongoing existence of the earth and all living beings is detached from, or made independent of, the actions of human beings, good and bad. The earth will continue to bring forth fruits, seasons will come and go, days and nights will not stop alternating. The law of the succession of the seasons and days will impose its rhythm on generations of human beings. It is the time of the earth which counts, and God is the guarantor of that.

A *new creation*

9.1   God blessed Noah and his sons
and he said to them,
     Be fruitful,
     become numerous
     and fill the earth.

2   Respect for you and fear of you shall there be among all life
     on the earth, among all the birds of the heaven, among
     everything that creeps upon the earth and among all the
     fishes of the sea.

Into your hand they are given.
3   Everything that moves and lives shall be your food,
likewise the green plants.
I give you everything.
4   Truly, flesh with its life or its blood in it you may not eat.
5   Truly, I shall require a reckoning of your blood and life.
From the hand of every living being I shall ask it.
From the hand of the human being,
from the hand of the man and his brother
shall I require a reckoning for the life of a human being.
6   Whoever sheds human blood,
his blood shall be shed by the human being,
for in the image of God he made the human being.
7   And you, be fruitful,
become numerous,
teem upon the earth
and be numerous there.

After God has confirmed that the earth will continue independently of human beings, he blesses Noah and his sons and gives them the task of being fruitful and numerous and filling the earth. This part of the blessing points back to Gen. 1, where God gave the same command. Here the command at creation is renewed: after the universal devastation the earth must be filled again. If in Gen. 1.22 a similar command was addressed by God to the fishes, the birds and the land animals, and in it the word 'teem' was used only for the fishes, now God uses it for the animals (8.17) and for the human beings (9.1 and 9.7). The surviving animals and human beings must teem over the earth. Within the framework of this renewed creation command God formulates two other commands.

> *be fruitful and fill the earth*
> all living beings shall have *respect* for you
> I give them into your hand
> you must have *respect* for life in others
> *from your hand* I shall require a reckoning
> *be fruitful and fill the earth*

In Gen. 1.26–28 the command is given to human beings to be fruitful and numerous over the earth, combined with the duty to care for the earth and the animals. Here this is taken up and filled in further. All living beings are to respect and fear human beings, and human beings must respect them. God gives human beings the animals and the plants. He gives both of these to human beings as food ('I give' points to 1.29), so that from now on human beings are not only vegetarians but carnivores. But at the same time the creation command of Gen. 1 is extended by the need for human beings to respect the life in other creatures. These others are not only given into the hand of human beings, but they have their own value and life-force. Human beings are to be called to account for their behaviour towards the creatures. Having been made wise by the evil that human beings have shown, God thus broadens his command at creation, not only to be fruitful and rule as in Gen. 1, but also to respect the life in other human beings and animals. The words 'the man and his brother', 'hand' and 'blood' (four times), explicitly establish a relationship with the story of Cain and Abel. If a man sheds his brother's blood, it is all up with the blessing. The filling of the earth and the recognition of the life principle in human beings and animals is what God requires of the human being.

The reader who so far has not understood why the wickedness of human beings was the occasion for the flood can now discover its implications from the conclusion of the story. Murder, bloodshed, the earth steeped in blood instead of being filled with new life, form the wickedness of which this text speaks. Over against this God sets his blessing, in which respect for all life is central. Human beings may indeed eat the animals, but not that part in which the life is concentrated, not their blood. Awareness of the independent worth of all life is what God aims at here with the supplement to his command at creation. Only then can the human being be 'the image of God' in relation to his fellow human being. This explicit reference to Gen. 1.26 shows that the anti-creation episode is over and creation has been recreated: anyone who wants to be a sign of God in the world will have to recognize and value the life of other creatures.

For a long time the evil in the world or the wickedness of human beings was wrongly derived from the disobedience of the human being towards God in the paradise story (Gen. 2–3). However, this text speaks more of a human process of growth than of a 'fall'. The sin which Genesis 1–11 certainly indicates is both the unfaithfulness of human beings to the earth and their unfaithfulness to other human beings and the animals. The shortcomings of the human being in relation to his fellow creatures are specified in Gen. 4 and Gen. 9 as a failure to recognize the principle of life in other creatures, in the man and his brother. This wickedness of human beings horrifies God and is the cause of his resolve to bring a great flood upon the earth. Through a new commandment which forms part of the blessing, God shows that blessing implies not only well-being for oneself but also respect for those others who have the same life in their blood. In short, the blessing which God gives to Noah and his sons at the end of the flood story shows that the three commands to 'be fruitful and fill the earth', 'call for respect' and 'respect the inhabitants of this earth' are the elementary conditions for the new creation.

A covenant

8   God spoke to Noah and his sons with him, saying
9   For my part,
         look, I make my *covenant* with you and with your seed after
             you,
10   with all living beings who were with you, with the birds,
         the animals and all life on earth with you, from all those who
             came out of the ark to all the life on earth.
11   I establish my *covenant* with you
         that all living beings shall never be cut off by the waters of the
             flood.
         No flood shall come to destroy the earth again.
12   God said,
         This is the sign of the *covenant* which I make between me and
             you,
         between all that life which is with you,
         for all following generations.
13   I have placed my bow in the clouds

and this shall be a sign of the *covenant* between me and the
earth.

14   It shall be that whenever I bring clouds over the earth,
the bow will become visible in the clouds.

15   Then I will remember my *covenant* between me and you and
all living beings,
and never again shall the waters of the flood destroy every
thing that lives.

16   When the bow is in the clouds
then I shall see it
to recall the everlasting *covenant* between God
and all living beings which are upon the earth.

17   God said to Noah,
This is the sign of the *covenant*
that I have made between me and all living beings
that are upon the earth.

God offers a completely and totally new covenant. Therefore he
uses the word *berit*, covenant, seven times: this is the beginning
of a new bond between God and the earth and its inhabitants.
Like the grace which God gave to Noah, this covenant too is
free and given for nothing. In the course of history it has been
constantly read as a covenant which God makes with Noah and
with Noah's descendants, and thus as a covenant between God
and all human beings. However, on a close reading it emerges
that each time God uses the word *berit*, covenant, he says that
this is a covenant between him and Noah, between him and all
living beings, and between him and the earth. The purpose
of this covenant is also clear, namely that all life shall not be
exterminated and that the earth shall not be destroyed. The
destructive work of human beings remains, but the destruction
of the earth by a flood will not happen again. That is the aim of
the covenant. God makes this covenant not only with Noah but
with everything that lives on the earth. Noah and his descendants constitute an important part of the living beings on earth,
but they form part of a greater whole.

    The sign of the covenant that God gives confirms this. God
puts a bow in the clouds as a sign. It remains unclear whether
this is a rainbow or another kind of bow. What is clear is that

the bow spans the earth and protects it. This bow is an 'all-embracing sign' which includes the whole earth. God therefore calls the bow the sign of the covenant 'between me and all of you' (9.9, 11, 12, 15), 'between me and the earth' (9.13), and 'between me and everything that lives on the earth' (9.16, 17). This sign points both to the autonomy of the earth and to the bond between God and the earth. Now that the earth has been washed clean of human faults and shortcomings by a great flood, God wants to guarantee and protect its ongoing existence. The seasons of the earth replace an eternal time or human immortality (see Gen. 6.1–4). They determine the rhythm of life. The new covenant between God and the (inhabitants of the) earth must prevent a new destruction. The all-encompassing sign in the clouds will remind him of that.

Names and faces of God

So far I have passed over the fact that in this flood story God is called by different names. Sometimes he is called *yhwh*, YHWH or Lord, and at others *elohim*, God. Anyone who reads through the text of Gen. 6–9 will see in succession: *yhwh* (four times), *elohim* (four times), *yhwh* (twice), *elohim* (twice), *yhwh* (once), *elohim* (three times), *yhwh* (three times), *elohim* (five times).

At the beginning of the flood story almost the same text appears twice. The first time it is connected with YHWH (6.5–8) and the second time with *elohim* (6. 11–13)

6.5   *yhwh* saw that the wickedness of the human being had become
          great on the earth,
       and that all the thoughts which he formed in his heart were
          sheer evil,
       all the days (of his life).
6   *yhwh* was sorry that he had made the human being on the earth
       and it gave him pain in his heart.
7   *yhwh* said,
          I shall sweep away the human being
          whom I have made
          from the face of the earth,

from human being to animal, from creeping beast to birds of
   the air.
For I am sorry that I have made them.
8   Only Noah found grace in the eyes of *yhwh*.

YHWH is directly involved with his creatures and shows an
almost human face: he has regrets and feels pain in his heart.
Only Noah finds grace in his eyes. YHWH's looking and his eyes
indicate that there is a clear bond between himself and the
creatures on the earth. This is not the case with *elohim*.

11   The earth was destroyed before *elohim*'s face
     and the earth was filled with violence.
12   *Elohim* saw the earth
     and look, it was destroyed,
     truly, all living beings destroyed their way on the earth.
13   And *elohim* said to Noah,
     The end of all living beings stands before my eyes
     for the earth is filled with violence through them.
     Look, I shall destroy them from the earth.

No words like regret, feel, heart, or anything of the kind occur
in connection with *elohim*. And what he sees and says does not
refer to human beings on earth, but to the whole earth and to all
living beings (*kol basar*). Nowhere in the text are human beings
mentioned by *elohim*. Even in 6.12, those who destroy the earth
are denoted by *kol basar*, 'all flesh', or 'all living beings', and
not by 'all human beings'. This is not meant to indicate that the
animals were also to blame for the destruction of the earth, but
to show that *elohim* is orientated on the whole earth with all its
inhabitants and is not limited to the human being. From these
two texts at the beginning of the story and the differences
between them we can infer that *yhwh* shows the aspect of God
by which God comes into contact with human beings on the
earth: one might perhaps call it the relational side of God.
Alongside this, the term *elohim* denotes the deity in himself, or
the non-relational side of God. The attention of *elohim*, this
God in himself, is directed towards the creation in itself.

At the end of the story we see something of this kind. After the waters have gone down and Noah and his animals have left the boat, Noah offers a sacrifice, and *yhwh* smells Noah's sacrifice. Immediately afterwards, *yhwh* says to his heart, 'I shall never again regard the earth as cursed because of the human being, although what is formed in the human heart is bad from youth up.' Thus *yhwh* puts his heart next to the human heart and lets his face (and his nostrils) speak. He takes the decision no longer to allow his actions towards the earth to be governed by human behaviour. This sensitive *yhwh* is followed (in 9.1–17) by *elohim*, who pays no attention to personal feelings and contacts, but to the whole creation. In what seems almost like a new creation story, he gives his blessing and offers a covenant. Here this blessing relates to the filling of the earth by human beings and to the recognition of the principle of life in all living beings. This principle of life belongs to *elohim*. Just as God requires human beings to honour his life principle, so God respects the life of all living beings (*kol basar*) by means of a covenant. This making of a covenant is not so much about human beings as about the earth and all the living creatures on this earth.

From all this, we can conclude that each time different aspects of God are brought to the fore, the name by which God is called is changed. If the name *elohim* is used, it stands for the deity in himself, for the transcendent God: *elohim* is God the creator and the one who relates to creation as a whole. By contrast YHWH stands for the immanent God, for the face of God which comes into contact with human beings and the other creatures on the earth. The choice of the name for God depends on the facet of God that the text seeks to represent.

What clearly emerges in Gen. 6–9 had already become clear in the earlier chapters of Gen. 1–11. In the creation story of Gen. 1 God is presented as absolute creator: God precedes creation, he stands above it and brings everything to life. This God is called *elohim*. The only relation between God and creation here is God's word and the creation which comes forth from it. Human beings are created to be in the image of *elohim* in a world in which God himself cannot be present as transcendent creator. Therefore as the image of God, human beings must preserve and continue this creation. The name *elohim* shows the primacy of God as the one who stands outside human beings and can never be reduced to a human image.

In the following story of paradise in Gen. 2–3, the name YHWH is added to this *elohim* to bring another dimension of God to the fore. This gives rise to the double name *yhwh elohim*. Here *yhwh* (as I mentioned earlier, this is a form of the verb 'be' or 'become') shows God in his relation to the being and becoming of creation, to the earth and the inhabitants of this earth. *yhwh*'s 'being' is connected with the 'becoming of creation'. As one divine name, *yhwh elohim* indicates at the same time both the transcendent and the immanent dimensions of God: God as creator who has made heaven and earth and stands outside creation and God as the one who is and becomes in the creation of the earth and the creatures on the earth.

In the story in Gen. 4.1–16 which follows Gen. 2–3, God is called *yhwh*, because he comes into contact with Cain and speaks to him directly about his relations with his brother. *yhwh* hears the blood that calls from the earth, and as a punishment dismisses Cain from his face and from the face of the earth. Here we can see the consequences for someone who has been banished from the face of *yhwh*: for such a person the breaking of the relationship with *yhwh*, with the brother and the earth is catastrophic. In the following texts, for a long time God is not named, although in Gen. 5, at the beginning of the genealogy, God is called *elohim*, a reference to the creation in Gen. 1. In the little myth in Gen. 6.1–4 which follows this genealogy the sons of god stand for the class of gods (*elohim*) which comes into contact with the daughters of men. However, this contact is short-lived. This is followed in Gen. 6–9 by the flood story, in which a distinction is always made between the different facets of God. Whenever God comes into contact with human beings and creatures he appears as the relational God, as *yhwh*, whereas when there is a reference to the creation story or when the content explicitly relates to the great totality of the earth, the term *elohim* is always used.

The conclusion is clear: depending on the aspect from which God is illuminated, as readers of Gen. 1–9 we see a particular aspect of this God. There are never complete images which make the nature of God tangible or possible to know. The divine names are rather a kind of window through which we look, which offers the writer and readers the possibility of making the unimaginable imaginable. The stories and names are the faces of God with which human beings come into contact. A recognizable face of God is indicated by the name *yhwh*. At the same time the 'generic' name *elohim* indicates that God cannot exhaustively be described by the name *yhwh*. Behind this is the deity as an entity which cannot be grasped, *elohim*, who is not to be thought of in relational terms (which by their very nature are also partly determined by human beings). And so here we see a recurrent feature of any thought about belief and the world. Anyone who thinks or believes makes a picture, but the picture does not exhaust what is being pictured. Just as there can be a reality which human beings picutre, although this notion does not cover reality or wholly disclose it, so there is a deity of whom many religions make images, to whom they give names, but without exhaustively describing the deity. Names are windows, but what is named slips through our fingers. At the same time, by combining *elohim* and *yhwh* Gen. 1–9 disseminates an awareness of both aspects: as *elohim* God is a creator standing by himself who is independent of the created world, and as *yhwh* God is a God of human beings who in contact with the creatures gives them meaning.

Conclusion: names and faces

The story of the flood has often been read in the light of the commandments at the end in 9.1–17. As a result of this, a good deal of the tension has disappeared from it. The whole destruction by the flood is then simply understood as an occasion for God's commandments and above all as an injunction to human beings to observe the commandments. However, these regulations and the concluding of a covenant function within a story in which the recognition of the principle of life, the preservation of the earth and respect for the living creatures on this earth are central. At the same time this story indicates a tension between creation and annihilation, between the mass of water and renewed creation. Stories tell of more than commandments; they tell the ambiguity of life in the pluriformity of a text.

This ambiguity grows and takes shape the more that names and faces are put into a narrative. That applies not only to the names of God but also to those of the other main figures, the earth and the human being. If we look back to Gen. 1–9 we discover a line in the naming of the earth. In Gen. 1 *erets* occurs almost exclusively, and together with heaven forms the cosmos, 'heaven and earth'. The *erets* is the dry land which appears when the waters gather in the seas. It is gradually overgrown with plants and populated by animals and human beings. Only once in Gen. 1 is the earth called *adama*, namely in connection with the creatures which creep upon the *adama* (1.25). After the fishes of the sea and the birds of the air, the creeping creatures are the first to populate the *adama*. In Gen. 2–3 the general approach to heaven and earth is focussed on one aspect: the human being, *adam*, on the earth, *adama*. Here, it becomes quite clear that the *adama* stands for the relational face of the earth: it is the earth as it functions in relation to human beings and to (land) animals. Just as the face of God is called *yhwh*, so the face of the earth is called *adama*. That does not mean that the earth would not exist without this face; in that case it is the *erets*, the earth in itself. To make this distinction clear in the translation, *adama* is always printed in italics, *earth*. From Gen. 2–3 it emerges that this face of the earth is not simply limited to the human being; the animals similarly maintain a relationship with the *adama*: both human beings and animals are made by YHWH God out of (stuff from) the *adama*, and in both cases this 'making' is called 'forming' (*yatsar*). Thus at their creation there is no difference between human beings and animals in relation to the earth. However, the human being is explicitly given the task of cultivating the earth, so that the *adama* can bring forth cultivated plants. In Gen. 1 the *erets* already brought forth wild plants, but for cultivated plants the *adama* is dependent on being cultivated by the human being.

The shift of attention from Gen. 1 with the emphasis on heaven and earth (*erets*) to Gen 2–3, about the relational face of the earth, *adama*, corresponds with the shift from the divine name *elohim* in Gen. 1 to the divine name *yhwh elohim* in Gen. 2–3. In the second text the subsidiary parts are in a much more direct relationship to one another. This focus is continued in Gen. 4.1–16, where Cain is the one who cultivates the *adama*. The murder of his brother is the cause of Cain's bond with the *adama* being broken; he is driven from the face of the *adama* and from the face of *yhwh*. Here too the explicit bond between the face of the earth and the face of God, *yhwh*, is evident. They are closely connected with each other.

The use of the names for the earth is most striking in Gen. 6–9. The word *erets* occurs fifteen times and the word *adama* nine. Where we have *adama*, the text is three times about creatures that creep upon the *adama* (6.20; 7.8; 9.20), three times about all creatures (from human being to animal) which YHWH has put on the *adama* (6.7; 4.23), twice about the dove and Noah who see the *adama* (9.9,13) and once about YHWH, who no longer regards the *adama* as cursed because of *adam* (8.21). Here too we also notice a relationally coloured earth which is called *adama*. If the *adama* is connected with God, then God is always called *yhwh*. By contrast, the divine name *elohim* occurs particularly with *erets*: above all at the end of the story *elohim* mentions this *erets* seven times with the conclusion of the covenant by the bow as a sign which encompasses the *erets*. Moreover *elohim*'s covenant and blessing are in the first place focussed on the *erets* and not on the *adam* or the *adama*.

Thus we see the relationships growing in our hands. God and the earth take on a colouring and a face of their own. Now we can discover that the human being too, is given different names in Gen. 1–9. In Gen. 1 he/she is still simply called 'human being' (*adam*), with a male and female component, and he/she is defined in relation to the earth as a whole (*erets*) and God (*elohim*). A more specific content is acquired only in Gen. 2–3. The human being seems to have his/her origin, end and fulfilment of life in the *adama*: as *adam* in relation to *adama*. Once divided into man and woman, the human being becomes *ish* and *issha*, although it is some time before the consequence of this difference becomes clear. But this does not exhaust all the aspects of the human being, since in Gen. 4 it proves that the human being who looks on his fellow human being is called *ach*, or brother. When a human being looks at his/her fellow human being or 'the other' (in Hebrew *acher*), he/she becomes 'brother', *ach*. When he does not look on the other, *yhwh* and the earth (*adama*) also disappear from view. We see this last facet of the human being, finally, in 4.26: the human being who calls on God by his name *yhwh* is there called *enosh* or human being. In short,

God seen in relation to human beings and the earth is called *yhwh*
God seen in himself is called *elohim*.

The earth seen in relation to human beings is called *adama*
The earth seen in itself is called *erets*.

The human being seen in relation to *adama* is called *adam*
The human being seen in relation to *yhwh* is called *enosh*
The human being seen in relation to *acher* is called *ach*
Man seen in relation to woman is called *ish*
Woman seen in relation to man is called *issha*
The human being seen in himself or herself does not occur.

In Gen. 1–9 the creation is recreated in language. We read how God made the heaven and the earth and how satisfied he was with what he had created. Then attention turned to relationships between human beings and the earth, man and woman, the human being and his fellow human being, the human being and God. Because the human being eventually has more trouble with himself than with controlling the earth or with his fellow human being, destruction begins. God responds to this destruction by a flood which sweeps everything off the earth. Thus the stories about the beginning show the reader how all that is made cannot exist in itself but only in reciprocal relationships. The changes in the names show that 'being' is always 'becoming in context'. Nothing and no one, not even God himself, is to be had separately. They are accessible the moment that they are looked at. Only when a human being looks another in the face and addresses him or her as fellow human being, brother or sister, as earth, as creature of this earth or as *yhwh*, does the human being get his or her own name and face.

Genesis 9–11: The Story of the Dispersion over the Earth[9]

9.18 The sons of Noah who came out of the ark
were Shem, Ham and Japhet.
Ham was the father of Canaan.

19 These three were the sons of Noah
and from them the whole earth was populated.

20 Noah began as a man of the *earth*
and planted a vineyard.

21 He drank of the wine
and became drunk.
He took his clothes off in the tent.

22 Ham, the father of Canaan, saw the nakedness of his father
and told his two brothers outside.

23 Shem and Japheth took the coat,
put it upon both their shoulders,
walked backwards,
and covered the nakedness of their father,
with their faces turned away,
so that they did not see the nakedness of their father.

24 Noah awoke from his stupor
and got to know what his youngest son had done to him.

25 He said,
Cursed be Canaan,
may he be a servant of servants to his brothers.

26 He said,
Blessed be YHWH, the God of Shem,
may Canaan be his servant.

27 May God make Japhet great,
may he dwell in the tents of Shem,
may Canaan be his servant.

28 Noah lived three hundred and fifty years after the flood.

29 All the days of Noah were nine hundred and fifty years
and he died.

10.1 These are the fatherings of the sons of Noah, Shem, Ham and
Japhet:

sons were born to them after the flood.

2 The sons of Japhet were Gomer, Magog, Madai, Javan, Tubal, Meshech and Tiras.

3 The sons of Gomer were Ashkenaz, Riphath and Togarmah.

4 The sons of Javan were Elishah, Tarshish, Kittim and Dodanim.

5 To these the coastal areas of the peoples in their lands were distributed, each according to his own language, their families, their peoples.

6 The sons of Ham were Cush, Mitsraim, Put and Canaan.

7 The sons of Cush were Sheba, Havilah, Sabta, Raamah and Sabteca
and the sons of Raamah were Sheba and Dedan.

8 Cush fathered Nimrod.
He began to be a ruler on the earth,

9 he was the ruler of the hunt before the face of YHWH,
therefore it has been said:
He is a ruler of the hunt before the face of YHWH like Nimrod.

10 ' The beginning of his kingdom was Babel, Erek, Akkad and Kalne in the land of Shinar.

11 From that land he went to Assyria.
And he built Nineveh, Rehoboth-Ir, Calah

12 and Resen between Nineveh and Calah;
that is the greatest city.

13 Mitsraim fathered the Ludim, Anamim, Lehabim and Naphtuhim,

14 the Pathrusim, Casluhim
from whom the Philistines came
and the Caphtorim.

15 Canaan fathered Sidon, his firstborn, and Heth,

16 and the Jebusites, the Amorites, the Girgashites,

17 the Hivites, the Arkites, the Sinites,

18 the Arvadites, the Zemarites, and the Hamathites.
Afterwards the families of the Canaanites spread.

19 And the frontier of the Canaanites ran from Sidon to Gerar near Gaza,
from Sodom and Gomorrah, Admah and Zeboim, to Lasha.

20 These were the sons of Ham by their families, by their languages, in their lands and in their peoples.

21 To Shem also were born,
the forefather of all the sons of Eber,
and Japhet's oldest brother.

22   The sons of Shem were Elam, Asshur, Arpachshad, Lud and
     Aram.
23   The sons of Aram were Uz, Hul, Gether and Mash.
24   Arpachshad fathered Shelah
     and Shelah fathered Eber.
25   To Eber were born two sons: the name of the one was Peleg,
     for in his days the earth was divided,
     and his brother's name was Joktan.
26   Joktan fathered Almodad, Sheleph, Hazarmaveth, Jerah,
27   Hadoram, Uzal, Diklah,
28   Obal, Abimael, Sheba,
29   Ophir, Havilah and Jobab;
     all these were sons of Joktan.
30   And their settlement ran from Mesha to Sephar, the hill country
     in the east.
31   These are the sons of Shem by their families, by their languages,
     in their lands and by their peoples.
32   These are the families of the sons of Noah by their fatherings in
     their peoples.
     From these the peoples divided over the earth after the flood.

11.1 The whole earth was of one language and one speech.
   2 It happened as they migrated from the east
      they found a valley in the land of Shinar
      and they settled there.
   3 They said to one another,
         Come!
         Let us make bricks.
         Let us bake them hard.
      And the bricks served them as stones
      and bitumen served them as mortar.
   4 They said,
         Come!
         Let us build a city for ourselves and a tower with its top in
            heaven.
         Let us make a name for ourselves,
         so that we are not dispersed over the face of the whole earth.
   5 YHWH descended to see the city and the tower
      which the sons of men built.
   6 YHWH said,
         Look!
         One people, one language for all.

This is the beginning of their doing,
and now nothing will stop them from doing
what they propose to do.
7 Come!
Let us descend.
And let us confuse their language there,
so that they may no longer understand one another's
language.
8 So YHWH dispersed them from there over the face of the whole
earth
and they stopped building the city.
9 Therefore its name was called Babel,
because there YHWH confused the language of the whole earth
and from there YHWH dispersed them over the face of the whole
earth.

10 These are the fatherings of Shem.
Shem was one hundred years old
and he fathered Arpachshad two years after the flood
11 Shem lived after his fathering of Arpachsad five hundred years
and he fathered sons and daughters.
12 Arpachshad lived thirty-five years
and he fathered Shelah.
13 Arpachsad lived after his fathering of Shelah four hundred and
three years
and he fathered sons and daughters.
14 Shelah lived thirty years
and he fathered Eber.
15 Shelah lived after his fathering of Eber four hundred and three
years
and he fathered sons and daughters.
16 Eber lived thirty-four years
and he fathered Peleg.
17 Eber lived after his fathering of Peleg four hundred and thirty
years
and he fathered sons and daughters.
18 Peleg lived thirty years
and he fathered Reu.
19 Peleg lived after his fathering of Reu two hundred and nine
years
and he fathered sons and daughters.
20 Reu lived thirty-two years

and he fathered Serug.
21 Reu lived after his fathering of Serug two hundred and seven
years
and he fathered sons and daughters.
22 Serug lived thirty years
and he fathered Nahor.
23 Serug lived after his fathering of Nahor two hundred years
and he fathered sons and daughters.
24 Nahor lived twenty-nine years
and he fathered Terah.
25 Nahor lived after his fathering of Terah one hundred and ninety
years
and he fathered sons and daughters.
26 Terah lived seventy years
and he fathered Abram, Nahor and Haran.
27 These are the fatherings of Terah.
Terah fathered Abram, Nahor and Haran
and Haran fathered Lot.
28 Haran died in the presence of Terah his father
in the land of his birth, in Ur of the Chaldaeans.
29 Abram and Nahor took wives for themselves.
The name of Abram's wife was Sarai,
the name of Nahor's wife was Milcah, the daughter of Haran,
the father of Milcah and the father of Iscah.
30 Sarai was infertile,
she had no child.
31 Terah took Abram his son, and Lot the son of Haran, the son of
his son, and Sarai his daughter-in-law, the wife of Abram his
son.
And he made them travel from Ur of the Chaldeans
to go to the land of Canaan.
They came to Haran
and remained there.
32 The days of Terah were two hundred and five years
and Terah died in Haran.

The naked Noah

In the course of time the story about Noah in his nakedness
has stimulated the imagination of many people. What seems
particularly to fascinate them is that Noah is drunk and lying

naked in his tent when his son Ham sees him. But it is unclear precisely what Ham's transgression was. The text says no more than

9.22 Ham, the father of Canaan, saw the nakedness of his father and told his two brothers outside.

One can get many things out of these lines, and people have done so. Some think that here Ham is being punished because he saw his father naked, others that he saw his father and mother making love; one writer thinks that Ham's fault was that he himself had sexual contact with his father and yet another that Ham castrated his father; finally, there are people who think that it is implied that Ham had sexual intercourse with his father's wife. These views come up fairly regularly. The story is filled in further depending on the time and the person concerned. At present it would perhaps be interpreted as incest.

There are yet more notable features about this story. Noah got drunk and lay naked and his son Ham saw him, but his grandson Canaan is punished for this, when he has done nothing wrong. Canaan has to atone for what his father and grandfather did and is condemned to a life as a slave of his brothers. The least one can say is that this is remarkable. This amazing fact stands out rather more against the background of the story.

The text opens in the first line by introducing the three sons of Noah: 'The sons of Noah who came out of the ark were Shem, Ham and Japhet. Ham was *the father of Canaan*' (9.18). It is striking that Ham is named *father* at the precise moment when he is introduced as son. Later, at the 'transgression' of Ham, exactly the same thing happens: 'Ham, *the father of Canaan*, saw the nakedness of his father' (9.22). It sounds rather stupid: doesn't Ham as a father see the nakedness of his father? Evidently the text wants to put all the emphasis on the father-hood of Ham or, rather, on the fact that he is the father of Canaan. In addition Ham is also the father of Mitsraim (Egypt), Cush (Ethiopia) and Put (North Africa), as emerges from Gen. 10.6. However, these sons do not count in the story of the naked Noah. Everything here turns only on Canaan. That similarly emerges from the words of Noah at the end of the story:

9.25 Noah said,
    Cursed be Canaan,
    may he be a servant of servants to his brothers.
  26 He said,
    Blessed be YHWH, the God of Shem,
    may Canaan be his servant.
  27 May God make Japhet great,
    may he dwell in the tents of Shem,
    may Canaan be his servant.

These are the very first words that Noah speaks. Throughout the flood he has not opened his mouth. So the first thing that he says is, 'Cursed be Canaan.' That doesn't sound very friendly; perhaps it would have been better had he been able to keep his mouth shut. So here Noah is not cursing Ham but Canaan. After that Noah says, 'Blessed be YHWH, the God of Shem.' So he is not blessing Shem, but YHWH the God of Shem. In other words, the opposition between the two brothers Ham and Shem takes on another colouring when Noah connects it with the opposition between Canaan and YHWH. The third and last sentence of Noah's statement confirms that: 'May God make Japhet great' equally refers to God and not just to Japhet. Certainly in the case of Japhet God is not called YHWH but *elohim*. Thus *yhwh*, the relational God, seems reserved for Shem, and the universal creator God *elohim* is simply named in the case of Japhet, not that of Canaan. All protection is withheld from him.

In short, the story of the naked Noah is told in a way which makes it clear that what is central is not Noah but the relationship between the father and the (grand)sons and the relationship between the sons and the grandsons in the light of the religious conflicts between the descendants of Canaan, Shem and Japhet.

Text in context

What is the function of a story about a drunken father and discordant sons within the totality of the primal history in Gen. 1–11? In the first place, it creates the conditions for the future relations between the brothers and their descendants, i.e. for the genealogy in Gen. 10. This story explains why there are hierarchical relations between the peoples on earth and why one people is superior to another. Because Ham has seen his father naked and has dishonoured him, his descendants are inferior to the descendants of Shem and Japhet. According to this story, human beings are not all the same but form part of peoples, some of whom shall rule over other peoples. The narrator tells this on the one hand in a way which means to say 'that is how it once was' and on the other hand includes himself and his readers in the one privileged group: they belong to the descendants of Shem. Therefore Canaan can reckon on little sympathy in this text.

The story in Gen. 9 points not only forwards, but also backwards to the previous chapter, and this gives it extra significance. Noah is described in the first place as 'a man of the earth' (*ish ha-adama*, 9.20). Earlier, as readers, we had already been able to make the acquaintance of two human beings who cultivated the earth, the first human being and Cain. The bond between the first human being, *adam*, and the earth, *adama*, was strong: coming from the earth, he/she had to cultivate the earth during his/her lifetime and return to it at his/her death. Cain was the first man-of-the-earth, *ish ha-adama*. He cultivated the earth and brought an offering of its fruits, but the earth, soaked in the blood of his murdered brother, accused Cain before YHWH. The result of this was that Cain ceased to become man-of-the-earth. After that Noah in turn is the first *ish ha-adama*. He plants a vineyard and makes wine from the fruits of the earth. Because the earth is no longer cursed, obviously it can bear abundant fruit – perhaps all too abundant, since the wine flows richly and makes Noah drunk. As well as this comparison between Adam, Cain and Noah as earthbound human beings there are further agreements between the story of Cain and Hevel, the paradise story and the story of the naked Noah.

The story of Noah is told in a way which makes the break between the brothers Shem and Japhet and their brother Ham central. The inequality between the brothers is even justified by putting it in a religious light. The story of Cain and Hevel also turns on a similar relationship between unequal brothers. Here Cain could not bear God looking on Hevel, his inferior brother, and even calling on him, Cain, to look at his brother. Here in Gen. 9 Noah cannot bear Ham seeing him in his nakedness. In both texts a 'revealing' look is the occasion for a break between members of the family. However, there is a difference in that God comes between the two in Gen. 4, but not in Gen. 9. The reason for this is given at the end of the story of the flood. There God makes a covenant with the earth, and commits human beings to honour the principle of life in all living beings. God concludes his blessing with, 'Whoever sheds human blood, his blood shall be shed by human beings' (9.6). Thus God will no longer appear as judge or avenger as in Gen. 4, but a human being will have to judge the behaviour of his fellow human being himself. In this sense God has withdrawn from inter-personal relations: the human being is himself responsible for his brothers (and sisters). On the first appearance of the human being Noah which follows this, Noah behaves similarly towards Cain. He may not murder his kinsman, but he does curse him and his descendants.

There are many facets to Noah's career. At his birth, Noah's father, Lamech, had said that his son 'will comfort us in our work and the labour of our hands on the earth which YHWH has cursed' (5.29). In 8.21 it is said after the flood and Noah's sacrifice that YHWH in fact removed the curse from the earth. At the same time YHWH has no illusions: the wickedness of all human beings (i.e. both righteous and unrighteous human beings) remains a fact. Both aspects are realized in the behaviour of Noah in Gen. 9.18–29. Noah cultivates the earth and his drunkenness bears witness to the fact that the earth has brought forth abundant fruit. This Noah, who hitherto was described as the prototype of a righteous man, here curses his own descendants. The result is that there is a certain hier-archy between the sons and the peoples: one people shall be stronger and better than the other; one brother shall be the servant of the other brother. What in Gen. 4 still happens on an individual scale here takes place on a larger scale, since the brothers have become peoples who are to rule over one another.

The story of the naked Noah functions as a parallel not only to Gen. 4 but also to Gen. 2–3. As well as the parallel, already mentioned, of a human being who cultivates the earth, in both texts we have the eating of the fruit of a tree or of a vine by which nakedness is uncovered. In Gen. 2–3 the eyes of the woman and the man are opened to their nakedness; in the case of Noah, first his eyes are closed, and then the eyes of his son are opened to the nakedness of his father. In both cases, the 'seeing' results in 'knowing'. One could call it knowledge by unveiling. In both cases the nakedness is covered by another: in the case of Noah it is his sons Japhet and Shem who subsequently clothe Noah with the cloak of love; in the case of the first human beings, God provides the clothing. Moreover a very apt parallel between the two stories is the role played by the mediator in the knowledge. In Gen. 3 that is the snake, and in Gen. 9 Ham. Both figures in the story have more knowledge and tell others about this revealing knowledge. This is indicated by the same word, *nagad*, tell. The consequence is identical: in Gen. 3.16 the descendants of the snake are cursed and in 9.25 the descendant of Ham. The mediator in knowledge, in revealing knowledge or knowledge about being naked, gets the heaviest penalty. Only here Canaan is punished in place of his father Ham. Just as the descendants of the snake are doomed to remain subject to the descendants of the woman, so Canaan and his descendants are doomed to remain subject to the descendants of Japhet and Shem.

The story of the naked Noah could be summed up as a renewed creation and an old tale. This story legitimates the inequality between human beings as caused by a transgression of Ham. The earlier paradise story is echoed here. The 'paradox of the fall' shows that the transgression by the human being shows both progress and the sense that this progress at the same time involves loss and has been possible only thanks to the transgression of a divine commandment. This is echoed in Gen. 9.18–29, in which a slight transgression has to explain the division of human beings into peoples and the existing differences between these peoples. The transgression is presented as the reason for an existing, unsatisfactory situation. Here need and transgression go hand in hand and in this way create a high degree of ambiguity in the text. This ambivalence cannot be reduced to simplicity, although people have done that all too often both in the paradise story and in the story of Noah and his sons.

Noah and his three sons

In the course of history this story has been read, supplemented, filled in, and adapted to people's own time. They have told it as a justification of their own views. The story has been reduced to a simple meaning which fits the interpreter's own view better than the ambiguity of the text. Earlier, we saw how people did this in different periods with the story of paradise. Now it will emerge that history has also left far-reaching traces on the interpretation of the story of Noah and his three sons.

In the genealogy in Gen. 10 the descendants of Ham are described as Mitsraim (Egypt), Cush (Ethiopia), Put (North Africa) and Canaan. In the rest of Genesis and the Bible the Hamites are identified with the Canaanites and with the inhabitants of the 'south', and later above all with the black people from Africa. From the beginning of Christianity Christians began to identify themselves with the descendants of Japhet. We have written evidence from the early Middle Ages (as in the historical work *Historia Brittonum* and the writings of Isidore of Seville, both from the seventh century CE), in which the descendants of Shem, Ham and Japhet are connected with the then known population groups on the three continents: the inhabitants of Europe descend from Japhet, the inhabitants of Africa go back to Ham, and the people in the Middle East are descendants of Shem. The European Christians infer from the blessing of Japhet in Gen. 9.27 the certainty that Japhet occupies a special position in the world. Therefore the Japhetites, viz. Christian Europe, must bring civilization and Christianity to the other population groups.

The stigmatization of the Negroes as Hamites had already begun earlier, and the story of Noah and his three sons was used for it. Here the Hamites are cursed by God through the mouth of Noah! Things were rather more difficult with the Shemites (we know them under the name Semites), since these are expressly blessed by the same Noah. However, Christians in Europe after the eighth century were quite clear. Because the Near East had been conquered by the Muslims, the Shemites were also cursed. Almost all the Shemites had become Muslims anyway. Here reference was made not so much to Gen. 9 as above all to Gen. 21, where Hagar and Ishmael are cast out. The Muslims were descendants of Ishmael, and thus they were also cast out by Abraham. In this way 'the Arab' was sufficiently qualified as an enemy. It was different with the Jews. These are also Shemites and are blessed by Noah, but in their case reference is made to another text: they were branded 'murderers' of Christ and so disqualified. Thus as descendants of Japhet and the bearers of Christianity the Europeans were the only ones who did not need to doubt their own important status on earth. Their relationship to the other peoples was nurtured and legitimated by their interpretation of the story in Gen. 9.18–29.

What had first begun as the interpretation of a story to explain a people's position in the world had far-reaching consequences. After Columbus' 'discovery' of America in 1492, the colonization of Central and South America by Spaniards and Portuguese began. Workers were needed as labour in the mines and on the plantations, and therefore a start was made on importing black slaves from West Africa. The slave trade grew and assumed enormous proportions. A justification was sought for this trade in human beings who had equally been created in the image of God, and was found in Gen. 9. The moral responsibility for the slave trade, which many people regarded as an economic necessity, called for a negative image of the Negro. Only in this way could Europeans justify what they, Christians, were to begin to practise to an increasing degree.

The story of Noah, the cursing of Canaan, and Noah's remark about the Hamites as slaves of their brothers were regularly quoted in preaching and in treatises to defend the European practice of slavery. So this story was not only reduced to one line, but was used to lull the conscience of Europeans who were concerned about the slave trade in their time. They did not need to worry: as Hamites, the Negroes had been cursed by Noah himself (and thus indirectly by God) and so were condemned to the existence of slaves. Beyond any doubt, as Japhetites who had been blessed, the white Europeans had the right to act in this way.

Slavery was abolished in the eighteenth century, though it was not to be until the nineteenth century that it disappeared completely. A new form of colonialism was developed, and Africa was divided between the leading European countries: England, France, Germany and Belgium. Again, a justification had to be sought for the economic and political domination by Europe. In accord with the more secular spirit of the time, this was no longer looked for in a story from the Bible but in the natural sciences. For scientific legitimation, reference was made to Darwin's theory of evolution. According to this view, the black race showed all the characteristics of a human species which was at a lower level of evolution than the white Europeans. Therefore whites had to do their best to bring up the less developed blacks in the Christian faith and in forms of European culture. As a colonialist the white man put the black man in a position to elevate himself.

Thus a view of the world seems to be attached to the story of Noah and his three sons, which has also contributed towards the world becoming as it now is. Apologies have already been made for the inhuman suffering that the children of Japhet have inflicted on the Jewish descendants of Shem, although the wrong that has been done has not been wiped out. However, people have not yet got this far over the black descendants of Ham. These still suffer to the same degree from the 'white stories', from the imagery of the whites in which the blacks are 'lesser gods'. Although reference is no longer made to Gen. 9, the notion behind it has still not disappeared: a child of Japhet is still always worth more than a child of Ham. The Europeans still regard themselves as 'the first world' and call others 'the third world'. And these others, who are called Hamites, may still only revolve as satellites around our first world.

A list of peoples

One story may be stimulating, and another seem dry. For most people, a genealogy or list of peoples belongs to the second category. But with some additional information it can still be more interesting than we might expect.

The beginning and end of Gen. 10 show the context of this chapter:

10.1 These are the *toledot* of the sons of Noah, Shem, Ham and Japhet:
sons were born to them after the flood.

10.32 These are the families of the sons of Noah by their fatherings in their peoples.
From these the peoples divided over the earth after the flood.

This chapter contains the *toledot* or fatherings of the three sons of Noah: Shem, Ham and Japhet. Here the line of the earlier *toledot* in Gen. 4 and 5 which had been broken by the flood is continued. This is the first genealogy for the time after the flood. However, now it is no longer about individuals but about peoples. Both processes are expressed by the word *toledot*.

Genesis 10 sums up the peoples as they were known at the time. A division was made of the peoples according to the sons of Noah, so that it could become clear that the population of the earth after the flood descends from one pair of ancestors, Noah and his wife. Perhaps it would be better to say that here they go back to one parent, since only Noah is mentioned, and not his wife. Noah gets his sons alone, just as his sons get their sons alone. Of course, we can infer from the voyage of the ark that women were needed for the procreation, for just as in the case of all the animals a minimum of one pair, husband and wife, were taken, so, too, human beings went into and out of the ark in pairs. However, in the actual procreation after the flood we hear only of men.

In a sense, this list has been written from the perspective of son Shem. The name 'Shem' means 'name'. He is called 'name' (compare the rabbinic tradition in which the name of God is pronounced as *ha-shem*, 'the name'; here the same word recurs). Of course you cannot give all three children the name 'name', so the two others are called 'Japhet' and 'Ham'. Japhet's name is explained in Gen. 9.27 with the words, 'May God make Japhet great' (*yapat elohim le-yapet*), with the word *yapat* being used for 'make great'. However, we do not know the meaning of Ham's name, nor are we given any explanation. From the names alone we can see that Shem is central and that Japhet is a good second. But in terms of descendants Ham surpasses his brothers, since he is the ancestor of the most prominent peoples.

Let's just run through the list of names, so that we get a picture of the ethnographic division of the known world of the time. That does not mean to say that all the people are equally known to us. We must guess at some names, but we do have an impression of most. The descendants of Japhet are Gomer, i.e. the Cimerrians, an Indo-European people in Turkey; Magog is Lydia, which is in Turkey; Madai are the Medes who live south of the Caspian Sea and north of the Tigris; Javan is the generally recognized name for Greece; Tubal and Meshech are inhabitants of eastern Turkey, and Tiras is also in Turkey and stands for Tyrene (a name which has been preserved in 'Tyrrhenian Sea'). The sons of the sons of Japhet are probably to be located on the islands near or in the coastal regions of Greece and Turkey. Thus the descendants of Javan (= Greece) are: Elishah or Cyprus; Tarshish, a port in southern Turkey; Kittim or Crete; and Dodanim, which can be a miswriting of either Rodanim, in which case it stands for the inhabitants of Rhodes, or of Donanim, in which case it stands for the Greeks generally (cf. the Greek *Danaioi*). So Japhet has seven sons: seven grandsons are mentioned in his case, and all these descendants are connected with the coastal regions or islands of Greece and Turkey.

The descendants of Ham are: Cush or Ethiopia, Mitsraim or

Egypt, Put or Libya, and Canaan. No further descendants of Put are mentioned, but all the more of Cush, Mitsraim and Canaan. The first, Cush or Ethiopia, fathers five sons who are all to be connected with Arab peoples on the Arabian peninsula (present-day Saudi Arabia). Of these, Sheba (present-day Yemen) is the best known, because of the Queen of Sheba who comes to visit King Solomon. Here we also find Havilah again, a name which we already encountered in the story of paradise (2.11). Both Sheba and Havilah are the locations of gold and precious stones. So the descendants of Cush stand for prosperous peoples and regions. The most notable son of Cush, however, is mentioned separately. He is the sixth son, Nimrod.

A great deal of attention is paid to Nimrod in this list of peoples. He is described as a mighty ruler and hunter. Although he, too, belongs to the Cush branch in Africa, he is so powerful that he founds a great kingdom which extends to Mesopotamia. He founds cities in Babylonia (Babel, Erek or Uruk, Akkad and Kalne) and in Assyria (Nineveh, Rehoboth-Ir, Calah and Resen). Moreover here Babylonia (present-day southern Iraq) is called Shinar, and that is the land where in Gen. 11 the tower of Babel is to be built. Nimrod must have been a very powerful ruler with such a great kingdom. We do not know whether Nimrod is a legendary figure or the description of a historical person. If the latter, Nimrod could possibly be compared with Nimmuri, the king who appears in the Amarna letters and who in Egyptian is called Amenhotep III; he lived from 1416 to 1379 BCE. This Nimmuri claimed that his kingdom stretched from Egypt to the Euphrates. We know that he built the enormous temples in Luxor and Karnak, at the remains of which we can still wonder. We also still have five scarabs with 'texts' which give an account of the life of Amenhotep III; one of them describes him as lord of the hunt, and contains a picture with one hundred and two lions. So it could be possible that Nimrod is the same as this Nimmuri or Amenhotep III. On the other hand, Nimrod could equally have been just a means of indicating that Cush had a powerful ruler as his son.

Ham has another son, Mitsraim or Egypt. His descendants are not as famous a Nimrod. No firm examples are known of them, since what follows is a dry summary of descendants who probably belong to the different population groups of Egypt. One of them is introduced as the forefather of the Philistines. From this it appears that the Philistines are seen as people who came from outside and settled in Canaan. Finally, the fourth son of Ham is Canaan. He has eleven sons, among whom Sidon stands for the capital of Phoenicia (present-day Lebanon), Heth for the Hittites, the Jebusites for the pre-Israelite population of Jerusalem, and the Amorites for the inhabitants of Syria and north-west Mesopotamia. All the descendants of Canaan live in Phoenicia, Syria, Jordan and Canaan. The last sentence in 10. 19 makes it clear that the frontier of the Canaanites runs from Sidon in the north to Gaza in the south-west, from Sodom and Gomorrah in the south-east (i.e. south of the Dead Sea) to Lasha in the north-east (though this last is uncertain, since the location of Lasha is unknown).

Finally, sons are born to Shem. The opening sentence is certainly different from that for his two brothers:

10.21 To Shem also were born,
        the forefather of all the sons of Eber,
        and Japhet's oldest brother.

Verse 21 does not say who is born to Shem, since the word 'sons' is missing. Nor does a summary of names follow immediately. Certainly we are told that Shem is 'the forefather of all the sons of Eber'. This Eber is evidently the most important of all Shem's descendants: all the sons descend from Eber, and Shem is their forefather. The formulation seems to make Eber almost more important than Shem. That is corrected to some degree at the end of the last sentence: Shem is the oldest of the sons of Noah, he is the oldest brother of Japhet. Of course he is also the older brother of Ham, but he is not mentioned again here.

Shem has five sons: Elam, or the mountain region east of Mesopotamia (present-day northern Iran); Asshur or Assyria (present-day northern Iraq); Arpachshad, the meaning of which is unknown; Lud or Lydia in south-west Turkey; and Aram or

Syria. Only further descendants of Aram and Arpachshad are mentioned. The sons of Aram (Uz, Hul, Gether and Mash) are unknown to us, but could have been population groups in Syria. All the emphasis then gets put on Arpachshad's line: through him and his son Shelah, the family of Shem is continued with Eber. This Eber is third in the line from Shem and the father of two sons, Peleg and Joktan. The name of Peleg is interpreted in 10.25 by the word *palag*, 'divide': 'for in the time of Peleg the earth was divided'. Joktan's name means 'the younger'; he is the younger brother of Peleg. It is striking that all the thirteen descendants of this younger brother (but not of Peleg) are named, all with Arab names, which probably stand for Arabian peoples. Peleg's descendants are mentioned only in Gen. 11. The areas in which all these descendants of Shem live lie in the east: from Mesha east of the Jordan to the frontier territory (Sephar) in Iran. It is typical that only Shem is connected with 'the east', and not the descendants of Japhet and Ham. Thus the Shemites are not the original inhabitants of Canaan, but people who come from the east.

So Genesis 10 gives a picture of the world. One might call the text an exercise in world cartography. From a global perspective the population is described as coming from the sons of Noah. Here the descendants of Japhet for the most part stand for the inhabitants of the north-west, Greece and Turkey. The sons of Ham represent the population groups of the south, North Africa, Ethiopia and Egypt, and those of the centre, Canaan, Lebanon and Jordan. Finally, the descendants of Shem are presented as 'the sons of the east': from Iran and Iraq to southern Turkey and Syria they form the line from which Abram eventually comes.

A socio-cultural description

However, Gen. 10 does not just give an ethnographic description of the population of the earth. This is evident among other things from some irregularities in the text itself. Thus we see that the descendants of both Japhet and Ham and those of Shem are situated in Turkey: the Medes, who live in the east and not in the west, are here coupled with Japhet, which argues against a western position for Japhet; Nimrod belongs in the west, but his kingdom includes all Mesopotamia; the same Arab peoples appear in the lines of both Ham and Shem. Moreover the narrator of the list himself indicates three times that it combines different things: it is about peoples in their lands, and peoples according to their languages or cultures (10.5, 20, 31). As well as an ethnographic ordering the text therefore offers a socio-cultural description of the then known world.

This is most visible in the somewhat more evaluative sentences which regularly conclude or introduce the lists. In the case of Japhet, in v. 5 we have:

10.5 To these the coastal areas of the peoples in their lands were distributed, each according to his own language, their families, their peoples.

The descendants of Japhet are the inhabitants of the coastal regions and the islands (the Hebrew word used means both coastland and island). These are population groups which not only live in the west but also belong to the seafaring nations. Whereas in the case of the descendants of Japhet above all the inhabitants of the islands or the coast are named, with Ham we have the great cultivated lands from Egypt to Mesopotamia. That is also why Nimrod is described at such length: he is presented as the founder of a kingdom. He builds the great cities in Mesopotamia, from Babylon to Nineveh, from Uruk to Akkad; these are the great cities of the then known world. Nimrod is a builder of cities and a hunter; the other descendants of Ham, like Egypt and Canaan, are also sedentary peoples: population groups which live in a vast area, in villages or cities.

10.19 And the frontier of the Canaanites ran from Sidon to Gerar near Gaza,
from Sodom and Gomorrah, Admah and Zeboim to Lasha.

The Canaanites fall under the same rubric as Egypt and Babylon: they live in an urban culture (compare the description in Deut. 1.28: the Canaanites are described as inhabitants of cities which were great and had walls up to heaven). Moreover their land of Canaan had a frontier, something which occurs only with settled areas. In short, the descendants of Japhet represent the coastlands and their seafaring population, and the sons of Ham form the sedentary population living in cultivated areas, in the great cities or fortified villages, the boundaries of which are known.

The descendants of Shem similarly appear in another light. It is not for nothing that the name of Eber is mentioned twice. Eber comes from the word *abar*, 'journey', 'travel', 'pass by', 'go past'. Eber thus means 'passer by', 'migrant', 'traveller', 'nomad'. The word for Hebrew, *ibri* or *ivri* (cf. *ivrit*, the name for the Hebrew language) comes from the same root. When elsewhere in the Pentateuch we read 'my father was a wandering Aramaean', the determining factors of a Hebrew are given, namely 'wandering' and 'coming from Aram'; in this case Aram stands for a land from the east: Syria or Mesopotamia. No cities or villages are mentioned in connection with the descendants of Shem, but only nomadic settlements or tents.

10.30 And their settlement ran from Nesha to Sephar, the hill country in the east.

The word used here in Hebrew for 'settlement' is *moshab*: this is not a village or city, a fixed dwelling place, but something movable. Therefore the word 'frontier' is not used here, as in the case of Canaan, since the area is not limited and fixed. As well as being a geographical and ethnographic division, Gen. 10 is thus a sociographic description of the social groups:

Shem is the father of all the children of Eber: the nomads
Ham is the father of all the inhabitants of kingdoms and cities: those who are sedentary
Japhet is the father of all the dwellers of the coasts and islands: the seafarers.

The strongest group is that of the settlers, the descendants of Ham who form the centre of the cultivated land: the Egyptians,

Canaanites, Babylonians and Assyrians. Eber, Shem's son, here represents the migrant part of the population which is distinct from the sedentary society. Shem is the father of all the sons of Eber, of all nomads. The story of the naked Noah and his three sons in Gen. 9 reflects the hostility which exists between Ham and Shem, between the sedentary and the nomadic population.

Thus Gen. 10 makes an essential contribution to the description of the development of the human being on the earth. Up till now the human being has been described as an individual, as a being who becomes human in relation to the earth, as man in relation to woman, woman in relation to man, human being in relation to fellow human being, human being in relation to God. Here the social aspect of the human beings is developed: a human being is a social being living in a people and a land, in a particular social group with its own language. Genesis therefore describes not only the development of human beings as individuals but also the development of human beings as social beings who form part of a social group or people.

This image is confirmed when we look at extra-biblical sources of Egyptian or Mesopotamian origin. In these texts the term *apiru* or *abiru* appears regularly as a description of a stratum of the population which appears in the different lands of the ancient Near East and forms the lowest social class in it. The *abiru* are the travellers, the nomads, the outsiders of this time. In one particular period these *abiru* have increased in number to such a degree that especially in Egypt they begin to form a threat to the indigenous population. They were therefore driven out of Egypt. Many biblical scholars are convinced that these *abiru* can be identified with the Hebrews, not only because the two words come from the same root *abar*, but also because this historical phenomenon is a reflection of the events described in Exodus with the departure of the Hebrew slaves from Egypt. The Hebrews, then, are travellers and nomads who form a social group which is distinct from the settled population. Their God is called YHWH, 'he who becomes what he is', and is a God who travels with them. It later emerges that this YHWH has no need for a fixed place or temple on earth: he simply wants to live in a portable ark of the covenant. Just as the story of Cain and

Hevel showed that God's concern was for Hevel, the worthless brother, so later in Genesis it will become clear time and again that YHWH, the God of Shem and of Eber, is a God of the outsiders, of those people who do not count as far as the settled inhabitants of a land are concerned. He is not so much the God of a people as the God of a particular social class: the have-nots. He will call them 'his people'. Whenever these Hebrews succumb to the custom of the settled peoples, he distances himself. YHWH sets out with the travellers.

The tower of Babel

11.1 The whole earth was of one language and one speech.
  2 It happened as they migrated from the east
    they found a valley in the land of Shinar
    and they settled there.

Anyone who goes on to read Gen. 11 directly after the list of peoples in Gen. 10 will be surprised. We have just had a description of how the world was divided up into peoples and languages, and now everything begins all over again in one place and with one language. Probably the relationship between Gen. 10 and 11 is to be compared with that between Gen. 1 and 2–3, where the paradise story highlights one aspect of the previous process of creation and describes it further. Something of the kind also happens here in Gen. 11.1. The camera zooms in on one moment of the preceding process of the *toledot* of the sons of Noah, 'when the earth was still of one language'. Then in Gen. 11 follows the story why more languages came into being.

The beginning and end of Gen. 11.1–9 present the framework of the story. Verse 1 gives the circumstances or situation which precedes the events that are to come: 'The whole earth was of one language and one speech.' The specific actions begin in v. 2, where the human beings find a valley and begin to build. Here YHWH rigorously puts an end to the spread of human beings over the earth. After that the narrator turns as it were outside the story and addresses the reader:

11.9 Therefore its name is called Babel (*babel*),
       because there YHWH confused (*balal*) the language of the whole
           earth
       and from there YHWH dispersed them over the face of the whole
           earth.

The narrator evaluates the event in the framework of the story
and in so doing gives a particular direction to the text. In the
first verse he describes the initial situation and in the last verse
the final situation of the whole earth:

1: the whole earth	*is one language*
9: yhwh confuses the language of	*the whole earth*
9: yhwh disperses them over	*the whole earth*

It is significant that the story of Gen. 11.1–9 has *kol ha-erets*,
the whole earth, as the first and last words. Thus the narrator
wants to make it clear that the whole earth is the framework of
reference for this text. He indicates this by barely referring to
the people concerned. The only time that they appear in these
verses is as the personal personal pronoun for 'they' (in the
Hebrew one letter which is attached to the verb). This third
person plural ('them') is only indicated and related to the whole
earth.
  We see something similar within the framework of the story.
Events begin in v. 2. But who is the subject of the action? The
grammatical subject is 'they'. It's a bit odd, 'when the earth . . .
they found a valley.' Who are the they? Beyond doubt 'the
human beings' is meant here. But it is striking that they are not
introduced with a personal or a generic name but as a third
person plural. Only in the transition from the mention of
human beings to that of YHWH is there one verse (v. 5) in which
the narrator denotes these 'they' for the first time with a generic
name: 'the sons of men' (*bene ha-adam*). The narrator says of
these sons that they build (*banu*): by means of the link between
bene and *banu* the narrator makes an explicit connection
between the sons of men and their building for themselves (*lanu*,
'for us', in v. 4). In short, in contrast to the framework of vv. 1

and 9, in which *kol ha-erets* appears three times, the narrator presents the active subjects as 'they' just once (when he puts the emphasis on the human beings and their building for themselves), as subjects who unlike 'the whole earth' are not described or specified further.

The human beings ('they') spur one another on:

3   They said to one another,
      Come!
      Let us make bricks.
      Let us bake them hard.
    And the bricks served them as stones
    and bitumen served them as mortar.
4   They said,
      Come!
      Let us build a city *for ourselves* and a tower with its top in
      heaven.
      Let us make a name for *ourselves*,
      so that we are not dispersed over the face of the whole earth.

All these human exhortations use 'we' (five times) and 'us' twice and have one aim: 'so that we are not dispersed over the face of the whole earth.' The human beings want to make sure that they are not dispersed all over the earth. They oppose dispersal over the whole earth with an action focussed on 'us'. So vv. 3,4 say nothing about human behaviour towards God, but only about human behaviour towards the earth. This behaviour is to be summed up as 'we not over the whole earth'.

In vv. 6–7 YHWH reacts to this human plan:

11.6 YHWH said,
        Look!
        One people, one language for all.
        this is the beginning of their doing,
        and now nothing will stop them from doing
        what they propose to do.
7   Come!
        Let us descend.
        And let us confuse their language there,
        so that they may no longer understand one another's
          language.

YHWH begins with, 'Look, one people, one language for all' and in so doing uses the word 'one' twice. Moreover, the unity of language is not the consequence of human action, for according to v. 1 this was already part of the situation of the earth at the beginning. Therefore this remark of YHWH's does not refer back to v. 4, either to the tower or the city. It is even questionable whether YHWH is blaming anyone in v. 6a. He is noting a fact: they are one people and all have one language. But through the actions of the human beings in vv. 3 and 4 it is as if YHWH is for the first time seeing the consequences of the 'fact' of v. 1: 'This is the beginning of their doing. Now nothing will stop them from doing what they propose to do.' YHWH fears that the behaviour of these people with their one language will lead to an even greater human orientation on 'we'. Therefore YHWH now formulates his own plan: 'Let us descend and let us confuse their language there, so that they may no longer understand one another.' Over against the 'us' and the 'we' that human beings use to spur one another on, YHWH sets the 'us' and the 'we' that he uses to spur himself on. Neither the narrator nor the human beings nor YHWH speak of a human striving which is directed against God. The only thing that is said there is that 'they' who through language are one and form one people are striving for more unity and do not want to be dispersed over all the earth.

After all this talk, YHWH goes into action:

11.8 So YHWH dispersed them from there over the face of the whole earth
and they stopped building the city.

In what he said, YHWH had been talking about confusing language, but afterwards he does not confuse language but disperses the human beings over the earth. Thus in what he says YHWH is addressing himself to the unity of language and in what he does YHWH is addressing himself to the unity of place (11.8). Finally, in v. 9 both aspects return in this action of YHWH: YHWH confuses the language of all the earth and disperses the human beings over all the earth. To be able to understand this mixing of language and place, the line which the story draws between the words *shem*, 'name', and *sham*, 'there', must be looked at more closely. In v. 2 the human beings move to a place which is steadily brought into closer focus, from the east, to the land of Shinar and to a valley in that land. They settle 'there', *sham*. Then they build in this spot a city and a tower which indicates yet a further concentration of place. At this spot they state their ideal: we want to remain in one place and make one name (*shem*) for ourselves, so that we are not dispersed all over the earth. This *shem* above all seems to stand for the name or the label of their unity in this place. Moreover an important point is that it is not the earth that gets a name from the people, but only the people themselves. The unity of language (v. 1) evidently leads to striving for one place and one name. The one place (city and tower), *sham*, is represented by the one name, *shem*.

YHWH takes action against this striving for one *sham* and one *shem*. First he states his plan to confuse their language there (*sham*) and for that purpose he disperses them from there (*missham*). This is summed up aptly in the words which the narrator addresses to the reader immediately afterwards, in v. 9: instead of one place (*sham*) and one name (*shem*) we now have 'its name Babel', in which the Hebrew word 'its name', *shemah*, indicates how language and place coincide there, since in this word there is both the a-sound of *sham* and the e-sound of *shem*. The name Babel also has the same significance: it is one name, which expresses plurality and confusion; here an explicit connection is made between Babel (*b.b.l*) and confuse (*b.l.l*). If we keep this line of meaning in mind, what YHWH says and does in vv. 7 and 8 becomes clearer. In what he says, YHWH addresses himself to the unity of language, and in what he does he addresses himself to the unity of place. The text makes this mixture of activities possible by using *sham* and *shem* in this text as counterparts, namely as signs of unity. Thus in Gen. 11.1–9 *shem* and *sham* are interconnected – both by the human beings (the persons who speak in the text) and YHWH, and by the narrator.

To sum up, in the framework of the story a reference is made to the changing situation of the earth. This change is brought about by the actions of the human beings and by YHWH in

vv. 2–8 inclusive. In these verses the human beings strive for more unity of place and language, and this is depicted by one valley, one city, one tower and one name. Subsequently YHWH strives for plurality or not-one: not one language, but many languages; not one place but a dispersal over the whole earth. With this second series of actions on the part of YHWH and the stop put to the human building, the final situation comes about: a multiplicity of languages and peoples, spread over the face of the whole earth.

The traditional interpretation of the story

In the Christian tradition, attention to Gen. 11.1–9 has always been focussed one-sidedly on human pride, which is said to want to be equal to God. In fact this interpretation of the story is based on two elements from v. 4a, namely the human plan to build a tower with its top in the heavens and the human wish to make a name for themselves. According to the usual view, a tower with 'its head in heaven' refers to the human striving to be like gods. The wish to make a name for themselves is therefore regarded as arrogance, indeed even as a striving for power, given that these human beings want to take power from God. God's reaction in v. 6 is always read in this sense. The desire for power is only the beginning of their villainous plans, for who knows what will come later? Perhaps human beings may even want to cast God out of heaven! The human activities of construction and concentration therefore call for a devastating counter-reaction on God's part: God cannot but oppose this human arrogance. In this connection a line is often drawn back to Gen. 2–3, and the story of the building of the tower is seen as a parallel to the story of paradise with the transgression of the divine prohibition against eating from the tree of the knowledge of good and bad. For their crime the builders of the city need to be punished, just like the first human being, man and woman.

In the Jewish tradition, Gen. 11.1–9 has long been read as the 'story of the dispersion of human beings'; moreover it has not been called the 'tower of Babel'. According to the Jews, God's dispersion of human beings over the earth is the main theme of this text. In contrast to the Christian tradition, in which the main emphasis has been put on human sin against God, the Jewish tradition has an interpretation of Gen. 11.1–9 as a story about languages on earth and the dispersal of human beings over the earth.

A positive interpretation

The problem with interpreting the story of Gen. 11.1–9 as a story about human arrogance is the exegesis of v. 4. The building of the tower with its 'top in heaven' does not refer at all to the wish to be like God. For the heaven (*shamayim*) in Gen. 1–11 does not stand for God's dwelling-place at all. The heaven is the vault between the waters, and God does not dwell in that vault, far less on the earth, since he remains outside creation. The heaven is not a sign of God, as is also evident from the fact that in v. 5 God has to descend in order to marvel at the tower with its top in heaven. So a later image of heaven has wrongly been connected with this text. Contrary to what the Christian tradition has read into it, Gen. 11.1–9 is not about the upward striving of human beings but about their horizontal striving: these people did not want to get to heaven or to God, but to remain on earth in one place. That is confirmed by the closing verses of the story, in which there is no more mention of the tower or the upward dimension. Verse 8 says that the people 'stop building the city' and the tower does not occur again. In v. 9, similarly, all the attention is paid to the city and the name Babel, and there is even less mention of the tower. To call Gen. 11.1–9 'the story of the tower of Babel' is thus really a misnomer; we would do better to call it 'the story of the dispersion of the human beings'.

Contrary to the Christian tradition, in which the main accent has been placed on human sin against God, with the Jewish tradition we do better to read Gen. 11.1–9 as a story about the difference of languages as a condition for the dispersion of human beings over the earth. This dispersion is not presented as a punishment for a sin which has been committed, but as a necessity. It is as if the hindrance which works against the dispersion, namely the one language, is done away because, thanks to the action of human beings, YHWH sees its consequences for the earth. Two indications in the text confirm this reading. The first is that alongside the phrase 'the whole earth', *kol ha-erets* (five times), the addition 'over the face of' (*al pene*) occurs three times in conjunction with the whole earth. So this passage is about people spreading over the whole surface of the earth and filling the whole earth. A second indication is that the people are called 'they' or 'them' by both the narrator and YHWH, who is a figure in the story: they are simply inhabitants of the earth, who are not specified further. Only the earth is defined, and is itself introduced five times as an independent subject, whereas the human beings remain in the shadow of the earth.

Despite the fact that the human beings are simply called 'they', both the Jewish and the Christian traditions are very human-centred in their exposition of this story. There is something ironic about this: people think that it is about them and their building of a city and tower, whereas God only puts emphasis on the earth and the dispersion of human beings. He is not concerned with the tower, nor even with the city. People assume that God looks through the same spectacles as they do, but he does not let the building of a tower make him put on human spectacles. Seen through God's spectacles, the question is one of the earth and the dispersion of human beings over the earth, since it is the earth that has to be filled and cultivated.

The descendants of Shem and Terah

After this enlargement of one facet in which the need for the many peoples and languages upon the earth is made clear, the text can return to the human beings. Now it is no longer about all human beings but only about the descendants of Shem. In Gen. 10 the *toledot* of Noah were central and the line of history was presented as the growth and distribution of human beings in three social groups: sedentary, nomad, and the inhabitants of the coasts or islands. In Gen. 11 attention is focussed exclusively on the nomadic population in the line of Shem and Terah.

The construction of the *toledot* of Shem is the same as those of Adam in Gen. 5, except that Gen. 5 has a more extended beginning and Gen. 11 a more extended end. However, in the main part of both chapters the fatherings by the fathers are central: father X lived for so many years, he had son Y, he lived after his fathering of Y so many years, and he fathered sons and daughters. If we compare that with the list in Gen. 10 we discover a difference. In Gen. 10 sometimes more sons are mentioned, each of which subsequently becomes the tribal ancestor of a people: with Shem we have the sons Elam, Asshur, Arpachshad, Lud and Aram (in 10.22), whereas in Gen. 11 only Arpachshad is mentioned as the son of Shem. The same thing happens with Eber, whose two sons Peleg and Joktan and the thirteen descendants of Joktan are mentioned in Gen. 10, whereas Gen. 11 contains only the oldest son, Peleg, followed by his son, Reu, his grandson Serug, his great-grandson Nahor, and his great-great-grandson Terah. In Gen. 5 and Gen. 11 only the firstborn sons are given a name; here everything turns on the individuals, fathers and oldest sons, whereas Gen. 10 is above all focussed on human beings as part of a people or a population group.

Genesis 11.10–32 also seems to have unexpected sides. In the list of Adam both the life and fathering and the death of the fatherers are mentioned: 'he was fathered', 'he fathered' and 'he died' is briefly what it amounts to. In the list of Shem, things are different. In it no one dies; there is so much emphasis on the continuation of life that the death of the (fore)fathers is not mentioned. With the genealogy of Terah things are different again. First of all, one of his three sons (Haran) dies very quickly (though his son, Lot, has already been born) and Terah's oldest son is married to an infertile wife. This last fact is even mentioned twice, because it is so important: 'she is infertile' and 'she can get no children' (literally, 'there was for her no child'). When soon afterwards Terah leaves Ur in Mesopotamia on his way to Canaan he takes his son Abram with him, and Lot the son of his son Haran and Sarai his daughter-in-law, the wife of his son Abram. Only Nahor and his wife Milcah remain behind in Mesopotamia. Thus Terah will not really live on through this Nahor. But Terah dies in Haran. This is the very last sentence of Gen. 11: 'Terah died in Haran.' Here is no hopeful end to a genealogy. Abram and his barren wife Sarai are the only ones left, with their nephew Lot. And to think that the *toledot* of Adam had begun so hopefully in Gen. 5 with a reference to the creation of human beings as the image of God! In the last list, the *toledot* of Terah end with the death and final extinction of the main line of Shem and Eber.

Thus two lines wind through the text: survival and extinction, remaining in a place and moving on. The amazing thing is that only the branch which travels on and the oldest son here threaten to die out. Abram's line does not go on, although his name *ab-ram* means 'exalted father'; he is not likely to become a father. Even the fixed rhythm of life and death in a genealogy can sometimes come to an end. But in the next chapter, what here seems to be at an end will prove to be the beginning of a new history of YHWH with Abram and the Hebrews. He will make a covenant with him and them. Even a so-called dead end, as in the case of Abram, seems to have more openness than we might think at this point. And therefore the primal history is not the end but the beginning of history.

Conclusion: *the story of the earth*

Imagine that we are standing on the tower of Babel and looking back over the landscape of Gen. 1–11. Far over the horizon we see how first the heaven is created and how after it the earth comes into sight. Then the heaven is populated with heavenly bodies and the earth with plants, animals and human beings. It is as if they are facets of one diamond: indissolubly bound together, each sheds its own light on the cosmos as a whole. One facet is that the inhabitants of the earth have the capacity to continue their own species and another that human beings have the task of filling the earth and ruling it. This creation of heaven and earth and the continuation of life on earth form the beginning of everything; they form the time and space of the landscape.

Rather closer, but still far away in the East, we see the garden of Eden. Rivers come out of this garden, and the garden forms a green oasis in the land. The story of this garden (in Gen. 2–3) shows how human beings are bound up with the earth. Not only the words *adam* and *adama* indicate that, but it is also brought out by the origin of the human being from the earth and his or her return to the earth. In the time between birth and death the human being is similarly bound to the earth because he or she constantly has to work on it to get food. Conversely, the earth is also dependent on human beings, since it does not produce any vegetation unless it is cultivated by them. Thus earth and human being are indissolubly connected. The other relations which determine human life are characterized in close connection with this relation between human being and earth. Thus the task of human beings, to rule over the earth, is described in analogous terms to that of the man towards the woman, and the life-giving task of the woman towards the man is described in analogous terms to that of the human being towards the earth. The relationship between human being and God is similarly dependent on that between human being and earth: God's care for the earth entails that he makes human beings who are in a position constantly to cultivate the earth. For this purpose God forms human beings who within the garden of Eden acquire the possibility for discernment and pro-creation. Then God sends them out of the garden to begin to work hard on the earth outside the garden.

We also see wandering around in the region of Eden a man who has just murdered his brother. His story, told in Gen. 4.10–16, is the story of a man who grudges his brother the light in his eyes. This man, Cain, has shed his brother's blood and the earth has accused him of having done so. Thereupon Cain's relationship with the earth and with God is broken, and after that he just wanders around. From Gen. 2–4 on, we there-fore know what the essential relationships for human beings are, namely those between human being and human being, man and woman, human being and earth, and human being and God.

A long series of people journeys through the landscape from Eden. Their names, even series of names, indicate that human beings are carrying out the task given in Gen. 1.28 to fill the earth and to rule over it. Sons of god come upon the earth, but their intercourse with the daughters of men does not result in their children (like their fathers) living for ever; immortality is excluded on earth. It is not immortality but immorality which prompts God's subsequent measures towards the earth. For human beings have filled the earth not only with new life and new human beings, but also with much misery, injustice and unrighteousness. The earth itself is in risk of perishing. Therefore God brings a great flood upon the earth, which swallows up all life on earth with devastating force. All drown, except for those who are voyaging in the ark. Fortunately, after the flood and after Noah's sacrifice God promises that the earth will continue, regardless of human evil. The water disappears and the earth reappears, and God makes a covenant with the earth and all its inhabitants. Now that everything has firm ground under its feet, the creation can begin again. The animals multiply, but we hear nothing of this. However, we do see that human beings procreate. Above all, Noah's sons are very fertile. As far as the eye can see, the earth is filled with their descendants, which differ somewhat from one another.

Close by and even around us we see a city rising. The tower on which we are standing lies in the centre of this city. The people speak one language and the result is clear: they begin to band together and form a group. They bake bricks, build houses for their children and a tower as a sign of their unity, since they want to avoid being dispersed over the earth. Languages, many languages, are necessary to disperse them, and God also sees to that, so that justice can be done to the earth. Babbling and gibberish fill the air, and people begin to set off. The earth can breathe again.

Standing on our somewhat ramshackle tower we see a great mass of people departing. They spread over the whole earth. Each speaks his or her own language. No one understands anyone else, and each goes to live in another place. There they set to work: they cultivate the earth and bring forth new life. Only in this way can the whole earth be filled and ruled.

From a survey of the creation story of Genesis 1–11 we can

conclude that it is a story about the cosmos, about the earth and its ongoing existence, and about human beings on this earth. Although progress and setbacks, development and destruction, alternate in this story, in the end God resolves on a covenant with all living beings on earth. In it God guarantees that the earth shall continue to exist. However, to populate and rule over the earth it is necessary for people to spread over its whole surface. Thus in the story of the tower of Babel the last condition is fulfilled for making the ongoing existence of the earth possible.

Part II

Other Stories of the Beginning

The Significance of Stories

Stories

In the beginning was the story. God created, and we have looked at God's creating through a story. Without that story we would have no ideas or no thoughts which we could fill with images. But without an actual beginning we would have no story. Not only is the creation of the world recreated in words, but so too is everything that happened afterwards. All experiences, emotions and events are time and again given new content by language, by stories in which again and again a new beginning is made in time and space and a new world is created. By reading, we step into these new worlds.

The world of the beginning has its own characteristics. A beginning presupposes continuity: everything develops from the beginning. A creation story therefore presupposes that time has begun and is continued up to the present. The story shows the connection between the beginning and what follows, and by this connection it can exercise influence, clarify the intention of the beginning and prove fruitful in any life afterwards.

A story gives structure to time by connecting a series of developments in a coherent way. The course of action shows a particular line in the event. Inspiring stories or 'true' stories are not inspiring or true because they happened precisely like that. Life is not a story, and does not contain any straight line of events. But precisely by the way in which the story creates a context and makes a connection between events from beginning to end, events take on meaning. Creation stories are about the absolute beginning, but other stories also create a beginning in time and go on to its specific end. A story tries to understand life by the way in which it orders time. Stories do not only reflect reality, but create a world of imagination. That moment of transformation at which the material takes form and becomes content, becomes the vehicle of an idea or an image, seems to

177

disclose something about what is going on within the reader. The best stories are those which have a naturalness about them, as if they had come into being in a moment rather than having been laboriously constructed. It is a question of simplicity, which in an experience of reading allows the complexity of experience to be seen and experienced.

Stories of the beginning are not only read as 'imaginings' of reality, but as forming part of reality. They do not function as fiction but as fact; they make it possible to relate and explain one's own past. The creation story in Gen. 1 has for centuries explained why the human being is the ruler of creation, and later provided support for technological control of the world. In the course of history the paradise story in Gen. 2–3 has determined the lives of millions of people; it has served as an explanation of the sinfulness of life, as a motive for rejecting sexuality and as reinforcement for making the wife the servant of her husband. Stories like this have constituted a picture of the world, human beings and God, and have demarcated an area within thought generally. In other cultures this space is demarcated in a different way, and disorder is ordered in a different structure of meaning. When we recognize that, we are given an insight into other peoples' thinking, and also into our own.

In all these creation stories, with language, with images expressed in language, and with words which sometimes stand at the very edge of what can still be said or understood, people try to understand something of another reality. For them it is a matter not just of belief, but also of a kind of sense of life. By contrast, others assume that the world as it is is pure matter. They think 'It's as it is and nothing more; as long as you live, you are there, and after that you aren't there any longer.' And they accept things only as things; their experience of reality stops at the material dimension. Creation stories are a counterbalance to such an approach. Their basis is wonderment at life and questions about it. Here matter is the vehicle of another order, and the stories create another form of reality which intensifies and deepens people's presence in the world or people's lives.

At the present moment there is a tendency to let the story be the story. Those in search of the core of belief and the core of life disregard everything which is on the 'fringe'. But what is core and what is form, and can there be content without a form or a message without a story? Suppose that instead of the story of the 'tower of Babel' we had just the core statement, 'Human beings had to disperse over the earth.' In one sentence this so-called message sums up what the story took almost thirty sentences to say. Of course such a summary is efficient, but it doesn't catch anyone's imagination. So a detached sentence has no power to convince. Moreover, those who follow the traditional exegesis of Gen. 11 and sum up its core as 'pride comes before a fall' do not achieve their aim. Would Brueghel ever have made a painting out of such a sentence? Have you ever considered changing your life on the basis of a poster at the station with the text 'God speaks'? The exodus story makes far more of an impression than such a slogan. The liberation from Egypt and the journey through the wilderness express in pictures how God goes along with people, how he frees slaves and rescues people. There is often also something moralizing and compelling about 'the' core; how could it be otherwise? By contrast, the story indicates more the ambiguity and plurality of life. It shows that life cannot be limited to one aspect; it shows the facets by which light falls on events from different angles. A story creates for readers the possibility of putting themselves in the positions of others. A story allows the reader to sympathize with the main characters, to share their perspective and so to experience what it is like to see things differently. Through a story we are addressed, whereas through a message we are merely spoken to.

This plea for stories goes further than a plea for language or for the literary dimension of a text. It is based on the conviction that it is an illusion to think that important things can be reduced to simplicity, when most things in life prove to be complex and ambiguous. Why should belief above all have to be reduced to cores, laws, fixed rules and statements of faith which are simple and unequivocal? Are convictions, idealism, faith and a view of life no more than a simple reproduction of the core of life? Stories are not just to be dismissed as fiction or fantasy, certainly not in older cultures in which generations of people have summed up their experiences in stories. In the course of time these 'solidified experiences' came to be regarded as a source of inspiration. To be supported by people's own experiences and guided by stories in which the experiences of others have been set down is more inspiring than to be guided by messages.

Perhaps we can make things clearer by looking at paintings. Someone has a portrait painted. The painter who makes such a portrait has a distinctive style. So a portrait by Rembrandt looks different from one from Van Gogh, and that in turn looks different from a portrait painted by Modigliani or Auerbach. Imagine that all four were to make a portrait of the same person. In other words, the 'object', or the 'reality', is a given for all four of them. But the way in which they treat that object differs: Rembrandt will have more light-and-dark shades, Van Gogh more bright colours, Modigliani will elongate the figure and Auerbach will use heavy daubs of oil. None of them could paint a portrait at all without the figure whom they portray, and in this sense they are all dependent on the object which stimulates them to give form and meaning. The person being portrayed exists apart from the portrait as a real human being, but a painter is needed if the portrait is to come into existence. This artist contributes all his or her own qualities and applies them to make a good portrait. Furthermore, an artist does not always work in the same way, since the young Rembrandt will paint a different kind of portrait from the older Rembrandt, and a 'potato-eater' portrait of Van Gogh differs from a portrait by Van Gogh painted in Arles. As those who look at the portraits, we only have the images to which form has been given, each of which in its own way points to the reality that is depicted. Our only possibility of getting at the subject is through the paintings. This person is the great absentee. He or she is present only in the portraits.

We could compare this with the portraits of Jesus that we find in the New Testament and which come from four evangelists.

The four Gospels give a picture of Jesus, each in its own way. They are motivated to do this by the life of Jesus himself. They are inspired by Jesus and seek to express what he meant for them so that others too should believe in him. We, readers and believers, have only their portrait, and cannot look behind the portrait to discover what Jesus looked like, whether he really had the kind of beard that all film directors give him, and whether indeed he had blue eyes. We cannot even answer more important questions, like precisely what his words or motives were. We have only the portrait of Jesus painted by Mark, which is similar to, but also different from, that of Matthew, and which in turn has somewhat different accents from Luke and John. For example, Matthew shows Jesus as messiah and son of God, and the disciples as people who (just like the later readers) are sometimes too blind to understand the consequences of the good news of Jesus for their own lives. It is even more difficult for the viewer or reader of the present day to look behind the portraits of the evangelists and encounter Jesus himself directly and hold out a hand to him than it is with the portraits by Rembrandt and other artists. Jesus is absent here and now, and we can only get to know him through the Gospels. But can we then say that these portraits or ideas have to be purged? I don't think so, since apart from these reproductions we cannot know or encounter Jesus.

The same thing happens with God. God is not present in the word in such a way that one can point and say, 'There he is! How attractive he is!' We only have stories, testimonies, poetry, images: pictures of him in the Bible, in the Qur'an, in the Buddhist tradition, in the testimonies of mystics, in our own experiences of faith. These experiences are sometimes summed up and crystallized in stories. We cannot look behind them or correct them; at best we can add new images which correspond more to our present-day experiences and insights. But we cannot require even these images to express the core more fully than the earlier pictures. Our notions, too, will be a mixture of right and wrong, and we shall not know which is which. God will not coincide with our images either. We shall never reach God as the purely transcendent God, as the one whom we can touch or embrace outside the portrait. And our image of God will always betray our artist's hand.

Philosophical reflections

We can put these considerations in a rather broader perspective and emphasize that any form of giving meaning, like belief, thought and interpretation, is at the same time a product of the world outside us and of ourselves. This leads to the conclusion not so much that everything is relative as that everything is relational. The reality of which we form a part is ordered by our culture and our language, and by the meaning and significance that we give it. Here the focus on the thing, the person, the reality or the experience is the crucial factor. Meaning is given from this perspective or standpoint. It is the same in graphic art, which invented the word perspective. Unless we occupy a standpoint, we see nothing. A particular perception is impossible without a standpoint.

At the same time this helps to explain how every form of thinking, believing and giving meaning comes into being as an interplay of three factors. The first factor is formed by the 'object': without a reality or experience of reality, an object or a person, no view or standpoint is possible. In that case you just stand there. There is nothing on which the gaze can be focussed. The second factor is the 'subject', the person who perceives, gives meaning and expresses himself or herself in language. Here the person-related perspective on the object, the person, the reality or the experience is determinative. Someone gives meaning from this perspective or standpoint. So meaning is not given beforehand but arises through and for human beings. However, giving meaning is not just a subjective expression of self, since both 'the thing itself', or the object that is the focal point, and the words used are not exclusively determined by the person. Words, language and culture are given beforehand. And these form the third factor which is a considerable influence on the meanings that we give. Therefore God, too, carries a history of words and concepts with him. So we cannot get outside history to be with God; we cannot get outside our culture to the thing itself or the heart of the matter. The relations between these three factors make it possible for us to give meaning: a subject with his or her own standpoint, the thing itself and the language and culture (and thus also the history) in which we live and with which or in which we give meaning.

If we go more closely into the last factor, the language and culture, we discover in it the role of stories (the great stories). Just as words have a meanings that we do not invent, but are given beforehand, what was written down first (and these are often the great stories) gives direction to a culture. Just as in bringing up a child the parents create material pointing in a particular direction with which the child can later work, so the first stories and texts create the necessary possibilities from which later interpretations can be produced. It is possible to revise only if there is something there in the first place. In this sense stories create the conditions through which it is later possible to give meaning. The creation story in Genesis has also been a directional text in this sense. We now think that the evolutionary model is a better account of the beginning than the creation story. But the theory of evolution is also an explanatory model, and is itself a story that creates coherence and provides connections between different detached perceptions. As a story it fits our present-day culture better, because this culture is one in which perception forms the highest epistemological category, and we regard the controlled perception or experiment as the most controllable form of truth. In keeping with this culture we find that the model of evolution offers a better explanation of the beginning and the formation of the world from the beginning. We even find it so good that we no longer notice its narrative character and regard it as reality. But even this form of explaining, thinking and believing is characterized by a certain transitoriness. Moreover it is an illusion to think that someone can step out of this transitoriness and say, 'Right, this is *the* account of the beginning or *the* truth.' Perhaps there are at most traces of the truth. So we have become seekers after truth, trackers.

Stories of the beginning have also been key features in every culture for forming a common language. They function as pointers to the way along which people must develop their lives. The narrative form shows that this way is characterized not only by rationality but also by imagination. A story offers an ambivalent approach which can make reflection possible. It provides an occasion for forming new images which give meaning and can inspire our world-view and actions.

Reading

Reading stories requires a certain openness from readers. They have to be in a position to look openly at the world, to acquire and assimilate new connections and ways of ordering. To demonstrate this I want once again to go into the way in which we perceive, give meaning and read.

People give meaning to the world around them. They perceive something that still has no form, and that compels them to seek forms and words with which to express it. The absence of form necessitates the giving of form, of meaning, but the existing culture means that the formless is given form in a fixed way, so that one does not have the sense of getting at the uniqueness, the individuality, of the thought or idea. Therefore perception is in the first place a matter of recognizing patterns: we recognize what we have seen or learned to see earlier. At the same time we are sometimes aware of the unique, the special or the specific, although we can only assimilate this when we relate it to what we know. Only by comparing the unknown with the known, or seeking a point of comparison, can we extend knowledge. An example may make this clear. When in 1492 Columbus arrived in Central America on a voyage to India, he saw the Caribbean islands for the first time in his life. This was totally new, and could not be included in what he already knew. And what does he write in his log? 'The Caribbeans are like Valencia in the spring!' He assimilates the unknown by associating it with the familiar. In more general terms, in order to be able to know and give meaning a person must on the one hand already have some knowledge, and have a culturally conditioned network for recognizing patterns, and on the other hand be in a position to correct and to fill in existing knowledge if something does not agree with what is thought to be knowledge. In this last instance the knowledge and images of the world are developed and one can talk of some growth.

Those who read are also confronted with something new. A certain flexibility is required to assimilate what is new in a text and to relate it to one's own experiences and knowledge. Some people do not have this, because their patterns of perception are too rigid. They only perceive the known truth, in which the other is dismissed as alien, odd, unsuitable. It is certainly one of the aims of this book to inspire more flexible thought about the beginning by both a new interpretation of Gen. 1–11 and a comparison with creation stories from other cultures. An awareness of other creation stories from America, Africa and Asia can help us to see our own thinking about the beginning in another perspective. In any culture, the creation stories are the royal ways to the foundatons of the order which people have created within their own culture. These ways make it necessary for us readers to embark on a long journey into other patterns of perception and worlds of imagination.

Stories from the Urals to the Andes

Stories and cultures[10]

Within a particular culture stories of the beginning are usually
the basis of the religious community. It is customary to call
other cultures' stories of the beginning 'myths'. The essential
feature of these religious convictions in story form is that they
are handed down orally from generation to generation and that
they are told especially at festivals or at particular landmarks in
life like birth, coming of age, marriages and funerals. Usually
these stories are accompanied by special rites which belong to
the particular occasion. 'Sacred stories' (myths) and 'sacred
actions' (rites) are in this sense indissolubly connected: the
story seals and explains the action; the action illustrates and
expresses the story. Often this also means that such a story may
not be told always and anywhere by just anyone. Only the
religious specialist or elder may tell such a story, on special
occasions and in particular places. Invited to such a context,
members of the religious community learn what the content of
their faith is, how they must behave and how the community
must be organized. The story of the beginning takes the believer
back to the beginning of time when God or gods inaugurated
the world order. The believer, moreover, need do no more than
follow this order instituted by God or the gods.

Usually those who study myths divide the texts according to a
particular typology (cosmogonies, theogonies, anthropogonies).
I shall not be doing that here, since this kind of classification
often says more about the scholar's desire for order than the
way in which the stories themselves order the world. It is even
more customary to tell these stories simply in order to go on
to compare them. In order to let the stories speak for themselves, here I shall not be making any comparisons either, since
unfortunately comparisons all too often lead to a quest for
agreements, for what is 'universal', and that fails to do justice to

the distinctive features of the story and the context. Moreover, the selection offered here is a very limited one: there are some thousands of creation stories from all over the world, of which only twenty are given here. To make a substantial comparison on that basis is impossible.

The selection of creation stories which now follows is based on a distribution over the parts of the world from which the texts come. Travelling from the Urals to the Andes, we first meet the stories from Asia, namely the ancient Babylonian account of creation, two Indian texts about creation and two Chinese texts. Then follow the stories from Australia, New Zealand and Hawaii. Crossing the ocean we get to America. The splendid creation story of the Quiché Indians (descendants of the Mayas) in Central America (Guatemala) which is called the Popol Vuh is given rather more space. After a shorter Indian story from North America we go from the Andes back in the direction of the Urals. First we come to the creation stories from Africa. Here there is a collection of eight shorter creation stories from Nigeria, Ghana, Zaire, Zambia, Rwanda and Tanzania. Finally we end up in Europe with a Greek creation story by Hesiod, part of the Icelandic Edda and a short extract from the Finnish epic, the Kalevala. As far as possible each story is first briefly located in its time of origin and context. The texts are based on various translations and have been worked over so as to produce a text which runs smoothly. Where many foreign names sometimes make them difficult to read, these names have sometimes been replaced by corresponding generic names: for example in the Popul Vuh 'Caculhá Huracán' has been translated 'Heart of Heaven'. But the use of these generic names is always derived from the texts themselves or from the explanatory indications which are given in the relevant text.

The stories collected here come one after another, although their characters are very different. These are independent texts, each of which is sacred within its own culture. Readers will fail to do them justice if they read them too quickly, one after another.

Stories from Asia

Babylonia: Introduction

The Babylonian creation epic is one of the oldest written creation stories in the world. This story is named after its opening words, 'when on high', *Enuma Elish*: 'When on high the heaven had not been named, firm ground below had not been called by name.' In its present form it presumably dates from the ninth century BCE, but it goes back to a version from the Old Babylonian kingdom which dates from the nineteenth century BCE, and was read each year on the fourth day of the New Year festival. The text as we now know it consists of seven clay tablets in cuneiform (Akkadian) which belonged to the library of the Assyrian king Asshurbanipal.

The Babylonian creation story comprises two parts: the beginning, with a short part about the origin of the powers of the cosmos, is followed by a longer part about how the present world order was established step by step. The opening describes the primal state at the beginning before the first gods were born: all is still a watery mass in which the sweet underground water, Apsu, and the salt sea water, Tiamat, had not yet been divided. There was nothing else, no other form. Even the notion of a heaven above had not yet occurred to anyone, and below there was no earth, not even an island, no marsh, and as yet there were no gods. Then two gods Lachmu amd Lachamu came into being from the mingling of these waters: they were fathered by Apsu and borne by Tiamat. The names Lachmu and Lachamu (from *l.h.m.*, silt, mud, mire) refer to the silt of which Mesopotamia is formed. At the mouth of the rivers Euphrates and Tigris, precisely where the sweet water (Apsu) flows into the salt water of the sea (Tiamat), new land was formed by deposits of silt. This situation in Mesopotamia is projected back on the very first beginning. Thus the land and the later gods emerge from the union of the waters.

After the material origin of land and gods (the description of all kinds of gods with Babylonian names has been omitted), there follows a dispute between the gods. This is a latent conflict between the representatives of two opposed tendencies: the gods who represent movement and activity, and the older generation of power which stands for inertia and rest. Marduk, the supreme god of Babylon, wins, and finally a new stable situation comes into being.

Enuma Elish[11]

When on high the heaven had not been named,
firm ground below had not been called by name,
nothing but primordial Apsu, their begetter,
and Tiamat, who bore them all,
their waters commingling as a single body;
no reed hut had been matted,
no marsh land had appeared,
when no gods whatever had been brought into being,
uncalled by name, their destinies undetermined.
Then it was that the gods were formed within them.
Lachmu and Lachamu were brought forth,
they were named by their name.
Endlessly they increased in years and greatness.
Other gods were brought forth . . .
The divine brothers banded together,
they disturbed Tiamat
as they surged back and forth,
yes, they troubled the mood of Tiamat
by their hilarity in the abode of heaven.
Apsu could not lessen their clamour
and Tiamat was speechless at their ways.
Their doings were loathsome,
unsavoury were their ways,
they were overbearing.
Then Apsu, the begetter of the great gods,
cried out, addressing his vizier, and spoke to him:
'My servant, you rejoice my spirit,

come, let us go to Tiamat.'
They went and sat down before Tiamat,
exchanging counsel about the gods, their firstborn.
Apsu, opening his mouth,
said to resplendent Tiamat,
'Their behaviour is loathsome to me.
By day I find no relief, nor repose by night.
I will destroy, I will wreck their ways,
that quiet may be restored. Let us have rest!'
As soon as Tiamat heard this,
she was angry and called out to her husband,
she cried out aggrieved, as she raged all alone,
injecting woe into her mood:
'What? Should we destroy that which we have built?
Their ways indeed are most troublesome, but let us attend
   kindly!'
Then the servant answered, giving counsel to Apsu.
Hostile and crude was the advice of the servant:
'Destroy, my father, their mutinous ways.
Then you will have relief by day and rest by night!'
When Apsu heard this, his face grew radiant,
planned plans against the gods, his sons.
As for the servant, by the neck he embraced him
as he sat down on his knees to kiss him.
Now whatever they had plotted between them
was repeated to the gods, their firstborn.
When the gods heard this, they were astir,
then lapsed into silence and remained speechless.
Surpassing in wisdom, accomplished, resourceful,
Ea, the all-wise, saw through their scheme.
A master design against it he devised and set up,
made artful his spell against it, surpassing and holy.
He recited it and made it subsist in the deep,
as he poured sleep upon him. Sound asleep he lay.
When he had made Apsu prone, drenched with sleep,
the adviser was powerless to stir.
He loosened his band, tore off his tiara,
removed his halo (and) put it on himself.

Having fettered Apsu, he slew him,
he bound the servant and imprisoned him.
Having thus established his dwelling upon Apsu,
he laid hold of the servant, holding him by the nose-rope.
After Ea had vanquished and trodden down his foes,
had secured his triumph over his enemies,
in his sacred chamber in profound peace had rested,
he named it 'Apsu', for shrines he assigned it.
in that same place his cult hut he founded.
Ea and his consort dwelled there in splendour,
in the chamber of fates, the abode of destinies,
a god was engendered, most able and wisest of gods.
In the heart of Apsu was Marduk created,
in the heart of holy Apsu was Marduk created.
He who begot him was Ea, his father,
and it was his mother who bore him.
The breast of goddesses he did suck.
The nurse that nursed him filled him with awesomeness.
Alluring was his figure, sparkling the lift of his eyes.
Lordly was his gait, commanding from of old.
When Ea saw him, the father who begot him,
he exulted and glowed, his heart filled with gladness.
He rendered him perfect and endowed him with a double
    godhead.
Greatly exalted was he above them, exceeding throughout.
Perfect were his members beyond comprehension,
unsuited for understanding, difficult to perceive.
Four were his eyes, four were his ears;
when he moved his lips, fire blazed forth.
Large were all four hearing organs,
and the eyes, in like number, scanned all things.
He was the loftiest of the gods, surpassing was his stature;
his members were enormous, he was exceedingly tall.
'My little son, my little son!
My son, the sun! Sun of the heavens!'
Clothed with the halo of ten gods, he was strong to the utmost,
as their awesome flashes were heaped upon him.
Anu brought forth and begot the fourfold wind,

consigning to its power the leader of the host.
He fashioned, stationed the whirlwind,
he produced streams to disturb Tiamat.
The gods, given no rest, suffer in the storm.
Their hearts having plotted evil,
to Tiamat, their mother, said;
'When they slew Apsu, your consort,
you did not aid him but remained still.
When he created the dread fourfold wind,
your vitals were diluted and so we can have no rest.
Let Apsu your consort, be in your mind
and the servant who has been vanquished.
You are left alone . . . .
Then Tiamat prepared for battle against the gods,
her offspring.
To avenge Apsu, Tiamat wrought evil . . .
While the gods of battle sharpened their weapons,
then joined issue Tiamat and Marduk, wisest of gods.
They strove in single combat, locked in battle.
The lord spread out his net to enfold her,
the evil wind which followed behind he let loose in her face.
When Tiamat opened her mouth to consume him,
he drove in the evil wind so that she did not close her lips.
As the fierce wind charged her belly,
her body was distended and her mouth was wide open.
He released the arrow, it tore her belly,
it cut through her insides, splitting the heart.
Having thus subdued her, he extinguished her life.
He cast down her carcase to stand upon it.
After he had slain Tiamat, the leader,
her band was shattered, her troop broken up.
And the gods, her helpers who marched at her side,
trembling with terror, turned their backs about,
in order to save and preserve their lives.
Tightly encircled, they could not escape.
He made them captives and he smashed their weapons,
snared them in a net,
placed them in cells . . .

192

And he turned back to Tiamat, whom he had bound.
The lord trod upon the legs of Tiamat,
with his unsparing mace he crushed her skull.
When the arteries of her blood he had severed,
the north wind bore it to places undisclosed.
On seeing this, his fathers were joyful and jubilant,
they brought gifts of homage, they to him.
Then the lord paused to view her dead body,
that he might divide the monster and do skilful works.
He split her like a shellfish into two parts:
half of her he set up and ceiled it as sky,
pulled down the bar and posted guards.
He bade them not to allow her waters to escape.
He crossed the heavens and surveyed the regions.
He squared Apsu's quarter.
As the lord measured the dimensions of Apsu,
the great abode, its likenesss he fixed,
the great abode, he made the firmament . . .
        . . .
When Marduk heard the words of the gods,
his heart prompted him to fashion skilful works.
Opening his mouth, he addressed Ea
to impart the plan he had conceived in his heart.
'Blood I will mass and cause bones to be.
I will establish a savage, "man" shall be his name.
Truly, savage-man I will create.
He shall be charged with the service of the gods
that they may be at ease!
The ways of the gods I will skilfully alter,
though alike revered, into two groups they shall be divided.'
Ea answered him, speaking a word to him,
giving him another plan for the relief of the gods:
'Let just one of their brothers be handed over;
he alone shall perish that mankind may be fashioned.
Let the great gods be here in assembly,
let the guilty be handed over that they may endure.
Marduk summoned the great gods to assembly;
presiding graciously, he issued instructions.

To his utterance the gods paid heed.
The king addressed a word to a god:
'If your former statement was true,
now declare the truth on oath by me,
Who made Tiamat rebel, and joined battle?
Let the one who contrived the rising be handed over.
His guilt I will make him bear. You shall dwell in peace.'
The great gods answered him,
the counsellor of the gods their Lord.
'It was Kingu who contrived the uprising,
And made Tiamat rebel and joined battle.'
They bound him, holding him before Ea.
They imposed on him his guilt and severed his blood vessels.
Out of his blood they fashioned mankind.
He imposed the service and let free the gods.

India: Introduction

India has many ancient creation stories. They can be found in
the Vedas, Brahamanas and Upanishads. A number of motifs
keep recurring: creation as the spilling of the seed of the creator
god, the cosmic egg, the primal waters and the like. But the
most dominant theme is that reality comes into being as a spirit
(*manas*) or soul (*atman*) from nothingness. The stories given
here come from the Rig Veda (c. 2000–1700 BCE) and the
Upanishads (sixth century BCE).

Rig Veda[12]

There was neither non-existence nor existence then;
there was neither the realm of space nor the sky which is
    beyond.
What stirred? Where? In whose protection?
Was there water, bottomlessly deep?
There was neither death nor immortality then.
There was no distinguishing sign of night nor of day.
That one breathed, windless, by its own impulse.
Other than that there was nothing beyond.

Darkness was hidden by darkness in the beginning;
with no distinguishing sign, all this was water.
The life force that was covered with emptiness,
that one arose through the power of heat.
Desire came upon that one in the beginning;
with no distinguishing sign, all this was water.
The life force that was covered with emptiness,
that one arose through the power of heat.
Desire came upon that one in the beginning;
that was the first seed of mind.
Poets seeking their heart with wisdom
found the bond of existence in non-existence.
Their cord was extended across.
Was there below? Was there above?
There were seed-placers; there were powers.
There was impulse beneath; there was giving forth above.
Who really knows? Who will here proclaim it?
Whence was it produced?
Whence is this creation?
The gods came afterwards, with the creation of this universe.
Who then knows whence it has arisen?
Whence this creation has arisen
– perhaps it formed itself, or perhaps it did not –
the one who looks down on it, in the highest heaven,
only he knows – or perhaps he does not know.

Brihadaranyaka Upanishad[13]

In the beginning this cosmos was self (*atman*) alone, in the
shape of a person. He looking round saw nothing but his Self.
He first said, 'This is I', therefore he became 'I' by name.
Therefore even now, if a man is asked, he first says, 'This is I'
and then pronounces the other name which he may have. And
because before all this he burnt down all evils, therefore he was
a person. Truly the one who knows this burns down every one
who tries to be before him. He feared, and therefore anyone
who is lonely fears. He thought, 'As there is nothing but myself,
why should I fear?' Thence his fear passed away. For what

should he have feared? Truly, fear arises only from a second. But he felt no delight. Therefore a man who is lonely feels no delight. He wished for a second. He was as large as man and wife together. He then made his Self fall in two, and thence arose husband and wife. That is why it is said, 'We two are thus like half a shell.'

Therefore the void which was there is filled by the wife. He embraced her, and men were born. She thought, 'How can he embrace me, after having produced me from himself? I shall hide myself.' She then became a cow, the other became a bull and embraced her, and hence cows were born. The one became a mare, the other a stallion; the one a male ass and the other a female ass. He embraced her, and hence one-hoofed animals were born. The one became a she-goat, the other a he-goat; the one became a ewe, the other a ram. He embraced her, and hence goats and sheep were born. And thus he created everything that exists in pairs down to the ants. He knew, 'I indeed am this creation, for I created all this.' Hence he became the creation, and he who knows this lives in this his creation.

China: Introduction

There are various kinds of creation story in China. There are more popular variants, like the story of the giant Pangu from whom the world came forth. Then there are more philosophical creation stories like those in the Taoist writings connected with Lieh-tzu. This Lieh-tzu is a legendary figure who is said to have lived between 450 and 375 BCE. The Book of Lieh-tzu was only compiled in the fourth century CE. The first chapter contains a splendid and profound reflection on the beginning of all things.

The giant Pangu[14]

In the beginning only dark chaos prevailed in the universe. This darkness took the form of an egg, and in this egg Pangu, the first living being, was born. Pangu slept, fed and protected by the egg. When he awoke after many years, Pangu had grown into a giant. He stretched himself, breaking the egg. The lighter, purer parts of the egg rose and formed the heaven; the heavier and impurer parts fell, and formed the earth. This was the origin of the forces which are called yin and yang.

Pangu was afraid that the heaven and the earth would fuse together again. To avoid that he propped up the heaven with his head and pressed against the earth with his feet. For the next eighteen thousand years Pangu grew three metres a day, so that the heaven and the earth were pushed further apart. Finally both the heaven and the earth seemed to remain fixed at a distance of fifty thousand kilometres, and Pangu fell asleep exhausted, never to wake up again. At his death the natural phenomena were formed out of the different parts of his body. His breath became the wind and the clouds, his voice turned into thunder and lightning, his left eye became the sun and his right eye the moon. The four points of the compass and the mountains arose from his limbs and trunk, his blood formed the rivers and his veins the ways and paths, his flesh became trees and earth, the hair on his head became the stars in the heaven, his skin and the hairs on his body turned into grass and flowers. Metals and stones arose from his teeth and bones, his sweat became dew and the parasites on his body formed the different races of human beings. Thus the giant Pangu created the universe.

Lieh-tzu[15]

Master Lieh-tzu was living in the game preserve of Cheng. For forty years no one noticed him, and the prince, the nobles and the high officials of the state regarded him as one of the common people. There was famine in Cheng, and he decided to move to Wei. His disciples said to him: 'Master, you are going away and have set no time for your return. What are you going to teach us before you go? Did not your master Hu-tzu tell you anything?' Lieh-tzu answered, smiling:

'These were his words:

There are the born and the Unborn, the changing and the Unchanging. The Unborn can give birth to the born, the Unchanging can change the changing. The born cannot escape birth, the changing cannot escape change; therefore birth and change are the norm. Things for which birth and change are the norm are at all times being born and changing. They simply follow the alternations of the light and the darkness (Yin and Yang) and the four seasons. The Unborn is by our side yet alone, the Unchanging goes forth and returns. Going forth and returning, its successions are endless; by our side and alone, its way is boundless.

The book of the Yellow Emperor says:

The Valley Spirit never dies:
It is called the dark doe.
The gate of the dark doe
Is called the root of heaven and earth.
It goes on and on, something which almost exists;
Use it, it never runs out.

Therefore that which gives birth to things is unborn, that which changes things is unchanging. Birth and change, shape and colour, wisdom and strength, decrease and growth, come about of themselves. It is wrong to say that it brings about birth and change, shape and colour, wisdom and strength, decrease and growth.'

Master Lieh said:

'Formerly the sages reduced heaven and earth to a system by means of the light and the darkness. But if all that has shape was born from the shapeless, from what were heaven and earth born? I answer, there was a primal simplicity, there was a primal commencement, there were primal beginnings, there was a primal material. The primal simplicity preceded the appearance of the breath. The primal commencement was the beginning of the breath. The primal beginnings were the breath beginning to assume shape. The primal material was the breath when it began to assume substance. Breath, shape and substance were complete, but things were not yet separated from each other; hence the name "confusion". "Confusion" means that the myriad things were confounded and not yet separated from each other.

Looking you do not see it, listening you do not hear it, groping you do not touch it; hence the name "simple". The simple had no shape nor bounds, the simple altered and became one, and from one altered to sevenfold, from sevenfold to ninefold. Becoming ninefold is the last of the alterations of the breath. Then it reverted to unity; unity is the beginning of the alterations of shape. The pure and light rose to become heaven, the muddy and heavy fell to become earth, the breath which harmoniously blended both became man. Hence the essences contained by heaven and earth, and the birth and changing of the myriad things.'

Master Lieh said:

'Heaven and earth cannot achieve everything; the sage is not capable of everything; none of the myriad things can be used for everything.' For this reason, it is the office of heaven to beget and shelter, the office of earth to shape and to support, the office of the sage to teach and reform, the office of each thing to perform its function. Consequently, there are ways in which earth excels heaven, and ways in which each thing is more intelligent than the sage. Why is this? Heaven which begets and shelters cannot shape and support, earth which shapes and supports cannot teach and reform, the sage who teaches and reforms cannot make things act counter to their functions, things with set functions cannot leave their places. Hence the way of heaven and earth must be either light or darkness, the teaching of the sage must be either kindness or justice, and the myriad things, whatever their functions, must be either hard or soft. All these observe their functions and cannot leave their places.

Hence there are the begotten and the Begetter of the begotten,
shapes and the Shaper of shapes,
sounds and the Sounder of sounds,
colours and the Colourer of colours,
flavours and the Flavourer of flavours.
What begetting begets dies,
but the begetter of the begotten never ends.
What shaping shapes is real,

but the shaper of shapes has never existed.
What sounding sounds is heard,
but the Sounder of sounds has never issued forth.
What colouring colours is visible,
but the Colourer of colours never appears.
What flavouring flavours is tasted,
but the Flavourer of flavours is never disclosed.

All are the offices of that which does nothing. It is able to reconcile the opposites in itself, make light and darkness, soften or harden, shorten or lengthen, round off or square, kill or beget, warm or cool, float or sink, bring forth or submerge, blacken or yellow, make sweet or bitter, make foul or fragrant. It knows nothing and is capable of nothing; yet there is nothing which it does not know, nothing of which it is incapable.

Stories from Australia and Polynesia

Australia: Singing the earth to life[16]

Once there was the Dreamtime, and the Ancestors of the
Aborigines created themselves from clay, hundreds and
thousands of them, one for each totemic species. A totem is
an animal (for example, a kangaroo or wallaby), a plant, a
stone or a natural phenomenon (rain, wind). Every phenomenon which occurs is sung to life and becomes a totem, the
emblem of a clan. Thus for example a wallaby man believes that
he is descended from a universal wallaby father, who was the
ancestor of all other wallaby men and all living wallabies.
Wallabies, therefore, were his brothers. To kill one for food was
both fratricide and cannibalism. Each totemic ancestor, while
travelling through the country, was thought to have scattered a
trail of words and musical notes along the lines of his footprints, and these Dreaming tracks lay over the land as 'ways' of
communication between the most far-flung tribes. A song was
both map and direction-finder. Providing you knew the song,
you could always find your way across country. In theory, at
least, the whole of Australia could be read as a musical score.
There was hardly a rock or creek in the country that could not
be or had not been sung. Together they form the story of the
sung earth. By singing the world into existence, the Ancestors
had been poets in the original sense of poesis, meaning
'creation'.

No Aborigine could conceive that the created world was in
any way imperfect. His religious life had a single aim: to keep
the land the way it was and should be. The man who went
'Walkabout' was making a ritual journey. He trod in the footprints of his Ancestor. He sang the Ancestor's stanzas without
changing a word or note – and so recreated the creation. People
form part of the land, and at the same time they sing it into existence. Without them there is no land, and without the land they

do not exist. Every invention that will ever be invented slumbers below the surface, waiting their turn to be called and sung.

New Zealand : Introduction

Among the Maoris in New Zealand Io (or Iho) is the supreme being, the eternal, omniscient creator of the universe, of the gods and of human beings. The story of the creation of the universe stands as the Maori's model for any form of creation: from the procreation of a child to the inspiration of a poet. So the creation story is recited at various rituals. The words with which Io brings the universe to life are used at the ritual of opening the womb of an infertile woman. Sometimes the words with which Io made the light shine in the darkness are used in the ritual of lightening a sombre and depressed heart.

Io and the creation of the cosmos[17]

Io dwelt within the breathing-space of immensity.
The Universe was in darkness, with water everywhere.
There was no glimmer of dawn, no clearness, no light.
And he began by saying these words,
'Darkness, become a light-possessing darkness.'
And at once light appeared.
He then repeated those selfsame words in this manner,
'Light, become a darkness-possessing light.'
And again an intense darkness supervened.
Then a third time he spoke, saying,
'Let there be one darkness above,
Let there be one darkness below.
Let there be one light above,
Let there be one light below.
A dominion of light,
A bright light.'
And now a great light prevailed.
Io then looked to the waters which compassed him about,
and spoke a fourth time, saying,
'You waters of Tai-kama, be separate.

Heaven, be formed.'
Then the sky became suspended.
'Bring forth Tupua-horo-nuku.'
And at once the moving earth lay stretched abroad.

Hawaii: Introduction

Originally the inhabitants of Hawaii came from other islands.
These Polynesians or 'people of many islands' travelled by
canoe and arrived at the place which they called 'Hawaii with
the green back'. They began to live there. So their stories of the
beginning are of mixed origin. There are stories which the
Polynesians brought with them from the islands from which
they came and there are stories which came into being on
Hawaii itself. These last stories of the beginning tried to give an
explanation for the sudden storms, the strange rock formations,
the man-eating sharks and the snow-covered mountains. These
stories were in the first instance handed down by word of
mouth. There was also only a spoken language and no written
Hawaiian. Later, when the need for a written language grew,
people began to write down in Latin script what was spoken. At
that time people proved able to write all the sounds of Hawaiian
with twelve letters (five vowels and seven consonants) from the
Latin alphabet. Four gods appear in this text: Kane or God of
Creation, Kanaloa or God of the Sea, Ku or God of the Forests,
and Lono, God of Growing Things.

The time of deep darkness[18]

In the time of deep darkness, before the memory of man, the
great gods came out of the night . . .
    The God of Creation picked up a vast calabash floating in the
sea, and tossed it high into the air. Its top flew off and became
the curved bowl, sky. Two great pieces of the calabash broke
away: one became the sun, the other the moon. The seeds scattered and became stars. The remainder of the calabash became
the earth and fell back into the sea. The God of Creation said, 'I
shall make a chief to rule the earth. Let us provide for his needs.'

The God of the vast, endless Sea said, 'I shall fill the waters with living things – sea creatures for the chief's use.' This he did.

Born was the coral,
Born was the starfish,
Born was the conch shell;
Born was the fish,
Born was the porpoise,
Born was the shark in the sea there swimming.

The God of creation said, 'I shall fill the earth with living things: flyers and crawlers, slow-movers and swift-movers; land creatures for the chief's use.' This he did.

Born was the caterpillar, the parent;
Out came the child, a moth, and flew.
Born was the egg, the parent;
Out came its child, the bird, and flew.
Land birds were born,
Sea birds were born,
Birds that fly in a flock,
Shutting out the sun.

The sea crept up to the land,
Crept backward, crept forward,
Producing the family of crawlers:
The rough-backed turtles,
The sleek-skinned geckos,
Mud-dwellers and track-leavers.

The God of the Forests said, 'I shall cause trees to grow; trees to give wood for the chief's use.' This he did.

Thick grew the forests,
Koa and candelnut;
Thick grew the forests,
Hau, wili.
Koa for paddles,

Hau for lashings,
Soft wiliwili for outrigger floats;
Woods for the chief's canoe, swift as an arrow.
Candlenut torches, to light the chief's way.

The God of Growing Things said, 'I shall cause food plants to grow; food for the chief.' This he did.

Green blades came sprouting,
Coconut, breadfruit, sweet potato, sugar cane,
Taro, banana, arrowroot, yam.

When all was ready the God of Creation said to the God of the Sea, the God of the Forests and the God of Growing Things, 'Now it is time. Go, find what is needed to make a chief.'

To the north and west, to the south and east went the gods. On the sunrise side of a hill near the sea they found rich red earth. This they took to the God of Creation, who made the figure of man and breathed life into it. The man walked about and spoke, and the gods were pleased.

The God of Creation said, 'We shall call him Red Earth Man.' Red Earth Man was happy. Soon he saw that wherever he went, something went with him. It walked when he walked, and rested when he rested. He was pleased to have company, and he called this thing Shadow. He talked to it, he laughed at it, and sometimes he even sang to it. But Shadow never answered. After a time the songs of Red Earth Man stopped. His laughter died away and he no longer spoke. The gods saw that he was lonely. 'He needs a living companion,' said the God of Creation. While Red Earth Man slept, the God of Creation breathed life into the shadow. When Red Earth Man woke he stretched and looked about. 'It's a fine day,' he said aloud. 'A fine day indeed,' a voice at his side agreed. Red Earth Man was startled, 'Shadow, you speak!' Shadow nodded, smiling. Then Red Earth Man laughed, and his laughter was good to hear. He sang, and Shadow sang with him. Their song was so beautiful that the birds flew down to listen. Red Earth Man said, 'You were my shadow but now you are alive! I shall call you Living Shadow.'

Then Red Earth Man and Living Shadow knelt and touched
their heads to earth, to give thanks to the great gods for the gifts
of life and companionship.

In time, men multiplied.
In time, men came from afar.
Born were the fair-haired,
Born the dark-haired.
Born were the broad-chested.
Born the big eaters.
Born were the song-chanters.
Born the family men,
Born were war leaders,
Born the high chiefs of long life.
Ever increasing in number, men spread abroad.
Man was here now.

Stories from America

Guatemala: Introduction

Guatemala is the home of the Quiché Indians, the descendants of the Mayas. Quiché literally means 'many (*qui*) trees (*che*)': Quiché is the land of many trees, and lies in the highlands of Guatemala. The Indians who inhabit this land have told their stories of the beginning for centuries. They call them Popol Vuh (from *popol*, 'together' or 'society' and *vuh*, 'book'), or the 'Book of the Community'. The Popul Vuh consists of four parts and is, by our standards, around 100 pages long. This book describes how the world, the gods and human beings came into existence, and gives an account of the history of the Quiché Indians. Possibly supported by illustrations, this book was handed down for centuries until the conquest of the Quiché territory by the Spaniards in 1524. After that the Spaniards exterminated a large part of the population, destroyed their cities and murdered their king. So as to prevent the final loss of the glorious history of the people, in the middle of the sixteenth century a learned Quiché Indian wrote down this history, which until then had been handed on orally – in his own language, but in the Latin alphabet. A Spanish Dominican, Francesco Ximénez, who was a missionary in this area at the end of the seventeenth century and knew the language of the Quiché Indians, translated this manuscript of the Popol Vuh into Spanish. Unfortunately the original manuscript of the sixteenth-century Quiché Indian, whose name is unknown, has been lost, so that all we have is Ximénez's Spanish translation. The first complete English translation of this appeared in 1950, and it is from that translation that the following passage has been taken.

In this version the names of gods have been paraphrased. There are four creator gods: Tzacol and Bitol, the Creator and the Maker, along with the Ancestors of human beings: Alom, the mother who bore all the sons, and Qaholom, the father who fathered the sons. Many other gods appear alongside these four creator gods. Those which appear in this passage are Tepeu, the King or Ruler; Gugumatz, the Snake who is decorated with green and blue feathers; Huracán, the Heart of Heaven or the God of Heaven. Sometimes series of names of lower gods, animals or plants appear in the original; these have been omitted here.

Popol Vuh[19]

This is the account of how all was in suspense, all calm, in silence; all motionless, still, and the expanse of the sky was empty. This is the first account, the first narrative. There was neither man, nor animal, birds, fishes, crabs, trees, stones, caves, ravines, grasses, nor forests; there was only the sky. The surface of the earth had not appeared. There was only the calm sea and the great expanse of the sky. There was nothing brought together, nothing which could make a noise, nor anything which might move, or tremble, or could make noise in the sky. There was nothing standing; only the calm water, the placid sea, alone and tranquil. Nothing existed. There was only immobility and silence in the darkness, in the night. Only the Creator, the Maker, the King, the Snake and the Forefathers were in the water surrounded with light. The Snake was hidden under green and blue feathers. By nature they were great sages and great thinkers. In this manner the sky existed and also the Heart of Heaven, which is the name of God and thus he is called.

Then came the word. The King and the Snake came together in the darkness and talked together. They talked then, discussing and deliberating; they agreed, they united their words and their thoughts. Then while they meditated it became clear to them that when dawn would break, man must appear. Then they planned the creation, and the growth of the trees and the thickets and the birth of life and the creation of man. Thus it was arranged in the darkness and in the night by the Heart of Heaven who is called the God of Heaven.

Then the King and the Snake came together; then they conferred about life and light, what they would do so that there would be light and dawn, who it would be who would provide food and sustenance. Thus let it be done! Let the emptiness be filled! Let the water recede and make a void, let the earth appear and become solid; let it be done. Thus they spoke. Let there be light, let there be dawn in the sky and on the earth! There shall be neither glory nor grandeur in our creation and formation until the human being is made, man is formed. So they spoke. Then the earth was created by them. So it was, in truth, that they created the earth. Earth! they said, and instantly it was made. Like the mist, like a cloud, and like a cloud of dust was the creation, when the mountains appeared from the water; and instantly the mountains grew. Only by a miracle, only by magic art were the mountains and valleys formed; and instantly the groves of cypresses and pines put forth shoots together on the surface of the earth. And thus the Snake was filled with joy and exclaimed: 'Your coming has been fruitful, Heart of Heaven.' 'My work and creation shall be finished,' the Heart of Heaven answered.

First the earth was formed, the mountains and the valleys; the currents of water were divided, the rivulets were running freely between the hills, and the water was separated when the high mountains appeared. Thus was the earth created, when it was formed by the Heart of Heaven, the Heart of Earth, as they are called who first made it fruitful, when the sky was in suspense and the earth was submerged in the water. So it was that they made perfect the work, when they did it after thinking and meditating upon it.

Then they made the small wild animals, the guardians of the woods, the spirits of the mountains, the deer, the birds, pumas, jaguars, serpents, snakes, vipers, guardians of the thickets. And the Forefathers asked: 'Shall there be only silence and calm under the trees, under the vines? It is well that thereafter there be someone to guard them.' So they said when they meditated and talked. Promptly the deer and the birds were created. Immediately they gave homes to the deer and the birds. 'You, deer, shall sleep in the fields by the river bank and in the ravines. Here you shall be amongst the thicket, amongst the pasture; in the woods you shall multiply, you shall walk on four feet and they will support you. Thus be it done!' So it was they spoke. Then they also assigned homes to the birds big and small. 'You shall live in the trees and in the vines. There you shall make your nests; there you shall multiply; there you shall increase in the branches of the trees and in the vines.' Thus the deer and the birds were told; they did their duty at once, and all sought their homes and their nests.

And the creation of all the four-footed animals and the birds being finished, they were told by the Creator and the Maker and the Forefathers: 'Speak, cry, warble, speak each according to your variety, each, according to your kind.' So it was said to the deer, the birds, pumas, jaguars and serpents. 'Speak, then, our names, praise us, your mother, your father. Invoke them, the Heart of Heaven, the Creator, the Maker, the Forefathers. Speak, invoke us, adore us.' But they could not make them speak like men; they only hissed and screamed and cackled; they were unable to make words, and each screamed in a different way.

When the Creator and the Maker saw that it was impossible for them to talk to each other, they said: 'It is impossible for them to say our names, the names of us, their Creators and Makers. This is not well,' said the Forefathers to each other. Then they said to them: 'Because it has not been possible for you to talk, you shall be changed. We have changed our minds: Your food, your pasture, your homes, and your nests you shall have; they shall be the ravines and the woods, because it has not been possible for you to adore us or invoke us. There shall be those who adore us, we shall make other beings who shall be obedient. Accept your destiny; your flesh shall be torn to pieces. So shall it be. This shall be your lot.' So they said, when they made known their will to the large and small animals which are on the face of the earth. They wished to give them another trial; they wished to make another attempt; they wished to make all living things adore them. But they could not understand each other's speech; they could succeed in nothing, and could do nothing. For this reason they were sacrificed, and the animals which were on earth were condemned to be killed and eaten.

For this reason another attempt had to be made to create and make men by the Creator, the Maker and the forefathers. 'Let us try again! Already dawn draws near: Let us make him who shall nourish and sustain us! What shall we do to be invoked, in order to be remembered on earth? We have already tried with our first creations, our first creatures; but we could not make them praise and venerate us. So, then, let us try to make obedient, respectful beings who will nourish and sustain us.' Thus they spoke.

Then was the creation and the formation. Of earth, of mud, they made flesh. But they saw that it was not good. It melted away, it was soft, did not move, had no strength, it fell down, it was limp, it could not move its head, its face fell to one side, its sight was blurred, it could not look behind. At first it spoke, but had no mind. Quickly it soaked in the water and could not stand. And the Creator and the Maker said: 'Let us try again because our creatures will not be able to walk nor multiply. Let us consider this,' they said. Then they broke up and destroyed their work and their creation. And they said: 'What shall we do to perfect it, in order that our worshippers, our invokers, will be successful?' Thus they spoke when they conferred again: 'Let us say again to the soothsayers, "Cast your lot again. Try to create again."'

The Creator and the Maker spoke to the soothsayers, the Grandmother of the Day, the Grandmother of the Dawn. And the Heart of Heaven, the King and the Snake said to the soothsayers, to the Maker: 'You must work together and find the means so that man, whom we shall make, man, whom we are going to make, will nourish and sustain us, invoke and remember us. Enter then into council, grandmother, grandfather, our grandmother, our grandfather, make light, make dawn, have us invoked, have us adored, have us remembered by created man, by made man, by mortal man. Thus be it done. Let your nature be known, twice mother, twice father, the master of emeralds, the worker in jewels, the sculptor, the carver, the maker of beautiful plates, the maker of green gourds, the master of resin, grandmother of the sun, grandmother of dawn, as you will be called by our works and our creatures. Cast the lot with your grains of corn, with a handful of red grains of corn. Do this and we shall know if we are to make, or carve his mouth and eyes out of wood.' Thus the diviners were told.

They went down at once to make their divination, and cast their lots with the grains of corn. 'Fate! Creature!' said an old woman and an old man. And this old man was the one who cast the lots and the old woman was the diviner. Beginning the divination they said: 'Get together, grasp each other! Speak, that we may hear.' They said, 'Say if it is well that the wood be got together and that it be carved by the Creator and the Maker, and if this man of wood is he who must nourish and sustain us when there is light, when it is day.' 'Come, fate, creature, get together, take each other,' they said to the corn, to fate, to the creature. 'Come to sacrifice here, Heart of Heaven: do not punish the King and the Snake.' Then they walked and spoke the truth: 'Your figures of wood shall come out well; they shall speak and talk on earth.' 'So may it be,' they answered when they spoke. And instantly the figures were made of wood. They looked like men, talked like men, and populated the surface of the earth. They existed and multiplied; they had daughters, they had sons, these wooden figures; but they did not have souls, nor minds, they did nor remember their Creator, their Maker; they walked on all fours, aimlessly. They no longer remembered the Heart of Heaven and therefore they fell out of favour. It was merely a trial, an attempt at man. At first they spoke, but their face was without expression; their feet and hands had no strength; they had no blood, nor substance, nor moisture, nor flesh; their cheeks were dry, their feet and hands were dry, and their flesh was yellow. Therefore, they no longer thought of their Creator nor their Maker, nor of those who made them and cared for them. These were the first men who existed in great numbers on the face of the earth.

Immediately the wooden figures were annihilated, destroyed, broken up, and killed. A flood was brought about by the Heart of Heaven; a great flood was formed which fell on the heads of the wooden creatures . . . The desperate men of wood ran as quickly as they could: they wanted to climb to the tops of the houses, and the houses fell down and threw them to the ground; they wanted to climb to the treetops, and the trees cast them far away; they wanted to enter the caverns, and the caverns repelled them. So was the ruin of the men who had been created and formed, the men made to be destroyed and annihilated; the mouths and faces of all of them were mangled. And it is said that their descendants are the monkey which now live in the forests; these are all that remain of them because their flesh was made only of wood by the Creator and the Maker. And therefore the monkey looks like man, and is an example of a generation of men which were created and made but which were only wooden figures . . .

Here, then, is the beginning of when it was decided to make man, and when what must enter into the flesh of man was sought. And the Forefathers, the Creators and Makers, the King and the Snake, said: 'The time of dawn has come, let the work be finished, and let those who are to nourish and sustain us appear, the noble sons, the civilized vassals; let man appear, humanity, on the face of the earth.' Thus they spoke. They assembled, came together and held council in the darkness and in the night; then they sought and discussed, and here they reflected and thought. In this way their decisions came clearly to light and they found out and discovered what must enter into the flesh of man. It was just before the sun, the moon, and the stars appeared over the Creators and Makers. [A passage about the origin of corn follows.] Of yellow corn and of white corn they made the flesh of our first mother and father; of corn meal dough they made the arms and legs of man. Only dough of corn meal went into the flesh of our first fathers, the four men, who were created.

These are the names of the first men who were created and formed: the first man was Balam-Quitzé, the second, Balam-Acab, the third, Mahucutah, and the fourth was Iqui-Balam. These are the names of our first mothers and fathers. It is said that they only were made and formed, they had no mother, they had no father. The were only called 'men'. They were not born of woman, nor were they begotten by the Creator nor by the Maker, nor by the Forefathers. Only by a miracle, by means of incantation, were they created and made by the Creator, the Maker, the Forefathers, the King and the Snake. And as they had the appearance of men, they were men; they talked, conversed, saw and heard, walked, grasped things; they were good and handsome men, and their figure was the figure of a man. They were endowed with intelligence; they saw and instantly they could see far, they succeeded in seeing, they succeeded in knowing all that there is in the world. When they looked, instantly they saw all around them, and they contemplated in turn the arch of heaven and the round face of the earth. The things hidden [in the distance] they saw all, without first having to move; at once they saw the world, and so, too, from where they were, they saw it. Great was their wisdom; their sight reached to the forests, the rocks, the lakes, the mountains, and the valleys. In truth they were admirable men, Balam-Quitzé, Balam-Acab, Mahucutah, and Iqui-Balam.

Then the Creator and the Maker asked them: 'What do you think of your condition? Do you not see? Do you not hear? Are not your speech and manner of walking good? Look, then! Contemplate the world, look, [and see] if the mountains and the valleys appear! Try, then to see!' they said to them. And immediately the four first men began to see all that there was in the world. Then they gave thanks to the Creator and the Maker: 'We really give you thanks, two and three times! We have been created, we have been given a mouth and a face, we speak, we hear, we think, and walk; we feel perfectly, and we know what is far and what is near. We also see the large and the small in the sky and on earth. We give you thanks, then, for having created us, O Creator and Maker! For having given us being, O our grandmother, O our grandfather!' they said, giving thanks for their creation and formation. They were able to hear all, and they examined the four corners, the four points of the arch of the sky and the round face of the earth.

But the Creator and the Maker did not hear this with pleasure. 'It is not well what our creatures, our works say; they know all, the large and the small,' they said. And so the Forefathers held council again. 'What shall we do with them now? Let their sight reach only to that which is near; let them see only a little of the face of the earth! It is not well what they say. Perchance, are they not by nature simple creatures of our making? Must they also be gods? And if they do not reproduce and multiply when it will dawn, when the sun rises? And what if they do not multiply?' So they spoke. 'Let us check a little their desires, because it is not well what we see. Must they perchance be the equals of ourselves, their makers, who can see afar, who know all and see all?' Thus spoke the Heart of Heaven, the King, the Snake, the Forefathers, the Creator and the Maker. Thus they spoke, and immediately they changed the nature of their works, of their creatures. Then the Heart of Heaven blew mist into their eyes, which clouded their sight as when a mirror is breathed upon. Their eyes were covered and they could see only what was close, only that was clear to them. In this way the wisdom and all the knowledge of the four men, the origin and the beginning of the Quiché race, were destroyed . . .

Then their women were made. God himself made them carefully. And so, during sleep, they came, truly beautiful, their women, at the side of Balam-Quitzé, Balam-Acab, Mahucutah, and Iqui-Balam. There were their women when they awakened, and instantly their hearts were filled with joy because of their wives. Here are the names of their wives: Cahá-Paluna was the name of the wife of Balam Quitzé; Chomihá was the wife of Balam-Acab; Tzununihá, the wife of Mahucutah; and Caquixhá was the name of the wife of Iqui-Balam. These are the names of their wives, who were distinguished women. They conceived the men, of the small tribes and of the large tribes, and were the origin of us, the people of Quiché.

North America: Father Earthmaker[20]

What it was our father lay on when he came to consciousness we do not know. He moved his right arm and then his left arm, his right leg and then his left leg. He began to think of what he should do and finally he began to cry and tears began to flow from his eyes and fall down below him. After a while he looked down below him and saw something bright. The bright objects were his tears that had flowed below and formed the present waters. Earthmaker began to think again. He thought, 'It is thus. If I wish anything it will become as I wish, just as my tears have become seas.' Thus he thought. So he wished for light and it became light. Then he thought: 'It is as I supposed; the things that I have wished for have come into existence as I desired.' Then he again thought and wished for the earth and this earth came into existence. Earthmaker looked at the earth and he liked it but it was not quiet. He thought again of how things came into existence just as he desired. Then he first began to talk. He said, 'As things are just as I wish them I shall make one being like myself.' So he took a piece of earth and made it like himself. Then he talked to what he had created but it did not answer. He looked upon it and he saw that it had no mind or thought. So he made a mind for it. Again he talked to it, but it did not answer. So he looked upon it again and saw that it had no tongue. Then he made it a tongue. Then he talked to it again but it did not answer. So he looked upon it again and saw that it had no soul. So he made it a soul. He talked to it again and it very nearly said something. But it did not make itself intelligible. So Earthmaker breathed into its mouth and talked to it and it answered.

Stories from Africa

Introduction

Africa has many creation stories. Each people has its own story
of the beginning, which is handed down by word of mouth from
generation to generation. To illustrate their significance for
those concerned, here is a story. Last century, the French priest
Fr Loupias spent quite a long time among the Tutses in
Rwanda. He describes how someone told him their creation
story. After he had heard the story, Fr Loupias thanked the
storyteller by saying that it was an interesting story. But his
informant was not satisfied with this: 'It may be a story for you,
but we Batutse know that this history is true. We really never
tell it to others, and when a father is old or sick, he hands this
story on to his son, but he makes sure that he is not overheard
by anyone.' The man swore Fr Loupias to secrecy over the story
and refused to return to the subject the next day: he was afraid
that he had spoilt the mystery of the story. So stories of the
beginning are not fiction, but true stories for those concerned.
However, in present-day Africa, which is marked by very rapid
changes, the stories of the beginning are starting to lose their
value for more and more Africans. Those living in big cities are
losing the original bond of community and the stories which
form the basis of this are losing their power to communicate.
Only where the connection with a social community has been
preserved do the stories still continue to function in close connection with rites and preserve their meaning.

Because there was no writing almost everywhere in Africa,
the stories were handed down for centuries by word of mouth.
Written sources became available only after Islam on the one
hand and Christianity and the colonial authorities in Africa
on the other introduced the Arabic and Latin alphabets respectively. This made it possible to write down stories from the oral
tradition. However, even now only a limited number have been

written down. There is also the problem that the older material has been written down exclusively by outsiders: missionaries, anthropologists, colonial officials or the military. That often makes the way in which they are told Eurocentric. Only where the original African text is given alongside the translation can some control be exercised here.

The eight stories which follow come from different peoples from different parts of Africa. The first is told in English; the other are translations from a collection of African stories made by Mineke Schippers and published in The Netherlands in 1983 under the title 'The Black Paradise' (*Het Zwarte Paradijs*). These texts are versions of French, English, German or Flemish translations which missionaries, officials and scholars of this century and the last have made of African stories that have been handed down orally. In the texts which follows, African proper names have been simplified as far as possible; sometimes there is some explanation of the translated names in the notes.

Nigeria: Why the sun and the moon live in the sky[21]

Many years ago the sun and the water were great friends, and both lived on the earth together. The sun very often used to visit the water, but the water never returned his visits. At last the sun asked the water why it was that he never came to see him in his house. The water replied that the sun's house was not big enough, and that if he came with his people he would drive the sun out. The water then said, 'If you wish me to visit you, you must build a very large compound; but I warn you that it will have to be a tremendous place, as my people are very numerous and take up a lot of room.' The sun promised to build a very big compound, and soon afterward he returned home to his wife, the moon, who greeted him with a broad smile when he opened the door. The sun told the moon what he had promised the water, and the next day he commenced building a huge complex in which to entertain his friend.

When it was completed, he asked the water to come and visit him the next day. When the water arrived, he called out to the sun and asked him whether it would be safe for him to enter, and the sun answered, 'Yes, come in, my friend.' The water then began to flow in, accompanied by the fish and all the water animals. Very soon the water was knee-deep, so he asked the sun if it was still safe, and the sun again said, 'Yes', so more water came in. When the water was level with the top of a man's head, the water said to the sun, 'Do you want more of my people to come?'

The sun and the moon both answered, 'Yes,' not knowing any better, until the sun and the moon had to perch themselves on the top of the roof. Again the water addressed the sun, but, receiving the same answer, and more of his people rushing in, the water very soon overflowed the top of the roof, and the sun and the moon were forced to go up into the sky, where they have remained ever since.

Nigeria: How men come to be on earth[22]

In the beginning the world was populated only by women. One day, the Earth God killed a woman by accident. When the other women heard about it, they met and asked him, if it was his plan to exterminate them, to bring destruction upon them all at once rather than killing them off slowly one by one. The Earth God was sorry that he had caused them grief. Therefore he asked them to indicate what they would choose from all his possession to make good for the fact that he had killed their fellow woman. They asked him to tell them what he had, and said that they would all shout 'Yes' when he mentioned something that they really wanted.

The Earth God began. He named all his fruits, birds and animals, but every time they heard one of these names they shouted 'No'. Finally he had almost finished. There was just one thing more on the list that he could offer. 'Will you take the man, then?', the Earth God finally asked. 'Yes,' they shouted in delight, and embraced one another and began to dance with joy at the thought of the gift that the Earth God would give them.

So they took the man as compensation for their lost fellow woman. Thereupon the men became subordinate to the women and have to work for them to this day. For although the woman comes under the influence of the man when she marries, she is her own mistress and has the right to ask any service of him and to expect him to do what she wants.

Rwanda: How the Creator created the world[23]

In the beginning the Creator created two lands, the land above the clouds, the sun and the stars, and the land below, which he made in the image of the land above but without beauty or happiness. That is the earth we inhabit, a land of misery, suffering, hard work, perplexing. Before this double creation there was nothing. Only the Creator existed. In the land above, the heaven, he created all sorts of plants and trees which were useful and good, and of every kind of animal he created both brother and sister. Human beings also dwelt in heaven, where they had free access to the Creator and without care enjoyed all the plants and animals that had been created. They knew nothing of suffering or sickness. After many years the human beings had multiplied.

However, in that paradise there were a man and a woman whose happiness was not complete. They had no children with whom they could enjoy their prosperity, and they could not have a family because the woman was infertile. So the woman made a gift of honey, pombe, milk, butter and animal skins and took it to the Creator. When she got to him she clapped her hands three times and said to him, 'Creator, you have given us everything: the bull and his sister, the ram and his sister, the hen and his sister, of every animal the brother and sister so that they should have descendants, should multiply and should serve us. I offer you this gift of the things that you have given us. You have made everything, you are almighty, everything belongs to you. You are good, generous, and you love us. Hear the prayer of your daughter: she has no children, though all your other creatures have them. Grant me, too, this happiness.' The Creator was moved: 'I am ready,' he said, 'to give you what you want, but can you keep it secret?' The woman promised that she would never tell anyone. Thereupon the Creator took clay, which he moistened with spittle; he kneaded the clay and gave it the form of a small human being, which he handed over to the woman. 'Take this,' he said. 'This is the child that the Creator has formed with his own hands and mouth; keep it in a pot and fill the pot with milk every morning and evening for nine months. When the limbs have developed completely you may take it out. It shall be your child. But never tell my secret, if you do not want to lose the child.'

The woman took the small figure home and put it in a pot, which she filled with milk morning and evening for nine months. The child grew. Every day the mother lifted the lid and looked with wonderment at the work of the Creator. Finally the moment came: she heard crying and howling. She immediately took the child out, washed it, and went to bed. When her husband, who had been away, came home, she showed him the newborn child. The husband was tremendously happy, congratulated his wife and showered her with gifts. We no longer know the name the child was given. We call it 'fallen from heaven', because it fell out of heaven. The Creator's child prospered, and came to the time of life when it had to be weaned. After that its mother again made a present of mead, milk, butter, honey and other things and went with it to the Creator to ask for a second child. He agreed on the same conditions. Again he kneaded the form of a child's body from clay and spittle. The woman took it home with her and put it in milk, which she changed every day. After nine months the child began to groan and howl, and the mother took it out of the pot. She went to bed and told her husband that she had had another child. The husband was happy and showered his wife with presents.

When the child was weaned, the woman went yet again to the Creator with gifts. 'Creator,' she said, 'you have given me two sons, but as yet I have no daughter. You are so good and generous, will you give me a daughter?' The Creator did not refuse her request. He formed the body of a girl and gave it to the woman, who took it home with her. She put it in milk, which she changed twice a day. When the child was fully grown, the mother warned her husband that she was on the point of giving birth. The husband quickly went outside to look for wood and green things for their home. Meanwhile the mother rapidly took the child out of the pot, washed it and suckled it. When her husband returned she let him see the child. It was a girl.

Years went by. The children surpassed everyone in their locality in understanding and beauty. They were the children of the Creator. The sons went hunting with their father and always hit the mark with their arrows and lances. They always returned from the hunt with rich booty. Their sister remained at home with her mother. She made the most beautiful mats and wove the most beautiful baskets of all the girls of her age. No one made such nice butter as she did. Everyone admired her and praised her lucky parents.

The woman had a sister who, like her, had not been able to have any children. This sister was jealous of the woman who had become a mother three times, but what intrigued her above all was that she had not noticed anything special about her sister before the birth of the children. She guessed that there was a secret here and wanted to know it at any price. She gave her every attention and brought gifts, but it was all in vain. The woman kept her promise and said that she had got her children just like all other mothers. However, one day the two sisters drank banana beer together and the woman got drunk. In her drunken state she threw all caution to the winds. 'O daughter of my mother,' she said to her sister, 'you have been pursuing me so long with your questions about my children. Today I shall tell you the truth. I shall give away my secret. When I had no children I was deeply distressed. One day I went to ask the Creator for children, and my prayer has been answered. Three times I have been to him, and three times he has heard my prayer. He took earth which he moistened with spittle and kneaded. In that way he made the body of a child, which he gave to me. I put this form in a pot into which I poured milk morning and evening. When the child was fully grown and I took it out of its bath, I told my husband and the neighbours that I had had a child, because the Creator had forbidden me to betray the secret.' So they talked until deep into the night, and then they went to sleep, side by side.

Before the dawning of the next day, the sons took their weapons and went with their father into the forest. They left their mother and their aunt sleeping. The woman's sister woke up quickly. Without saying good-bye to her, she decided to go home. She only greeted her niece, who had not been there during their conversation the previous evening. She was in a hurry; she wanted to make a present as quickly as possible and go to ask the Creator for children. When the woman finally woke up, she was surprised that her sister had gone away so quickly. She asked her daughter why she had not stayed. The girl replied, 'Mama, she went to make a present to take to the Creator today.' Then the mother remembered her indiscretion of the previous evening. She wailed and scratched her face with her nails. 'I have killed my children,' she said, 'I have insulted the Creator. I have killed my children.' Grieving and in a frenzy, she went to her sister. 'Child of my mother, I have committed a great sin. I have betrayed the Creator's secret, I have killed my children.' 'Your fault and your sorrow are your concern. I am glad that I know your secret. I shall now go the Creator myself to ask for children and he will give them to me.' said her sister. 'Sister, child of my mother, don't do that, don't say to the Creator that I have betrayed him.' 'Why shouldn't I go?' 'Do you think that the Creator will listen to you if he is annoyed? My fault is also yours. Let me go first, and if he has not heard our words of last night, you go afterwards.' So that was agreed.

The woman went with a gift to the Creator. He was angry. She was not allowed to come close. He called her. She came forward and clapped her hands. 'With whom have you spoken?', he immediately asked her. 'You have violated my secret. You children will be taken from you. They must go to the underworld to suffer and toil there. I will not accept your present. I think obedience more important than the gift of things which I myself have made.' The woman left in tears.

Tanzania: The origin of woman[24]

Long ago, there were no women. There were only two men, who lived on honey. One man climbed a tree. There was honey in this tree, and he wanted to get the honey out with his axe. The iron head of the axe dropped off and hit his companion, who was sleeping on his back underneath the tree. The falling axe hit him in his private parts and cut them off. A bloody wound was made, just as with a woman. His companion looked down and asked, 'What is that?' He replied, 'The axe has clipped me there.' Then they slept with one another and a girl was born. They slept with one another again and a boy was born. Since that day all women have to lose blood, as was the case with this first woman. Yes, they all lose blood from below.

Tanzania: How two people from heaven learned to live on earth[25]

There were many people above with the God of heaven. One day the God of heaven said, 'Many people must also come to earth.' He threw two people down, two adults. One was a man and his companion was a woman. With them he also threw down seeds, a bit of every kind. Their food consisted of a grain of corn. The God of Heaven said to them, 'Mill the one grain of corn and cover the flour with a winnow.' When they took off the cover later, they discovered that there was much more, enough for them to eat for two days. In addition, they had spinach, calabashes and beans. The God of Heaven also gave them two fishes, which they put in the water. So they farmed many fish to eat.

In the beginning they did not know how to get children. One day the woman said to the man, 'I have a wound in my groin, boil water for me to wash my wound.' He boiled water and washed and washed and washed, but the wound would not heal. He said, 'Why is the wound not healing?' The God of Heaven saw the people and what they were doing and said, 'They are so stupid! I shall give them the son of wisdom to impart knowledge to them.' Immediately the woman's knee began to swell and swell and swell. After a day, a child appeared, wise and understanding. The moment he fell to earth from the knee, he began to speak. He said, 'What you are washing there is not a wound. You must have intercourse with this woman there, so that she gives birth.'

The man went to the woman and slept with her. And she gave birth to a child, a girl. When this girl had grown up, she was given in marriage. One day the mother-in-law gave the bride a grain of corn and said, 'Mill this one grain on the stone and cover the flour with a winnow.' The mother-in-law went into the field and the bride was left behind alone. She said, 'How shall we be satisfied from a single grain of corn? I shall take lots of grains, a basket full.' And so she did. When the mother-in-law returned to the village, she saw what the bride had done. She howled and said, 'Oh, oh, oh! You have brought the earth and its people to ruin! Now we shall have to labour all our days and perish of hunger.' Then the God of Heaven came down. He said, 'You have made a mess of the earth. From now on you will have to work and die the death.'

Zaire: The origin of black and white people[26]

In the beginning the Supreme Being lived completely alone. But it was not long before he began to get tired of his loneliness, so he looked for a way of entertaining himself. He created a chicken, and from then on held it in his right hand. He set off like this, but nowhere did he find another being or creature. Then he said to himself, 'Where shall I live? Where shall I find water and wood to burn, and who will bring all that to me and serve me?' Thereupon he created the earth with its mountains and made his dwelling-place there.

On the third day he said to the chicken, 'I am the Lord of all and I have no one to serve me. Lay eggs and let each of them bring forth a human being.' That same day the chicken laid no less than forty eggs. Later the chicken laid yet more eggs. She is the mother of all the chickens in this world. On the fourth day the forty eggs burst open and forty human beings appeared. Now the Supreme Being was content. He had subjects and servants. He spoke to them as follows: 'We shall all live together here, but I am the Lord of all and I want you, human beings, to populate the whole world. This man must leave this place and settle elsewhere on the cape by the sea. I shall make him a consort and he shall be the father of all creatures on earth.' The Supreme Being immediately made a woman, and the man left the place with her and went south. He chose the cape as a dwelling place, as the Supreme Being had commanded him. He lived there happily and he was blessed with numerous descendants. They produced no less than one hundred children, who are the ancestors of all kings and all human beings.

All these children lived with their parents, grew up and prospered. When they were adult, it was resolved that they should go away: each was to seek his dwelling place elsewhere in order to live in accord with the commandment of the Supreme Being and populate the whole earth. Unfortunately the father was poor, and he could give no inheritance to his children. However, the Supreme Being came to the help of his creatures. What happened? We do not know, but one thing is certain: in the morning when they woke up, all the children were clutching a present from God in their hands. One had a cow, another an ox, another a goat, and so on. The tribal ancestor of the Bashi awoke with a pot of milk in his hand. That is why the Bashi love milk and cows so much.

However, the human beings found that the Supreme Being had given gifts to them unequally. Envy led to disputes among the children of the man. One of the most privileged was banished by his brothers. Then the man showed his father's heart: he took his son and his servant and his dog into his house. Since then he has never been seen again among human beings.

The tribal ancestor of the Europeans, whose name has been lost, hardly recognized himself when he woke up. He had not only received a special gift from the Supreme Being, namely instruments for writing and shooting, but his skin had turned from black, like that of his brothers, to white, like that of Europeans today. When his brothers saw this, they said to him, 'Where do you come from? You are not a son of man as we are. Our mother did not give birth to you, and who knows what things you have in your hand?' It was decided to slaughter a young chicken and read the meaning of all this in its entrails. They perceived that the Supreme Being himself had changed him in this way and that to this creature alone he had revealed the secret of the gifts which had been given to him. He too was banished from his birthplace like the other son. He went away to a distant land called Bulayi (Europe), but by which way he went is unknown. Did he die first and rise again, and was he then transported invisibly to his land? Was he carried through the clouds, or did he follow the way of the rains? That is a secret. One thing is certain. He carefully took with him the gifts which God had given him. And therefore his descendants, the Europeans, are still the only ones who have instruments for writing and shooting.

Zambia: *The first human beings and the origin of the two sexes*[27]

The Creator created two human beings; in the beginning they were not man and woman, but sexless persons. Moreover not only did they have no sexual organs, they did not even have an anus. This anatomical lack caused them discomfort, so one of them went to consult the Creator. He said that his work of creation was incomplete. He took two packages and gave them to the human being, saying: 'Look, here are two packages, one for you and one for your fellow human being. Take them both. Put one packet in your crutch in the night-time and give the other to your fellow human being, who must do the same thing.' This human being returned to the earth, but the way was long and he had to spend the night somewhere. He lay down and before he went to sleep he put one of the packages between his legs, as he had been instructed. The next morning he discovered that he was a man and was complete in every respect. He picked up the other package, but when he happened to smell it, he found the smell so unpleasant that he thought it had gone bad, so he threw it away. He returned to his fellow human being, who immediately saw that he was changed, and asked how that came about. The man told how the Creator had changed him, but made no reference to the second package.

The other human being decided to go to the Creator, too, to ask for help. When this human being arrived, the Creator said.

'But I sent a package for you as well. Didn't you receive it?' The human being replied, 'No, I saw no package, nor did he say anything to me about one. He only told me about his own package.' The Creator said nothing, but gave a fresh package to this man with the same instructions. These were followed, and when the human being woke up the following day, she was a woman.

Sexual desire arose in their hearts and the man had sexual intercourse with the woman. After that they both felt terribly afraid. They did not understand the new experience that they had had. So they went to the Creator and told him of their anxiety. The Creator listened, and said to the man, 'When you were last here, did I not give you two packages, one for yourself and one for your fellow human being? And did you not throw away her package?' The man conceded that this was the case. The Creator assured him that this new experience was nothing to be afraid of, because he himself had given it to them. However, he said to the man, 'You acted wrongly and threw away the package which I intended for the woman. And although it is true that you have done it together and each desired to know the other, as I intended, you must give your wife a bride-price because you have slept with her. And from now on in every generation the young man shall pay a bride-price to the girl if they want to marry.' 'And that is how it has come about,' they say, 'that the man has to pay a bride-price.'

Ghana: How man and woman came together[28]

It was the Great Spider who created the world. She created the men and the women. When she had finished this creation, she said to them that there was still one thing to do, but that she was now going away and that they should wait three years. When she came back after this, she would finish what she still had to do. After these words she took sand and scattered it between the men and the women. She repeated that one thing still had to happen, but that she would first go away and would be back in three years. No one, she said, man or woman, must set foot on the sand that she had put between the land of the men and that of the women. After that she took big banana leaves and covered the beautiful white sand with them. Then she said farewell and departed. It is said that two and a half years went by after her departure without men or women setting foot among their neighbours. It would only be six months before the Great Spider returned. In this time the men were naked; they only wore ornaments of gold and beads. The women were also naked; they wore no clothing whatsoever and had never yet tasted salt.

Six months still separated the human beings from the return of the Great Spider, when one of the men had the idea of going hunting. Walking along, he ended up near the women's village. He heard voices. He was dumbfounded, kept as quiet as a mouse and asked himself what he was going to see. He listened keenly, kept his eyes peeled and wondered at the white strip just in front of him. A slave girl of the queen of the women came to dispose of refuse in this place. The man asked the name of the place where he was. Without saying a word the woman fled and went to the queen to report what she had seen. 'Just imagine. There is a great animal by the dunghill!' In fact the women had never seen a man before, just as the men had never seen a woman before. The queen instructed her slave girl to go and get the animal and bring it to her. The slave went back to the dunghill and cried: 'Hey, animal! Hey, animal! Our mother says that you must come.' He stood up and went with her. When he was in the village the women began to crowd round him and exclaimed: 'Indeed, you did not lie, it really is an animal. He has hairs on his face, and look at all those hairs all over his body!' Meanwhile the queen had something cooked for him to eat. She offered him an excellent meal which he enjoyed very much. Very soon it was evening. The serving girl of the queen made a bed of bark for him in front of the hut and told him that he had to sleep there. He lay there for a while, but then he began to complain, 'I'm cold, I'm cold. Let me in to sleep.' The girl went to tell her mistress, 'Mother, he says that he's cold and that he wants to sleep in the hut.' 'Let him come in, then,' replied the queen. The man got up and went into a corner of the hut to sleep, while the serving maid slept in another corner. Just after midnight, he began to moan again, 'I'm cold, I'm cold, let me sleep with you.' But the serving girl said, 'Dirty beast, let me rest. You are much too ugly to sleep with me. Go to sleep and keep still.' The man replied, 'I have gold dust with me, I have a gold pin, and I have beads.' 'What am I to do I with your gold dust, your gold pin and your beads?,' she replied. The man went on, 'If you don't know what to do with these things, then surely you're not so silly that you don't know what to do with salt, which is so nice to eat. Look at this salt; I have handfuls of it. Nothing is nicer for the palate. I put it on all my food.' But the woman said sharply, 'It's only because you are a beast that you put these little stones on your soup.' 'All right,' said the man, 'tomorrow I shall put some in your soup and you will notice it. You will also want to give it to the queen.' And he kept on pestering the woman until she finally agreed with his request. The next day she told everything to her mistress, who in turn wanted to risk the adventure. So it happened that the man remained a few days and . . . the colony expanded! Later, the man went home and trod on the sand that the Great Spider had scattered.

At the appointed time the Great Spider returned. The first thing she did was to look to see whether anyone had walked on the sand. And behold, there were footprints! 'Who has walked on the sand?', she asked the men and women. 'The men,' said the women, 'they came to us.' 'What a lie!' replied the men, 'It was the women who walked on the sand.' The Great Spider investigated, and discovered that it had been the men who had visited the women. Thereupon she spoke with the voice of an oracle: 'I told you that I had one more thing to do, that I should go away and return after three years. I gave you one command to live by. You have violated that command, and you shall be punished for it. This shall be the punishment for the man: when he sees a woman and desires her in his heart, he shall first give her gold and clothes and pretty things before he can get her. And this is the punishment for the woman, for she has been equally disobedient: when you see a man and desire him in your heart, then you will not be allowed to say that straight away. You must keep it to yourself. Moreover you must pound the fufu and do all the rest of the work before you yourself may eat.' She also said to the woman. 'The days of your pregnancies shall be nine or ten months, and you shall bear your children with great pain.' That is why a man must always reconcile himself to so much difficulty and trouble if he desires a woman and wants to marry. All that is the result of the fact that he was disobedient to the Great Spider, the creator of the world.

Stories from Europe

Greece: Introduction[29]

By comparison with the great riches and many facets of Greek religion generally, ideas of creation do not occupy a particularly prominent place. That can partly be attributed to the fact that philosophy began to develop in Greece at a very early date. From the beginning the Greeks also concentrated on the questions of the origin and derivation of the world, and in this way took over one of the functions of religious narratives.

The two most important cosmogonies in Greece are those of Hesiod and of the so-called Orphic (mystical) creation hymns. The poet Hesiod lived in the eighth century before Christ in the country district of Boeotia. We know little or nothing of his life, but among the poems he has left behind is a 'theogony' of around a thousand lines. He begins with the existence of a primal matter and makes the further development of the cosmos take place in the form of fertilization and birth. Hesiod opens his work with an extensive invocation of the Muses and the god Zeus, for which he needs more than a hundred lines. Then he begins to explain clearly that chaos existed first of all things, and from this Gaia, the earth, and Eros, love, 'the most beautiful of the immortal gods', came forth. The earth and love in a sense fall outside order, for now two beings emerge from chaos which are much more central. The first is called Erebos, a word which can indicate both darkness and the underworld and the depths of the sea; the second is Nux, night. From darkness and night, air and daylight are born. After that things happen on earth: it first brings forth heaven, then the mountains, and finally the sea.

Hesiod's Theogony[30]

At the beginning of everything was Chaos. Next, broad-bosomed earth, the solid and eternal home of all, came into being, and Eros, the most beautiful of the immortal gods, who in every man and every god softens the sinews and overpowers the prudent purpose of the mind. Out of void came Darkness and black Night, and out of Night came Light and Day, her children conceived after union in love with Darkness. Earth first produced starry Sky, equal in size with herself, to cover her on all sides. Next she produced the tall mountains, the pleasant haunts of the gods, and also gave birth to the barren waters, sea with its raging surges – all this without the passion of love. Thereafter she lay with Sky and gave birth to Ocean with its deep current, and other gods. After these came cunning Chronos, the youngest and boldest of her children; and he grew to hate the father who had begotten him.

Earth also gave birth to the violent Cyclopes – Thunderer, Lightener and bold Flash – who made and gave to Zeus the thunder and the lightning bolt. They were like the gods in all respects except that a single eye stood in the middle of their foreheads, and their strength and skill were in their hands. There were also born to Earth and Sky three more children, big, strong and horrible. This unruly brood has a hundred monstrous hands sprouting from their shoulders, and fifty heads on top of their shoulders growing from their sturdy bodies. They had monstrous strength to match their huge size.

Of all the children born of Earth and Sky these were the boldest, and their father had them from the beginning. As each of them was about to be born, Sky would not let them reach the light of day; instead he hid them all away in the bowels of Mother Earth. Sky took pleasure in doing this evil thing. In spite of her enormous size, Earth felt the strain within her and groaned. Finally she thought of an evil and cunning stratagem. She instantly produced a new metal, grey steel, and made a huge sickle. Then she laid the matter before her children; the anguish in her heart made her speak boldly: 'My children, you have a savage father; if you will listen to me, we may be able to take vengeance for this evil outrage: he was the one who started using violence.' This was what she said, but all the children were gripped by fear, and not one of them spoke a word. Then great Chronos, the cunning trickster, took courage and answered his good mother with these words: 'Mother, I am willing to undertake and carry through your plan. I have no respect for our infamous father, since he was the one who started using violence.'

This was what he said, and enormous Earth was very pleased. She hid him in ambush and put in his hands the sickle with jagged teeth, and instructed him fully in her plot. Huge Sky came drawing night behind him, and desiring to make love: he lay on top of Earth stretched out all over her. Then from his ambush his son reached out with his left hand and with his right took the huge sickle with its long jagged teeth and quickly sheared the organs from his own father and threw them away. The drops of blood that spurted from them were all taken in by Mother Earth, and in the course of the revolving years she gave birth to the powerful Spirits of Vengeance and the huge Giants with shining armour and long spears. As for the organs themselves, for a long time they drifted around in the sea just as they were when Chronos cut them off with the steel edge and threw them from the land into the waters of the ocean.

Then white foam issued from the divine flesh, and in the foam a girl began to grow. First she came near to holy Cythera, then reached Cyprus, the land surrounded by sea. There she stepped out, a goddess, tender and beautiful, and round her slender feet the green grass shot up. She is called Aphrodite by gods and men because she grew in the froth . . . Eros and beautiful Passion were her attendants both at her birth and at her first going to join the family of the gods. The rights and privileges assigned to her from the beginning and recognized by men and gods are these: to preside over the whispers and smiles and tricks which girls employ, and the sweet delight and tenderness of love.

Iceland: Introduction

The Edda is a loose collection of Old Icelandic songs of heroes and gods which was written down in Iceland at the beginning of the thirteenth century. However, it goes back to a much earlier oral tradition. The way in which Christianity was introduced in the year 1000 had a lasting influence on the text. Christianity was not imposed from above, but accepted by the Icelanders of their own free will. Moreover Christianity very quickly influenced existing ideas and customs, and thus also the Icelandic poems about heroes and gods. The first song, the Voluspa, is the most famous song in the Edda, and the extract chosen here is the first part of it.

The Voluspa was pronounced by a seer, who was a woman. The old sagas often mention such seers, who were highly respected. On the great festivals the seer went through the land accompanied by a group of maidens, and wherever she went, she was the highlight of the feast. Sitting on an elevated throne in the great hall, she uttered her spells, sang songs and predicted the fortunes of each of the guests. The first part of the Voluspa is clearly an inspired song. The seer addresses Odin, while other gods listen in. She tries to illuminate the obscure past for her audience. As she goes far back before the first origin of things, when chaos, the great void, prevailed, she experiences anew the first fortunes of the world, the giants who first nurtured her, the world's destruction and rebirth. In the passage cited here she tells of the ordering of the universe (strophes 4 and 5), the loss of the first innocence with the coming of the goddesses of Fate (strophe 8), the creation of the Dwarves (strophes 9–17), the appearance of gods and the coming of human beings (strophes 18–20).

Edda. The vision of the seer[31]

[1] Hearing I ask from the holy races,
From Heimdall's sons, both high and low;
As Valfather wills, I shall relate
Old tales I remember of men long ago.

[2] I remember stil the giants of old,
who gave me food in days gone by.
Nine worlds I knew, the nine in the tree
With mighty roots beneath the mould.

[3] Once there was a time when Roarer lived;
Sea nor cool waves nor sand there were;
Earth had not been, nor heaven above,
But a yawning gap, and the grass nowhere.

[4] Then Bur's sons lifted the level land,
Mithgard the mighty there they made;
The sun from the south warmed the stones of the earth,
And green was the ground with growing leeks.

[5] The sun, the sister of the moon, from the south,
Her right hand cast over heaven's rim;
No knowledge she had where her home should be,
The moon knew not what might was his,
The stars knew not where their stations were.

[6] Then sought the gods their assembly seats,
The holy ones, and council held;
Names then they gave to noon and twilight,
Morning they named, and the waning moon,
Night and evening, the years to number.

[7] At the Field of Deeds met the mighty gods,
Shrines and temples they timbered high;
Forges they set, and they smithied ore,
tongs they wrought, and tools they fashioned.

[8] In their dwellings at peace they played at chess,
Of gold no lack did the gods then know, –
Till thither came up daughters of trolls,
A mighty three, from the realm of the giants.

[9] Then sought the gods their assembly seats,
The holy ones, and council held,
To find who should raise the race of dwarfs,
Out of Brimir's blood and the legs of Blain.

[10] Motsognir was the mightiest made,
Of all the dwarfs, and Durin second.
Many a likeness of men they made,
the dwarfs in the earth as Durin said.

[11] Washing and Sleeping Man, North and South,
East and West, Mighty Thief and Loiterer,
Bifur, Bofur, Bombur, Nori,
Friend and fighter, Europa and Mead-Wolf.

[12] The Star, Gandalf, Wind Elf, Thrain,
Thekk and Thorin, Sage and Blusher,
The Body and the Striver, now I have told
– Wise Man and Swift in Counsel – the list aright.

[14] Now shall I tell from Loiterer's throng
the host of the dwarfs, right down to Lofar.
They sought a place far from the stony earth
in fields of land and plains of sand . . .

[16 . . .] So for all time shall the tale be known,
The list of all the forbears of Lofar.

[17] Then from the throng did three come forth
From the home of the gods, the mighty and gracious;
Two without fate on the land they found,
Ask and Embla, of uncertain fate.

[18] Soul they had not, sense they had not,
Heat nor motion, nor goodly hue,
Odin gave them breath, Hoenir a spirit,
Lothur gave them colour and a good complexion.

[19] I know where an ash stands, Yggdrasil its name,
With water white is the great tree wet.
Thence come the dews that fall in the dales,
Green by Fate's well does it ever grow.

[20] Thence come the maidens mighty in wisdom,
Three form the dwelling down under the tree;
Past one is called, and present the next,
Future the third; they carved on staves.
They made laws, and life they allotted
To the children of men, and set their fates.

Finland: Introduction

In the first half of the nineteenth century, the Finnish artist Elias
Lönnrot travelled round the rural areas of Finland in search of
the remains of a living song culture. At this time in remote dis-
tricts there were still singers who understood the art of singing
old mythical proverbs and songs. In former times these songs
were handed down orally from generation to generation. They
all had common features in both form and content. In this way
Lönnrot collected a veritable treasury of songs and finally
succeeded in bringing together the various mythical motifs and
figures. By assembling many ancient texts into one composition
he created a great epic work. He called it Kalevala, publishing a
first version in 1835 and a second, definitive version in 1849.
This definitive version comprises fifty 'runes' or songs. Thus the
Kalevala is an epic composed of different songs.

The Kalevala tells of the great singer Vainämöinen and the
world-smith Ilmarinen who go in search of a wondrous young
maiden in the mythical Northland. The wicked rulers of that
land require the forging of the mysterious Sampo, a magic mill,
which only Ilmarinen can do. The rulers of the Northland shut
up this magic mill, which brings blessings, in a mountain, but
after a long journey the heroes finally recapture it. This is the
greatest blessing for the land, since every part of this magic mill
brings life, happiness and prosperity. Only the first rune tells of
the beginning of the world, and in this sense forms a creation
story.

Kalevala. The origin of the world[32]

Great and mighty is Ukko, the god of gods, the king of kings. White is his hair and white his beard; a fiery cloud is his garment, the lightning is his sword, the rainbow his bow, heaven and earth are subject to him. Many spirits dwell in rocks and streams, in the forest and in the trees, large and small, good and evil. The Fair God rules in the air; the Wild God in the water; the Dark God in the realm of the dead. But above them all stands Ukko.

This was the primal beginning, when sun and moon did not shine, there was no vault of heaven, and no winds defied the earth. There was nothing but the foaming sea and the clouds hanging above it. Then Ilmatar, who ruled in the air, launched herself from the heights into the sea, was borne up by the waves, and played in their foaming caps. A bird came, a wild duck flew, seeking a place where she could settle. But she saw only the foaming sea, and the storm wind ruffled and plucked at her wings. The Fair God lifted her knee from the water and the duck settled on it and built her nest there. When the nest was finished, she laid seven eggs in it, six of gold and one of iron, and began to sit on it to hatch them. For three days the wild duck sat, and the knee of the Fair God became hotter and hotter, so that finally she thought that her joints were on fire and her veins were melting. Then she jerked her arms and legs, so that the seven eggs fell into the water and broke in pieces. But the fragments did not sink into the deep. The lower half of the largest golden egg became the round earth, and the upper half the high vault of heaven. The yellow yoke began to shine as a very bright sun, and from the egg-white arose the moon, shedding its gentle light. The many golden pieces became the stars in the heaven, and the dark pieces of iron became the grey clouds. The Fair God lifted her head from the water, stretched her arms and legs, and spread out her arms. Wherever her foot rested, bays full of fish arose, and wherever she turned her hips, flat shore appeared. And the earth brought forth grass and moss, shrubs and trees, animals and human beings.

Part III

Scientific Approaches to the Beginning

The Natural Sciences

Introduction

In our time, at the end of the twentieth century, the scientific approach has become the dominant view of existence. This approach is based on 'seeing' as the highest category of knowing. The sciences also influence our daily life. Many of us believe only what we ourselves have seen, and think that only what can be perceived is true. Things which have not been, or cannot be, perceived cannot be controlled and therefore are not objective. That even applies to our view of the past: only what can be recovered as a trace of the past in the present is a historical event. 'Seeing' has become the only approach to 'being'.

Twentieth-century thought about the beginning is similarly dominated by this scientific way of thinking. If we reflect on the beginning, we do so usually in the form of theories of the Big Bang and/or evolution. Although these theories have produced order and created coherence on the basis of detached, controllable facts, we regard such scientific views of the beginning as those which come closest to the truth. They are not fiction like stories, tales or myths, but provide a perspective on what really happened. These views are no longer seen as pictures of the world but as an objective account of it. Moreover on the basis of the many discussions which have been held, we tend to see creation and evolution as opposites: one or the other view is true, since both cannot be true at the same time. In this chapter we shall examine some elements of the scientific approach to the beginning.

Looking at the stars[33]

Anyone who looks into the starry sky at night can see how the firmament stretches in all its splendour from horizon to horizon. The Pole Star can be clearly seen, as can the Great Bear. The longer you look, the more stars you see light up. Sometimes the starry heavens seem to emanate a peaceful rest. It is as if the vault of heaven were solicitously bending over the earth. Everyday worries seem futile when one is confronted with this timeless reality. And then to think that this heaven is almost no different from the starry heaven of yesterday or that of two thousand years ago! Aristotle, Copernicus and Einstein let their gaze dwell on the same constellations. The only thing that has changed is the way in which we look at the starry heaven and picture the place of human beings in the universe. Aristotle believed that the earth formed the immovable centre of the universe; Copernicus thought that the sun occupied the central place in the cosmos. It was only a few centuries ago that people became aware that the stars in the heavens are all suns, some far greater and fiercer than our own sun. They discovered that the earth is only a small planet in an orbit around one of the stars in the Milky Way. We know that even the Milky Way is no more than one of the countless stellar systems in the universe.

If we can derive this knowledge about the solar system from the starry sky, why didn't the Greeks succeed in doing so? The most important reason is that they began from some unconscious presuppositions. Thus in their eyes the earth had to form the centre of the universe, and all the other heavenly bodies had to move in perfect circular orbits around the earth. If we had not learned at school how things really are, after a look at the starry sky in all probability we would have drawn the same conclusion. Almost two thousand years ago this Greek thought put a stamp on the human view of the heavens. But just because a view lasts for a long time, that does not mean that it is right; in the sixteenth century, Aristotle's geocentric view of the world had to give place to Copernicus's heliocentric view. However, the latter was not easily accepted, since the old mistaken notions seemed so obvious that no one could imagine that they did not agree with reality. When it was discovered later that the universe does not even revolve around the sun, but that the sun and the solar system form only a small part of one of the stellar systems, the heliocentric view of the world had to be abandoned as as well. The question is, of course, what the unconscious presuppositions are in our present-day picture of the universe. It is even questionable whether our human standard of observations and categories is any use in providing a trustworthy picture of the whole universe. For example, is our way of ordering things by means of the Einsteinian categories of time and space the only possible one? These are questions to which we have no answer, but which clarify somewhat the limits of our knowledge.

Looking with the natural sciences

In the natural sciences, people engage in a particular type of research. A researcher perceives a specific phenomenon within a particular experimental situation. He (or she, but for convenience let us just say he) links his perception to magnitudes or measurable units, like the scientific properties of temperature, velocity, mass, time, length, or the chemical elements of hydrogen, oxygen and carbon. In other words, the researcher makes the things that are observed comprehensible by describing them as measurable units with simple measurable relations. In fact the researcher is then arguing 'inductively': he describes the relation between a specific phenomenon which is observed and a general rule. An illustration will make this clear. If someone sees one black crow, then another one, and later still several hundred, he can connect this with the general rule 'all crows are black'. The observer concerned has no certainty; this rule works only until the contrary has been proved, i.e. until a white crow has been observed. An inductive investigation describes what is observed by means of quantities and measurable relations, and formulates these in general rules. The result of such an inductive investigation can never be an absolute truth, but is only a possibility. This possibility offers the researcher the means for making predictions for similar phenomena until these have been falsified by subsequent experiments.

If we were to argue in this way within a non-scientific context, we would quickly discover that this kind of argument has its limitations. Suppose that we were living in the southern states of America at the end of the eighteenth century. We might look around us and see a Negro who was a slave. Looking round further, we would see more Negroes who were slaves. We would see Negro slaves hundreds and thousands of times. By an inductive argument, in that case we could state the rule 'all Negroes are slaves'. This rule would itself have a certain predictive force. There is a Negro, so he must be a slave. It should be clear that such reasoning has many shortcomings. An inductive form of reasoning generalizes, and acts as if simple explanations underlie similar phenomena. It reduces things to simplicity and measurability, and generalizes this into a rule. This kind of approach is very useful for the natural sciences, and it has expanded our knowledge of the world enormously, but these scientific arguments do not provide any objective knowledge, far less absolute truth. They describe and generalize on the basis of possible relations.

In the natural sciences, not only inductive but also deductive arguments are used. In the latter an explanation is given by drawing conclusions for specific instances from a general rule. Take, for example, the general rule that all planets in the solar system move round the sun in an elliptical orbit. To give a specific example, Jupiter is a planet within that solar system. So the conclusion must be that Jupiter moves in an elliptical orbit around the sun. This argument next has to be tested experimentally. Deductive arguments are logical explanations which explain these necessary relationships. If the rule is true, and a specific phenomenon comes under this rule, then the phenomenon must behave in accordance with the rule. If the earth is part of the solar system, and thus revolves around the sun, then the earth cannot one day begin to revolve around the moon. This form of explanation shows how a particular event has one particular cause. The rule formulates this causal relation. The moment that someone formulates an acceptable explanation on the basis of concrete cases, this can be investigated and tested. Thus a century after Copernicus, Kepler formulated the general rule that planets move in ellipses round the sun, and later again Newton, with his universal law of gravity, offered a scientific explanation for these elliptical movements. Only when they had established these rules could people test new perceptions by them. Once such rules have been verified, it can be assumed that they are universally valid laws. With the help of these laws scientists then began to observe things differently; they discovered new phenomena that they would not have observed without them. So any observation is guided by a particular picture and a particular knowledge of things. Therefore observation by itself is not enough. Science is observation coupled with logical argument. The arguments develop, and through them observations can also develop.

Thus the natural sciences provide a useful insight into reality. The only surprising thing is that in the twentieth century people began to think that this approach was the only, or the only reliable, approach to reality. But what justifies the presupposition that the natural sciences, which always limit themselves to a very specific and well-defined area, are the only possible perspective for all areas? One of the starting points of the scientific way of thinking is that there is only one possible right answer to a meaningful question. In every experiment, if a question is asked, the answer must be one and the same result; if not, then no laws or general rules can be based on it. But does this simplicity apply to everything? The great importance attached to the simple logical explanation is probably connected with the linear Western view. Simple truths are connected with one another logically and this, it is assumed, offers a growth in insight, a line of development in history, progress in the economy and in human thought. The question is very much whether this simplicity and this linear thought are valid for all aspects of reality. Suppose one were to apply this kind of thinking to the human view of history. If history showed clear progress, Bach would be a rudimentary version of Beethoven, Monet an improvement on Michelangelo and Heidegger a deeper thinker than Aristotle. It is possible to describe phenomena by simple causal relations in the natural world, but in other spheres it is more a question of pluralism and relations. In this connection pluralism means that there are different ways of giving an answer, and that sometimes there are several possible answers to one question which at the same time can be argued over in a valuable and meaningful way. Relations means that each of these views is connected with a particular stand-point that is in part defined by historical, cultural and personal factors and in part by the object, phenomenon and person being observed or stated. The natural sciences do not deny this pluralism, but limit themselves to the non-pluralistic and non-relational aspect of the world, and therefore show only part of reality from a particular perspective. The fault then does not lies with the natural sciences, but with those who think that they are the only approach to reality and the only form of knowledge.

The beginning in astronomy: the Big Bang theory

The Big Bang theory is a recent theory about the origin of the universe, the beginning of everything. It is part of cosmology; it shows what the universe looks like and from that deduces how everything has come into being. To describe this picture of the beginning I shall use the model of enlargement as used in teaching cosmology. It shows the position of human beings within the universe using an enlargement factor of ten. Suppose we take your, the reader's, back garden as the starting point. With a helicopter I take a picture of you in your back garden. In the next photograph, taken ten times further away, we see how the garden is part of a city; you yourself are no longer visible. Another factor of ten higher, and we see the city in question lying in the middle of the surrounding countryside. Another factor of ten higher gives us a picture of the earth as a planet with clouds round it. This is how Armstrong saw the earth from the moon. Another factor of ten higher we see a photograph of the earth with the moon going round it, and we see just a bit of the orbit that the planet Mars takes round the sun. Another factor of ten higher and we see the whole solar system, with the sun as a blinding centre. Unfortunately we have to go another factor of ten higher, and then we discover that the solar system is part of an untidy collection of stars. One factor of ten higher we discover that this mass is an organized spiral, a stellar system: the Milky Way. The solar system forms only a very small part of this, and is almost on the edge of the Milky Way. Another factor of ten higher and we see that there are even more stellar systems than the Milky Way. Our Milky Way seems to be just an 'island' in space, a flattened disc of billions of stars, outside which there are many more billions of such islands or stellar systems. The closest system is Andromeda, which has as many stars as the Milky Way. Another factor of ten higher, and we discover yet more of these stellar systems. And yet another factor of ten higher we see many clusters of stellar-systems which are moving millions of years away from the Milky Way. One last factor of ten higher and we see how unimaginably many stellar systems are dispersed through space in an irregular way. Together they form the space that we call the universe.

If we survey this universe, it becomes clear in a flash that we human beings are only a mini-minuscule part of this universe, a peripheral phenomenon. If we use human measurements (for example metres or kilometres) to express the distances, we get nowhere. Even with the unit of time which needs light to bridge space, we still arrive at astronomical figures. If we apply human measurements to the dimensions of the universe, we ourselves vanish from the picture. Astronomers usually start with a measurement derived from light: the distance which light travels in a particular time. Light travels through space at a velocity of 300,000 kilometres per second. That means that a light-minute corresponds to 300,000 x 60 kilometres or 18 million kilometres. If we know that the distance between the earth and the sun is eight light-minutes, that means that the rays of the sun have taken eight minutes to reach us. The distance to Pluto, the most remote planet in our solar system, is five light-hours from earth. If astronomers look at Pluto through a telescope, in reality they are looking back five hours in time. In other words, the image of Pluto takes five hours to get here. If we look at a star in the Milky Way which is 50,000 light years away from the sun, we are looking back 50,000 years in time. The only way in which we can see the whole of the universe is thus by looking back in time. We never know how the universe *is*, only how it *was*. If we look at a star which is thousands of light-years away, then in reality we are travelling back thousands of years into the past. Take Andromeda, for example, the stellar system which is two million light-years distant from earth. When a person on earth sees Andromeda high in the heavens, he or she is looking back two million years in time. Conversely, suppose that someone on a star in Andromeda were looking back on the earth, this person would at best see a few ape-like forerunners of human beings. So someone on a star 300 million light-years from the earth could see dinosaurs walking around on earth. The most remote stellar systems are about ten billion light years away from us. If we receive signals from these systems, we are thus looking back ten billion years in the history of the universe.

Anyone who stands on earth and looks into the heavens will very quickly notice that all the stars are in continuous movement. It seems that not a single stellar system in the universe is standing still. All the stellar systems in the universe are moving away from one another with incredible velocity. The further they are from us, the more rapidly they seem to move. That means that the distance between the stellar systems is gradually getting larger. In other words, the universe is expanding. Here the systems are not moving through space; it is space itself which is expanding: the stellar systems are being as it were carried along with space. But how did this expansion come about? Where there is expanding movement there must have been a beginning. Because Einstein had made it clear that time and space are connected, scientists could explain how space expands going forwards in time and shrinks going backwards in time. It was even possible to calculate back to the time when there was no space in the universe. The closer one gets to zero point in time, the higher the density of the mass and energy becomes. All the energy and mass which were later in the universe were already present in its very first second. This primal plasma or primal soup contained all the elements from which protons, electrons and atoms emerged, and yet later stars and other heavenly bodies.

Thus in the middle of this century, on the basis of the expansion of the universe, the Big Bang hypothesis was formulated: the universe is expanding because of a primal explosion which took place right at the very beginning. Later, in the 1960s, scientists found a weak background radiation all over the universe. This radiation was regarded as the tangible proof, as it were the electromagnetic fossil, of the hot primal matter from which the universe had emerged. From this moment the Big Bang hypothesis was regarded as a theory which explained what the very first beginning of all had looked like. In short, this theory implies that fifteen billion years ago or, to put it more cautiously, between ten and twenty billion years ago, a explosion took place which was tremendously rich in energy, and through this the universe came into being. At that time all matter was so condensed that the force of gravity made it excessively warm; this matter was so hot and compressed that it exploded. As a result of this explosion the matter spread, and then it gradually cooled down. First a baby universe of subatomic dimensions came into being, which gradually swelled to the size of a football. Aeons went past and this universe expanded. Millions, billions of years elapsed. Millions of stars and stellar systems came into being out of the revolving clouds, which kept cooling down. One of them was the solar system, with the earth as one of its planets. So the earth came into being 4. 6 billion years ago.

The Big Bang theory as a creation story

When the Big Bang theory was formed half way through the twentieth century, it was a hypothesis by which a number of astronomical observations could be explained. It was not regarded as the revelation of the ultimate secret of the universe. After the hypothesis had attained the status of a generally accepted theory among cosmologists, a wider public gratefully accepted it. This theory about the beginning fitted amazingly well into the linear picture of the beginning that people had in the West, and gave the impression of being a scientific version of the creation story in Genesis 1.

However, the Big Bang theory does not seem to be the definitive solution of the mystery of the origin and structure of the universe. In the euphoria of this century people were almost to forget that like its predecessors, Aristotle's geocentric picture of the world or Copernicus's heliocentric universe, the Big Bang is no more than a theoretical model. This model is based on two observations: of the expanding universe and of the uniform weak radiation dispersed all over the universe. But just like these earlier models, which were finally overturned by observed contradictions, so too, as time goes on, the Big Bang model is being confronted with problems and inconsistencies. Too many observations contradict it. In the 1970s stars were discovered which are at least fifteen and perhaps sixteen billion years old. These stars are possibly older than the universe itself. Of course that cannot be. Moreover there seemed to be far more matter than could be explained from the theory. Under the pressure of these observations, the Big Bang theory had to undergo major adaptation. To achieve this, the so-called 'inflation hypothesis' was formulated. This hypothesis predicts the existence of enormous quantities of dark matter, the composition of which deviates from any known form of matter. On the basis of this, hundred of times more dark, invisible matter than visible matter is being predicted. However, this dark invisible matter has never yet been found, no matter how hard it has been sought . . .

When the Hubble telescope investigated space in the 1990s, scientists hoped for objective facts which would restore the Big Bang theory to its earlier status. But the opposite proved to be the case. The observations did not seem to correspond with the theory. On the basis of the Big Bang theory it is necessary to assume an universe which is expanding equally, but from the results provided by the Hubble telescope, it proved that the distribution of the stellar systems is far from being as equal as was expected. In place of an equally expanding universe, a 'lumpy' universe is becoming visible, with both great clusters of stellar systems and superclusters and wide areas where there is virtually no matter. Moreover, in 1994 the journal *Nature* wrote that the present measurements by the Hubble telescope had to be examined, and that it had to be recognized that there is something wrong with the Big Bang theory. There is too little support for it in observations. Nevertheless, the majority of astronomers and 'ordinary people' cling to the basic idea of the Big Bang theory, although a great deal of the matter cannot be found; its distribution over the universe is unequal; and the life-times of stars and the universe are incompatible. It is the grip on things which the theory offers, the hope for order in a cosmos which cannot be an inexplicable chaos, that makes people cling to the model. In the Big Bang theory they seek the explanation which will demonstrate that the history of the universe is a logical and chronological development.

Therefore the Big Bang theory can be said to be the most recent and most scientific creation story. It has one theme in common with its historical predecessors. It speaks of a time before time, of space before space, with categories of thought which are purely and simply based on our time and space. It describes both inductively and deductively how pure energy emerged from sheer nothingness. Like any other story, it creates unity and development on the basis of detached elements. These elements are often measurable entities and their relations, but the connection between them is constructed. This is a way of working which in a sense is to be compared with historical investigation: the past is reconstructed on the basis of facts which are encountered in the present and on the basis of natural processes as they have now been perceived. These steps are presented as a story with a logical sequence of events, actions or states (i.e. one that can be understood in terms of human logic). This emerges, for example, from what the Big Bang model assumes about the very first beginning. Reasoning back in time, scientists have arrived at the first fraction of a second in which elementary particles were moving around in a primal soup. Secondly, it is assumed that this fraction of a second was preceded by an absolute beginning. That was the zero point, and in it the leap from nothing to something took place. How have scientists and cosmologists come to say that something must always come out of nothing? The ancient Greeks, for example, could not imagine that something could come out of nothing. Thus this scientific approach from point zero is not an insight, but a presupposition which has been taken over on the basis of the cultural history in which the creation story of Genesis (with its creation from nothing) has played an important role.

The Big Bang theory has given us pictures of the beginning and development of the universe. These are created orderings,

253

made on the basis of comparisons with our world. The pictures are added to the objective or measurable perceptions. This is science extended with a story. Perhaps no strict science about the beginning is even possible. That is no bad thing. The only problem is when people attribute an absolute validity to a theory about the beginning and reject other ways of talking about the beginning as irrelevant.

The beginning in biology: the archive of the earth[34]

Another recent theory about the process of the coming into being of all things and the changes in them is the theory of evolution, which is above all concerned with life on earth. Based on the insights of this theory, the development of life looks like this.

More than four billion years ago the geological history of the earth began. There was life, and at that time life consisted bacteria and primitive monocellular organisms. A billion years ago, for the first time complex organized forms of life like plants and animals appeared. But the bacteria and other monocellular organisms continued to exist. Before today, people were perhaps hardly aware that these bacteria and single cells form the essence of life on earth. Alongside this microworld, living nature as we know it in plants and animals has played only a modest role. Moreover, these complex multicellular organisms which give form to visible nature can only exist by virtue of their symbiosis with the bacteria.

The archive of life that is stored in successive layers of sediment all over the earth shows that in the course of time the plants and animals have been constantly subject to changes. Two processes give form to these changes: *evolution*, the origin of new forms of life from old species, and *extinction*, the disappearance of existing species of plants and animals. The term 'extinction' can amount to either real dying out, in which a species disappears without leaving offspring, or replacement, in which over the course of many generations the offspring change to such a degree that they form a new species. In general, the species of complex organisms have a short life-span. On average a species of plant or animal exists for only around four million years. All species are doomed to disappear again. They then give place to new forms of life which in turn flourish for a period and then disappear.

Between five and three millions ago, hominids, man(and woman)-like beings, evolved within the order of primates (which now includes apes, ape-like and human beings). The first beings to fashion stones into tools appeared in Africa around 2.5 million years ago. On the basis of this skill and the characteristics of their skeletons, this species is regarded as the earliest representative of the genus *Homo*, human being. Differing species of this genus have populated the earth for a shorter or longer period. At present the whole human race belongs to one single species, *Homo sapiens*. There is still vigorous controversy over the origin of this species. Fossil remnants are scarce and incomplete, and do not offer a clear answer. There are no fossils of our species which are older than around 130,000 years. Until around 34,000 years ago a closely related being, *Homo sapiens neandertalensis*, the Neanderthal, lived in Europe and the Middle East. As well as this Neanderthal man, *Homo sapiens sapiens* came into being within the species *Homo sapiens* in Africa or Asia between 300,000 and 150,000 years ago, and from there spread all over the world. Fossils show that he was present on all continents around 30,000 years ago. In biological terms, *Homo sapiens sapiens* is an extremely successful being who has formed great populations. But there is no reason to suppose that in the end this species will not suffer the same fate as the countless other forms of life which have lived on earth and disappeared again. Then the human being, too, will be stored in the archive of the earth.

The theory of evolution

It has been possible to formulate this twentieth-century view of the process of the origin and development of life on earth on the basis of the theory of evolution which was developed in the nineteenth century. In 1859 Charles Darwin laid the foundation for it with his book *On the Origin of Species*, in which he was able to explain the causes and background to changes which have taken place on earth. Darwin described the developments of the species of living beings as a series of irreversible changes based on interaction with their environment and determined by natural selection. This natural selection is the result of a struggle for life which each individual of a species has to wage against rivals in the search for food and sexual partners, against predators, parasites, infections and so on. Here the individual best adapted to conditions will ensure its ongoing existence. Its offspring will inherit the advantageous properties. Thus as a result of natural selection unfit individuals will disappear and the fit, which are equipped with new properties, will survive and multiply. In this way new breeds and finally new species come into existence.

How did Darwin arrive at these insights? As a young man he made a voyage on the frigate 'Beagle' which took him from England via the Cape Verde Islands to South America and Brazil. In particular his observations of finches on the Galapagos Islands and his capacity to draw conclusions from his observations led him to ask the question which became the starting-point for his investigation. Then he read Lyell's *The Principles of Geology*, and got from it the model for putting his observations in a specific theoretical framework. In that book, Lyell described the present landscape of the world as the result of an infinitely long and slow development. Lyell's theory was that very small changes in weather, wind, ice floes or temperature could lead to great geographical shifts, provided that they lasted long enough. By reading Lyell, Darwin learned to see nature through historical spectacles, and the idea occurred to him that the changes in the organic world could also be explained by means of causes which were still constantly at work. Darwin could use them to interpret his observations.

For example, on the Galapagos Islands Darwin had observed clear variations in the shapes of the beaks of the finches from the different islands. From this he drew the conclusion that these differences were closely connected with what the finches ate on the different islands. The finch with a sharp beak lived on the seeds from pineapples, the small songfinch on insects, the woodpecker on insects in trunks and branches. Each species had a beak which was perfectly adapted to its food. Darwin asked himself how all these finches could have descended from the same species of finch, and how this species of finch could have adapted over the course of time to the circumstances on the different islands, so that eventually a number of new species of finches came into being. Closer investigation, for example of foetuses in mammals – a dog, a bat, a rabbit and a human being – led Darwin to the discovery that almost no differences were visible between the foetuses at a very early stage. Could that mean that they were distantly related to one another? Darwin formulated the hypothesis of natural selection. By selection, nature determines which examples survive. Too large a number of animals of one species leads to the disappearance of other species, simply because these can best adapt to the environment and produce offspring. He further showed that the struggle for existence is often fiercest between those species that are most closely related. These have to fight for the same food. As a result, the small advantages (like the beaks of finches) come into their own. The harsher the struggle for existence, the quicker new species develop. Only those examples which are best adapted survive; the others die out.

When Darwin presented these views in 1859, they caused a great shock. Not only was there criticism from the churches, but there was also scientific criticism, since Darwin could not give an adequate explanation on the one hand of why new species came into being (and not just new variations within a species) and on the other of how heredity worked. He did not have a sound theory of heredity. On the basis of an investigation into heredity by Mendel, at the beginning of the twentieth century it proved possible to go a step further and describe how heredity works and new varieties come into being, namely through 'recombination'. In other words, hereditary factors or 'genes' can form new combinations which make both continuity and variation possible. Later again, it proved possible to explain the sudden transition to new species by the concept of 'mutation'. The last great development in the modern theory of evolution took place in 1953, when the DNA molecule was discovered. In it the hereditary substance was present which fulfilled all the important functions of heredity that were being sought. The structure of DNA explained both the stability and the possibility of mutation and recombination, and also the capacity for exact reproduction. This insight forms the molecular, genetic foundation of the modern Neo-Darwinian 'synthetic' theory of evolution, in which a synthesis is forged between Darwin's old theory of evolution and the insights of the modern theory of heredity.

The present-day Neo-Darwinian approach differs in a couple of points from the classical Darwinian theory of evolution. Researchers after Darwin regard evolution on earth as a totality of chemical reactions lasting over four billion years with the world as a reactor. Here the sequence of reactions can be calculated and predicted. As an approach, this way of thinking is as deterministic as that of creationism, in which God is seen as a great watchmaker and the watch of creation is running according to his plan. The Neo-Darwinians, however, think that there have to be changes or mutations to explain the progress in evolution. Their basic assumption is that mutations take place purely by chance. According to them, the chance that anything meaningful is evolving out of this biological roulette has become very small indeed. 'The whole of evolution is based on sheer chance,' says Jacques Monod. In an analogous sense God has changed from being a clockmaker to someone who plays dice. Today the Neo-Darwinian view has become standard.

Over the last few years more and more criticisms of this standard view have been expressed, for example by people like Riedl and Eigen. These writers are not Darwinians and therefore do not follow any deterministic, far less Neo-Darwinian view of nature, since they do not regard evolution as a process involving chance factors. Riedl in particular shows that the synthetic theory of evolution fails because it pays to little attention to the connection between the different levels (genetic, embryogenetic, ecological, ethological). Neo-Darwinians speak of 'chance' or 'arbitrariness' because they concentrate too much on one level and ignore the connections within the greater whole. Riedl's criticism is perhaps to be compared with that of modern health care, in which the specialists are criticized for concentrating on only one element and losing sight of the connection between the parts. Eigen, another theoretician of evolution, wants to show above all that the picture of a 'chance' or unguided evolution is wrong. On his view evolution is guided by the environment. If the environment changes, this will entail a particular adaptation of individuals or mutants. It should be possible to attribute a capacity to direct to the environment and a capacity to select or adapt to the mutants. The essential difference between his view and that of the Neo-Darwinians relates to the chance character of mutation: it is the difference between blind experiment and the intelligent quest for a goal.

The theory of evolution as a creation story

Since the last century the theory of evolution has put its stamp on biological thinking and from there on the whole of Western thought. For many people in Western Europe the creation story in Genesis has been 'outdated' since the development of the theory of evolution. That happens above all because this theory is often no longer regarded as a model or a view, but as a fact. And since previously the creation story of Genesis had also been read as 'fact', or as an account of actual events, people faced the problem that either Genesis or the theory of evolution was true, but not both. Most opted for the theory of evolution; those who still believed in the creation story in Genesis were dismissed by the others as creationists, fundamentalists or orthodox conservatives.

This general acceptance of the theory of evolution is understandable against the background of developments in Western thought in the last few centuries. Since the Renaissance a development has taken place in the modern picture of human beings and nature as a result of which the human being has come to occupy a central place, and nature has begun to be approached as a mechanism. Since then, what is quantitatively definable, measurable and calculable has been regarded as the essential aspect of nature which determines knowledge. Only the quantitative aspects of reality are still objective facts. Thus nature has increasingly been reduced to an object to be investigated scientifically and to be controlled. This has ultimately even resulted in a fundamental reduction in the concept of nature: only what appears relevant within a scientific explanation is regarded as authentic. Reality is 'no more than' what is scientifically relevant, in other words the quantifiable, the repeatable and the regular. Furthermore, scientific knowledge is coming to occupy a monopolistic position. Thus among other things the question of purpose, 'To what end does everything behave like this?', is declared irrelevant and is replaced by the causal question, 'As a result of what does everything behave like this?'.

This way of thinking was extended in the Enlightenment by a sense of historicity: nature, human beings and society are not immutable facts, but the result of a process of historical change which is still constantly going on. The very insight that nature, too, has undergone a historical development led Darwin to his theory of evolution. Therefore he could begin to see the living organization as the result of a mechanical succession of natural laws, and no longer as the consequence of God's purposefulness. Neo-Darwinianism has extended this view and argues that this process is not only historical, but also chance, arbitrary and without purpose. As a result of this the concept of 'meaning 'or 'significance' has also become meaningless: the process of evolution takes place by chance; there is no great director, and even the participants are there by chance. Everything has come into being under the influence of more or less chance circumstances. Thus it is an inexplicable coincidence that human beings exist. According to the Neo-Darwinians, no other meaning is to be attached to our human life than that we are the chance result of an ongoing process of becoming.

It is amazing that the most fervent adherents of the theory of evolution do not recognize that this theory, too, simply reproduces a particular state of affairs and is the result of a particular perspective. It has unproven presuppositions, like the basic assumption that regularities and natural processes work in the same way today as they did millions of years ago. People assume, without knowing or even being able to know, that the changes which took place in the past derived from specific causes that are still at work today in the same way and therefore can be studied through experiments now. Another starting point is the use of human causal arguments, in other words arguments and rules which have been accepted as scientific since the Enlightenment. As a result the theory of evolution can reduce the variety of biological facts to a few fundamental principles and can give a causal explanation of the origin of life on earth. In this way it can give an answer to the questions how the great diversity in forms of life and their striking purposefulness and adaptability have come into being, what regularities are to be discovered in this course, and what causal mechanisms underlie the changes. This approach has proved very valuable as an instrument or working model: by putting a particular spotlight on matter, scientists have created a particular form of order and gained insights. But that does not mean that this partial truth is the whole truth, far less that the spotlight coincides with the whole of reality. For where argument turns into the requirement that reality must coincide with the argument, theory is being turned into a fact.

Theory has become a net in which not only the world but also human beings have been trapped. That emerges very clearly in the use of the term 'chance' by the Neo-Darwinians. By 'chance' they mean 'not on purpose', 'unnecessary', 'unpredictable' or 'arbitrary'. But all these terms above all say something about their own human expectations about evolution, and nothing about the process of evolution itself. If nothing runs according to plan, that means that it does not run according to our plan; if something is not necessary, that means that it does not run in accordance with our laws of cause or logic. But as far as we know, nature may have other laws which (so far) still lie outside our principles of ordering. It is arrogant to state that what one does not understand as a human being is a shortcoming in nature. To say 'There is no order' or 'The evolution of life knows no purpose' instead of saying 'I do not know the order and the purpose' bears witness to a lack of awareness of one's own partial perspective. In this way theories become ideologies.

So it is preferable to have other perspectives and approaches alongside the theory of evolution with its meaningful partial perspective, like those which are expressed by stories, poetry, music and expressions of faith. Then nature can again be given a qualitative side as well as its quantitative side. Then stories are given the opportunity to show another side of reality, human beings and life. These stories do not replace science, but they supplement it where the scientific theories fall short. If they do, a story like that of Cain and Hevel can show that there is more than 'the survival of the fittest'. Whereas the theory of evolution shows nature as something in which the strongest survives, a story of Cain and Hevel can show that the weaker, the worthless, have a right to life. *That is the story which religions have to tell*, whether they are called Judaism, Christianity or Islam. In their stories, in principle they take a stand against the mentality in which all are concerned for their own survival. Whereas nature and the natural sciences concentrate on the 'winners', the religions and their stories display a preferential option for all the others, the weaker and those who seem to be of no importance for the progress of history. They opt for the supernumeraries in the arena of life.

Epilogue

The story of Earth

In a collection called 'The Story of Earth', indigenous people talk about their view of the earth and of white people from Western Europe and the United States.[35] Here are two fragments of stories about and by Indians from Brazil and North America.

'An old Indian in the Amazon region once asked me: Why do you travel so far in search of wood with which to warm yourself? Don't you have wood in your own land? I replied that we had a great deal of wood, but not of the same quality, and that we did not burn brazil wood but got dyes from it. I added that in our land there were merchants who had more fabrics, scissors, mirrors and other goods than he could imagine and that these merchants all bought up pau-brazil (the tree from which Brazil takes its name, but now completely extinct) with many ships laden with such goods. What a wonder you are telling me, said the savage. But this rich man you're talking about, will he never die? Yes, of course he will die like anyone else. And when he dies, to whom does he leave all his possessions? To his children, if he has them. Well, went on the Indian, I can see that you are all crazy. You cross the seas, suffer every kind of hardship and work so hard to amass riches which you leave to your sons and other relatives. Don't tell me that the land that you feed cannot in its turn feed you! We have our fathers, mothers and children whom we love, but we are convinced that when we die, the earth which has fed us will also continue to feed them. So we love our family and we stay at home.'

. . .

'An Indian chief recently paid us a visit in the Brazilian capital: it was his first acquaintance with the centre of a great city. Hardly had he set foot on the street when it occurred to us that

263

the man almost certainly did not have enough money. So we took him to an 'electronic bank' to show him the technology of the white people and how they kept their money. When we opened the door of the cabin, to our great surprise we found in it a poor and neglected child, six or seven years old. The child didn't say a word, but his sleepy eyes seemed to ask forgiveness for the fact that he was not in his own home but in the house of money. Only hours later, as though he could not believe what he had seen, the Indian chief asked us for more explanation of this incident. Then he said: "No one is advised to want to penetrate to the brain of civilized man. He has television, telephones, automobiles and enormous buildings, but is not in a position to feed and house his children. Those of us who come from the villages have nothing of all these riches: we hunt, fish, plant, look after the area where we live and protect it, and children are always the centre of our interest. When our children come into the world, it is our people that is being reborn. When that is no longer possible, then we shall have come to the end of everything. The day that the white man reached our village, we talked with one another and he gave us all kinds of presents to lure us into a new form of existence that he called 'civilization'. But it was all a cheat, since we do not live on presents. So I often sit and ask myself: What does it mean to be civilized? What do riches stand for? What does it mean to be developed?"

The school books which are used to teach children the history of the heroic "taming" of the wild Brazilians regularly relate how a certain Portuguese adventurer, when he noticed that the Indians were not interested in gold mines or money, and far less inclined to give these to the invaders, decided on a certain day to present the recalcitrant people with an ultimatum. He poured brandy into a basin in the sight of the whole village, and set the liqueur on fire so that it looked as if water was burning. In their terror at this the Indians immediately showed him the place where their gold mines were. For them it was of the utmost importance to keep the water that quenches our thirst, and of no importance at all to collect grains of gold which were absolutely useless except to make the white men crazy. We aborigines often asked ourselves: What way do the white people want to follow?

If we regard the earth as the web of life that supports us, then it is clear that the web has been weakened, that the earth is sick. But if we look at the other side, from the living earth itself, then the planet is not sick, but human beings are the embodiment of the sickness. The conclusion of this absurd argument must be that it is not sickness that will destroy the earth, but we ourselves. Human arrogance is an important part of the problem. It is because we human beings have a capacity that no other single creature has, namely the capacity to destroy the equilibrium of nature, that we are such a danger to ourselves. Precisely because we have this capacity, we have ceremonies and instructive stories to remind us of our proper place. We are not the strongest beings in the creation. In many respects we are even the weakest. We were originally given a task by the Creator. Very simply, it was to be friendly to one another and have respect for the earth. Because human beings have a tendency to forget this, the Creator gave us stories to remind us of our task and to put us once again on the right path of the good spirit.'

Notes

1. The most important literature used for this chapter is: Barr 1968, 1972; Cassuto 1964; Clines 1967; Hamilton 1990; Jacob 1934; Perry 1993; Sarna 1966; Tsumura 1989; Wenham 1983 and White 1991.
2. The most important literature used for this chapter is: Barr 1992; Buchanan 1956; Cassuto 1964; Combs 1988; Hauser 1982; Humphreys 1985; Naidoff 1978; Ska 1984; Tsumura 1989; Turner 1991; Vogels 1978, 1983; Wolde 1994.
3. Based, *inter alia*, on: Baskin 1989; Pagels 1989; Schürer 1973; Segal 1986.
4. The material in this section is chiefly based on: Burghardt 1947; Pagels 1983, 1989.
5. The content of this section is chiefly based on: Augustine 1985, 1992; Pagels 1985, 1989.
6. Based, *inter alia*, on: Holman 1986; Pagels 1989.
7. The literature used for this chapter is: Anderson 1978; Brongers 1995; Bryan 1987; Cassuto 1964; Cole 1991; Combs 1988; Friis Plum 1989; Hamilton 1990; Hauser 1980; Jacob 1934; Kugel 1990; Spina 1992; Wenham 1983; Wolde 1994.
8. This chapter is based, *inter alia*, on: Barré 1984, 1988; de Boer 1962; Cassuto 1964; Clark 1971; Hamilton 1990; Hulst 1958; Jacob 1934; Molina 1980; Peterson 1976; Rendtorff 1961, 1989; Robinson 1986; Schwarzbaum 1957; Steinmetz 1994; Tomasino 1992; Wolde 1990, 1994.
9. This chapter is based, *inter alia*, on: Cassuto 1964; Friis Plum 1989; Jacob 1934; Oded 1986; Rietbergen 1994; Robinson 1986; Steinmetz 1994; Tomasino 1992.
10. See e. g. Beck 1994.
11. The translation of the Enuma Elish is from E. A. Speiser, 'Enuma elish', in *Ancient Near Eastern Texts*, ed. J. B. Pritchard, Princeton 1968, 60–72.
12. Rig Veda X, 127, from R. C. Zaehner (ed.), *Hindu Scriptures*, London 1972, 1f.
13. Brihadaranyaka Upanishad I, 4, 1–4, translated by F. Max Müller, *The Principal Upanishads* I, London 1884, 85f.

14. After C. Whitaker, *Oosterse Mythologie*, Amsterdam 1992, 20–1.
15. From *The Book of Lieh-tzu*, translated by A. C. Graham, London 1961, 17–20.
16. From B. Chatwin, *The Songlines*, London 1987, 14–17.
17. From M. Eliade, *From Primitives to Zen. A Thematic Sourcebook of the History of Religions*, London 1967, 86f.
18. From Vivian L. Thompson, *Hawaiian Myths of Earth, Sea, and Sky*, Honolulu 1988, 11–14.
19. From D. Goetz and S. G. Morley, *Popol Vuh. The Sacred Book of the Ancient Quiché Maya*, London 1950, 81–94, 165–70.
20. From Eliade, *From Primitives to Zen* (n. 17), 83f.
21. This story is from the Efik-Ibibio people in Nigeria, text in P. Radin, *African Folktales*, New York 1983, 41.
22. This story is from the Ekoi-people in Nigeria. Two gods appear in the stories of the Ekoi, Obassi Osaw (the god of heaven) and Obassi Nsi (the god of earth). Originally Obassi Nsi was a goddess but in the long run she was no longer called 'mother earth' but 'father earth'. However, there are also indications that the Ekoi saw Obassi Nsi more as a mother god and Obassi Osaw as the father god. Obassi Nsi appears in the story 'How men come to be on earth'. In the translation this god is rendered as 'earth god'. The translation is based on the version in M. Schipper, *Het Zwarte Paradijs, Afrikaanse Scheppingsmythen*, Heerlen 1980, 104.
23. In this story from the Tutses in Rwanda the name of the creator god Imama is translated 'the creator'. The text is taken from Schipper, *Het Zwarte Paradijs* (n. 22), 104.
24. This story is from the Saramo people in Tanzania. The text is taken from Schipper, *Het Zwarte Paradijs* (n. 22), 103.
25. In this Tanzanian story from the Kulwe people the name of the god Nguluwi is translated 'god of heaven'. The text is taken from Schipper, *Het Zwarte Paradijs* (n. 22), 88.
26. In this story from the Bashi people in Zaire the supreme being is called Nyamuzinda. Here this is translated Supreme Being; some names of places and persons have also been omitted in this story. The text is taken from Schipper, *Het Zwarte Paradijs* (n. 22), 32–3.
27. This story from the Kaone people in Zambia has Lesa as the name of the creator god. Here Lesa is translated 'the Creator'. The names of the first man (Mulonga) and first woman (Mwinambuzhi) have been omitted in this translation. The text is

taken from Schipper, *Het Zwarte Paradijs* (n. 22), 97–8.

28. In this story from the Ashanti people in Ghana the Great Spider plays an important role. Here he takes over the role of God as creator. The names of the mother of men, Amali, and the mother of women, Amasia, have been omitted, as has the name of the servant girl Okra. The text is taken from Schipper, *Het Zwarte Paradijs* (n. 22), 99–102.

29. This introduction is based on T. P. van Baaren, *Scheppingsverhalen. De schepping der Wereld volgens het geloof der volken*, Amsterdam 1964, 166–7.

30. The Hesiod text is taken from M. Eliade, *From Primitives to Zen* (n. 17), 114–16.

31. The text is based on *The Poetic Edda*, translated by Henry Adams Bellows, New York 1936, 3–9, with some alterations and modernizations of language.

32. See *The Kalevala*, translated by Keith Bosley, London 1989; cf. also *Kalevala, The Land of Heroes*, translaed by W. F. Kirby, London 1977, 16–17.

33. The information about the stars in this chapter is based on: Beekman 1986; Boslough 1993; van Calmthout 1993a, 1993b; Delft 1993; Gaarder 1994; Gleick 1993; Schilling 1993a, 1993b, 1994a, 1994b.

34. This section on the theory of evolution is based, *inter alia*, on Van den Beukel, 1991, 1995; Gaarder 1994; Priem 1993; Prigogine 1993; Soontiëns 1988.

35. From M. Terena, 'De zingende stem van het bos', and J. Bruchac, 'De cirkel is de manier van kijken', in *Het verhaal Aarde. Inheemse volken aan het woord over milieu en ontwikkeling*, Novib 1992, 41–56: 21.

Bibliography

Anderson, B. W., 'From Analysis to Synthesis: The Interpretation of Genesis 1–11', *Journal of Biblical Literature* 97, 1978, 23–39

Ankersmit, F., Doeser M. C., and Varga, A. K. (eds.), *Op verhaal komen. Over narrativiteit in de mens- en culturwetenschappen*, Kampen 1990

Augustine, *Confessions*, translated by H. Chadwick, London 1992

—, *City of God*, translated by H. Bettenson, Harmondsworth 1984

Baaren, T. P. van, *Scheppingsverhalen. De Schepping der Wereld volgens het geloof der volken*, Amsterdam 1964

Barr, J., 'The Image of God in the Book of Genesis – A Study of Terminology', *Bulletin of the John Rylands Library, University of Manchester* 51, 1968, 11–26

—, 'Man and Nature – The Ecological Controversy and the Old Testament', *Bulletin of the John Rylands Library, University of Manchester* 55, 1972, 9–32

—, *The Garden of Eden and the Hope of Immortality*, London 1992

Barré, L. M., 'The Riddle of the Flood Chronology', *Journal for the Study of the Old Testament* 41, 1988, 3–20

Baskin, J. R., 'Rabbinic Reflections on the Barren Wife', *Harvard Theological Review* 82, 1989, 101–14

Beck, H., *Fenomenologie van de godsdiensten*, lecture notes, Tilburg Theological Faculty 1994

Beekman, G., 'Punt Nul. Theorieën over het onstaan van het heelal', *NRC Handelsblad*, 14 October 1986

Bellow, H. A., *The Poetic Edda*, New York 1936

Berlin, I., *The Crooked Timber of Humanity. Chapters in the History of Ideas*, London 1991

Beukel, A. van den, *More Things in Heaven and Earth*, London 1992

—, 'Zin of geen zin, dat is de kwestie', in *Harde wetenschap: Waar blijft de mens?* (ed. W. Drees), Baarn 1994

Boer, P. A. H. de, *Gedenken und Gedächtnis in der Welt des Alten Testaments*, Stuttgart 1962, 12–64

Boslough, J., *Meesters van de tijd*, Amsterdam 1993

Brongers, H. W., 'Die Wendung $b^e sem$ *yhwh* im Alten Testament',

Zeitschrift für die alttestamentliche Wissenschaft 77, 1965, 1–20

Bryan, D. T., 'A Re-evaluation of Gen. 4 and 5 in Light of Recent Studies in Genealogical Fluidity', *Zeitschrift für die alttestamentliche Wissenschaft* 99, 1987, 180–8

Buchanan, G. W., 'The Old Testament Meaning of the Knowledge of Good and Evil', *Journal of Biblical Literature* 75, 1956, 114–20

Burghardt, W. J., *The Image of God in Man according to Cyril of Alexandria*, Washington 1957

Calmthout, M. van, 'De natuurwetenschap is in verval geraakt', *Volkskrant* 24, December 1993a

Calmthout, M. van, 'Wetenschap vertelt wat we zien, niet wie we zijn', *Volkskrant*, 31 December 1993b

Cassuto, U., *From Adam to Noah. A Commentary on the Book of Genesis. Part One*, Jerusalem 1964

Cassuto, U., *From Noah to Abraham. A Commentary on the Book of Genesis. Part Two*, Jerusalem 1964

Chatwin, B., *The Songlines*, London 1987

Clark, M., 'The Righteousness of Noah', *Vetus Testamentum* 21, 1971, 261–80

Clines, D. J. A, 'The Image of God in Man', *Tyndale Old Testament Lecture* 19, 1967, 53–101

Cole, T. J., 'Enoch, a Man Who Walked with God', *Bibliotheca Sacra* 149, 1991, 288–97

Combs, E., 'Has JHWH cursed the Ground? Perplexity of Interpretation in Genesis 1–5', in *Ascribe to the Lord. Biblical and Other Studies in Memory of Peter C. Craigie*, ed. L. Eslinger and G. Taylor, JSOTS 67, Sheffield 1988, 265–87

Delft, D. van, 'Alexander Friedmann. De vader van het uitdijend heelal', *NRS Handelsblad*, 14 October 1993

Eliade, M., *From Primitives to Zen. A Thematic Sourcebook of the History of Religions*, London 1967

Friis Plum, K., 'Genealogy as Theology', *Scandinavian Journal of the Old Testament*, 1989, 66–92

Gaarder, J., *Sophie's World. A Novel about the History of Philosophy*, London and New York 1995

Gleick, J., *Chaos: Making a New Science*, London and New York 1989

Hamilton, V. P., *The Book of Genesis. Chapters 1–17* (NICOT), Grand Rapids 1990

Hauser, A. J., 'Genesis 2–3: The Theme of Intimacy and Alienation', in

Art and Meaning: Rhetoric in Biblical Literature, ed. D. J. A. Clines, D. M. Gunn and A. J. Hauser, JSOTS 19, Sheffield 1982, 20–36

—, 'Linguistic and Thematic Links between Genesis 4. 1–16 and Genesis 2–3', *Journal of the Evangelical Theological Society* 23, 1980, 297–305

Holman, J., 'D(i)e verdraaide erfzonde', in *Bij de put van Jacob. Exegetische Opstellen*, ed. W. Weren and N. Poulssen, Tilburg 1986, 19–45

Hulst, A. R., 'Kol Basar in der priesterlichen Fluterzählung', *Oudtestamentische Studiën* 16, Leiden 1958, 28–58

Humphreys, W. L., *The Tragic Vision and the Hebrew Tradition*, Philadelphia 1985, 73–81

Jacob, B., *Das erste Buch der Tora, Genesis*, Berlin 1934

Kalevala, the Land of Heroes, translated by W. F. Kirby, London 1977

Kugel, J., 'Why was Lamech Blind?', *Hebrew Annual Review. Biblical and Other Studies* 12, 1990, 91–103

Leeming, D. A., *The World of Myth. An Anthology*, New York 1990

Lieh-tzu, The Book of, translated by A. G. Graham, London 1961

Molina, J. P., 'A Man to Work the Soil: A New Interpretation of Genesis 2–3', *Journal for the Study of the Old Testament* 5, 1978, 2–14.

Oded, B., 'The Table of Nations (Genesis 10) – A Socio-cultural Approach', *Zeitschrift für die alttestamentliche Wissenschaft* 98, 1986, 14–31

Pagels, E., 'Adam and Eve, Christ and the Church', in *New Testament and Gnosis: Essays in Honour of R. McL. Wilson*, ed. A. Logan and A. Wedderburn, Edinburgh 1983, 146–75

—, *Adam, Eve and the Serpent*, London and New York 1989

Perry, T. A., 'Poetics of Absence: The Structure and Meaning of Genesis 1. 2', *Journal for the Study of the Old Testament* 58, 1993, 3–11

Petersen, D. L., 'The Yahwist on the Flood', *Vetus Testamentum* 26, 1976, 438–46

Popol Vuh, *The Sacred Book of the Ancient Quiché Maya*, translated by D. Goetz and S. G. Morley, London 1950

Priem, H. N. A., *Aarde en Leven. Earth and Life*, Amsterdam 1993

Prigogine, I and Stengers, I., *Order Out of Chaos. Man's New Dialogue with Nature*, London and New York 1985

Radin, P., *African Folktales*, New York 1983

Rendtorff, R., 'Genesis 8, 21 und die Urgeschichte des Jahwisten',

Kerygma und Dogma 7, 1961, 69–78

—, '"Covenant" as a Structuring Concept in Genesis and Exodus', *Journal of Biblical Literature* 108, 1989, 385–93

Rietbergen, P. J., 'Na de zondvloed: Noachs zonen en het Europese wereldbeeld', *Schrift* 153, 1994, 94–9

Robinson, R. B., 'Literary Function of the Genealogies of Genesis', *Catholic Biblical Quarterly* 48, 1986, 595–608

Sarna, N., *Understanding Genesis. The Heritage of Biblical Israel*, New York 1966, 37–80

Schilling, G., 'De jacht op de scheppingsdatum', *Volkskrant,* 13 March 1993a

—, *De salon van God. Speurtocht naar de architectuur van de kosmos*, Amsterdam 1993b

—, 'Het grootstse deel van het heelal is zoek of bestaat niet', *Volkskrant,* 30 April 1994a

—, 'Scheppingsverhaal blijft heilig', *Volkskrant,* 24 December 1994b

Schipper, M., *Het Zwarte Paradijs. Afrikaanse scheppingsmythen*, Heerlen 1980

Schürer, E., *The History of the Jewish People in the Age of Jesus Christ*, Vols. 1–4, revised and edited by G. Vermes, F. Millar and M. Black, Edinburgh 1973

Schwarzbaum, H., 'The Overcrowded Earth', *Numen* 4, 1957, 59–74

Segal, A., *Rebecca's Children. Judaism and Christianity in the Roman World*, Cambridge, Mass. 1986

Ska, J.-L., '"Je vais lui faire un allié qui soit son homologue" (Gen. 2. 18). A Propos du terme '*ezer* = "aide"', *Biblica* 65, 1984, 233–8

Soontiëns, F. J. K. J., *Evolutie en finaliteit*, Nijmegen 1988

Speiser, E. A., 'Enuma Elish', in *Ancient Near Eastern Texts*, ed. J. B. Pritchard, Princeton 1968

Spina, F. A., 'The "Ground" for Cain's Rejection (Gen 4): *adamah* in the Context of Gen. 1–11', *Zeitschrift für die alttestamentliche Wissenschaft* 104, 1992, 319–32

Steinmetz, D., 'Vineyard, Farm and Garden: The Drunkenness of Noah in the Context of Primeval History', *Journal of Biblical Literature* 113, 1994, 193–207

Thompson, V. L., *Hawaiian Myths of Earth, Sea, and Sky*, Honolulu 1988

Tomasino, A. J., 'History Repeats Itself: The "Fall" and Noah's Drunkenness', *Vetus Testamentum* 42, 1992, 128–30

Tsumura, D. T., *The Earth and the Waters in Genesis 1 and 2: A*

Linguistic Investigation, JSOTS 83, Sheffield 1989

Turner, L. A., *Announcements of Plot in Genesis*, JSOTS 96, 1991

Vogels, W., 'It is Not Good that the "Mensch" Should Be Alone: I Will Make Him/Her a Helper Fit for Him/Her' (Gen 2:18)', *Église et Théologie* 9, 1978, 9–35

—, 'L'être humain appartient au sol. Gn 2, 4b–3, 24', *Nouvelle Revue Théologique* 115, 1983, 515–34

Wenham, G. J., *Genesis 1–15*, Word Biblical Commentary, Waco 1983

White, H. C., *Narration and Discourse in the Book of Genesis*, Cambridge 1991

Whittaker, C., *Oosterse Mythologie*, Amsterdam 1992

Wieger, L., *Les pères du system Taoiste*, Paris ²1983

Wolde, E. J. van, 'Van tekst via tekst naar betekenis. Intertekstualiteit en haar implicaties', *Tijdschrift voor Theologie* 30, 1990, 331–61

—, *Words become Worlds. Semantic Studies of Genesis 1–11*, Leiden 1994

Zipor, M. A., 'A Note on Genesis VI 13', *Vetus Testamentum* 51, 1991, 366–9